# Kierkegaard and Theology

*Murray Rae*

t & t clark

**Published by T&T Clark International**
*A Continuum Imprint*
The Tower Building
11 York Road
London SE1 7NX

80 Maiden Lane,
Suite 704,
New York, NY 10038

www.continuumbooks.com

**British Library Cataloguing-in-Publication Data**
A catalogue record for this book is available from the British Library.

ISBN 13: 978-0-567-03312-3 (Hardback)
       978-0-567-03313-0 (Paperback)

Typeset by Newgen Imaging Systems Pvt Ltd, Chennai, India
Printed and bound in Great Britain by the MPG Books Group

# Contents

# Contents

# Preface

As always in a work of this nature, many people have contributed to its development and final realization. I thank in particular Tom Kraft of Continuum who suggested I write this book in the first place and who, with great patience, has guided it through the various stages of production. I am grateful too, to Cynthia Lund and Gordon Marino for their warm welcome and generous provision at the Hong Kierkegaard Library at St Olaf College, Minnesota. This book began at the Hong Library where I was surrounded by the volumes of Kierkegaard's own work, both in their original language and as they have been lovingly translated into English by Howard and Edna Hong. To these latter, all Kierkegaard scholars working in English owe an enormous debt of gratitude. Finally, I was also surrounded in the Kierkegaard library by the accumulated wisdom, set down in writing, of scholars who have worked on Kierkegaard over the years. To them I am grateful, even where I take issue with their conclusions about, or, indeed, their approach to, Kierkegaard's work. One's own thoughts are commonly generated, developed and refined by engagement with those with whom one disagrees. Should such interlocutors chance upon this book, I hope that it will provide the same service for them. And to those fellow readers of Kierkegaard from whose writings I have learned and accepted much – especially Stephen Evans, Robert Perkins, Sylvia Walsh, David Gouwens, Simon Podmore and the late Julia Watkin – I hope that this book offers something to which you can consent.

Three of the following chapters draw upon and sometimes recast the work that I have published elsewhere. I am grateful to editors and publishers for permission to re-present parts of the following:

'The Risk of Obedience: A Consideration of Kierkegaard's Fear And Trembling', *International Journal of Systematic Theology* 1.3 (November, 1999), 308–21.

'Kierkegaard, Barth and Bonhoeffer: Conceptions of the Relation Between Grace and Works', *International Kierkegaard Commentary: For Self Examination and Judge for Yourself!* (ed. Robert L. Perkins; Macon, GA: Mercer University Press, 2002), 143–67.

'The Forgetfulness of Historical-talkative Remembrance', *International Kierkegaard Commentary: Practice in Christianity* (ed. Robert L. Perkins; Macon, GA: Mercer University Press, 2004), 69–94.

# Chapter 1

# Introduction and Disclaimer

This book does not offer an introduction to all that the Danish author Søren Kierkegaard has to say, much less to all that his scholarly readers would have him say. It is directed rather to those who want to understand something of Kierkegaard's theology. This limitation of scope should not alarm readers who might suppose themselves to be missing out on the 'main thing' that Kierkegaard has to say. For Kierkegaard, theology *is* the main thing. Kierkegaard was, above all, a Christian thinker, and to think Christianly is precisely to do theology, to consider all questions of human life, that is, in light of the Truth that is disclosed in Christ. Many scholars who study Kierkegaard do not agree with this assessment.[1] It is not my intention to argue the point in any detail, however. The warrant for the claim will be furnished in the end only by reading Kierkegaard's work and by taking seriously his own 'report to history'[2] concerning the primary intentions of his authorship. There, in 'The Point of View of My Work as an Author' Kierkegaard reports that '. . . I am and was a religious author, that my whole authorship pertains to Christianity, to the issue: becoming a Christian, with direct and indirect polemical aim at that enormous illusion, Christendom . . .'[3] Later in the same work he tells us that he was 'duty-bound in the service of Christianity' and that he 'dedicated himself to it from the first moment'. Kierkegaard anticipated that many would find this uninteresting: 'And now', he writes, 'now I am not at all interesting any longer. That what it means to become a Christian should *actually* be the fundamental idea in the whole authorship – how boring!'[4]

Whatever legitimacy there might be in the scholarly work of appraising Kierkegaard's contribution to a vast range of other disciplines, Kierkegaard himself insisted that his authorship was directed to the single purpose of making it 'clear what Christianity is'.[5] This is a theological matter. The fundamental concerns of Kierkegaard's authorship are God's paradoxical self-disclosure in the 'God-man', the manner of our being brought into relation with the truth uniquely instantiated in him and the 'practice of Christianity' or the obedience that is the sole mark of Christian faith. Much in Kierkegaard's authorship that appears to address other themes is in fact an analysis of the ways in which we are prone to avoid that encounter and to take offence both at the divine command and at the paradox of faith. To the question of what it means to become a Christian, Kierkegaard writes, even 'The Seducer's Diary' belongs. It too 'signifies in a deeper sense how infinitely important it is to become a Christian'.[6] The 'Diary' referred to here appears as the concluding section in the first part of *Either/Or* and tells of the life of Johannes, a Don Juan type figure who lives the life of an aesthete, having no goal in life other than the gratification of his desires. So far as women are concerned Johannes takes his pleasure from the excitement of the chase, but once the catch is made and the gratification secured, it is time to move on to another pursuit. While there may be much to learn from the Diary, as scholars have sought to do, about developmental psychology, the aesthetic sensibility, morality and so on,[7] we must not overlook the hermeneutical clue Kierkegaard himself gives. This work too belongs to the project of signifying 'how infinitely important it is to become a Christian'.

Given Kierkegaard's attention to the central questions of human existence, his scathing critiques of Christendom, of particular trends in philosophy, and of the ecclesiastical establishment of his day; given also his poetic genius, and his deep psychological insight, all of these forged on the anvil of his own suffering, it is not at all surprising that his work should be of interest to scholars from a vast range of disciplines. There is much to be learned from their labours, but in the midst of all the scholarly engagement with Kierkegaard we must remind ourselves that the reader he himself sought was one who was prepared to engage, not with his genius as an author, but with the existential challenge of the paradoxical self-presentation of God, and thus also with God's call upon every individual to a true realization of the self. In face of that challenge, Kierkegaard repeatedly reminds us that the self-important industry of the scholar can very easily become just one more form of evasion. An 'introduction' to the thought of Søren Kierkegaard ought to serve, in the end, therefore, merely as an encouragement to become one of Kierkegaard's 'readers', willing to 'read aloud', and with 'only yourself to consider' – yourself, that is, before God.[8]

Kierkegaard's overriding interest in what it means *to be* a Christian means that we do not find in him anything remotely resembling a systematic presentation of Christian doctrine. There is no discussion of the Trinity, though he frames his thought in Trinitarian terms. He says little of the resurrection, though the theme of giving up one's life in order to receive it back again is returned to again and again. He has nothing resembling a doctrine of creation, but consistently presupposes the divinely bestowed goodness of the created order. There is very little by way of eschatology except for the reminder that the decisions of faith bear upon the individual's eternal destiny. In these and in most other matters of theological interest, Kierkegaard has little argument with the standard doctrinal presentations of Christian faith. 'The doctrine in the established Church and its organization are very good', he says. 'But the lives, our lives – believe me, they are mediocre'.[9] Kierkegaard's interest, and the task of his authorship, lies in the accurate portrayal of what Christian *existence* entails. The doctrine is not in dispute. What matters is the degree to which the lives of those who claim to be Christian 'reduplicate' what is confessed with their lips. 'My thesis', he says, 'is not that the substance of what is proclaimed in Christendom as Christianity is not Christianity. No, my thesis is that the *proclamation* is not Christianity. I am fighting about a *how*, a reduplication. It is self-evident that without reduplication Christianity is not Christianity'.[10]

It would not do justice to Kierkegaard, therefore, indeed it would be a grave disservice to the reader of a work such as this, to attempt something resembling a systematic presentation of his theology. The approach I take instead is to try to let the central theological concerns of Kierkegaard emerge through the reading of his texts. The central concern with what it means to exist Christianly will be ever present, but as we circle around that theme, revisiting it again and again as it is developed through particular texts, we will gain some understanding of what he believes about God, about Christ and about the Spirit. We will discover what he thinks about the divine command to love your neighbour as yourself, about the relation between grace and works, about revelation, about Scripture, about prayer and about the sacrament of communion. We will learn something of Kierkegaard's conception of the atonement, and about the priestly role that Christ undertakes on our behalf. We will consider his account of the formation of the self, and learn what he has to say about anxiety and about sin. But in each case, the focus will be not on how best to formulate the Christian understanding of these things, as is the legitimate concern of systematic theology, but on how to give faithful expression to the Christian theological affirmations in the manner of one's existence.

Pursuit of that goal requires that we read not only the usual and most commonly studied works of Kierkegaard's corpus, principally the pseudonymous works, but also the works published under his own name, the several series of Discourses, the Journals of course, and also the prayers. Most of the Discourses are preceded by a prayer and these prayers, collectively, are as valuable a source of insight into Kierkegaard's theological convictions as any of the more celebrated works. The importance I will attach to the Discourses, including those published in the volumes *Works of Love*, *Judge for Yourself!* and *For Self-Examination* reflects Kierkegaard's own estimation of their importance.

Finally, and to reiterate, Kierkegaard's purpose as an author will be betrayed if this book is taken as a summary of his theological thought. Kierkegaard loathed the prospect of being treated as an object of scholarly attention. We conform much better to his own intentions if the reading of his work becomes an aid to devotion, to 'upbuilding' and to discipleship. If there are theological objections to be made to his particular construal of the Christian gospel, so be it. But Kierkegaard would urge, I suggest, that attention to his own failings not stand in the way of the much more important matter of reckoning with the gospel itself.

# Chapter 2

# A Life Directed by Governance

Søren Aabye Kierkegaard was born in Copenhagen in Denmark on 5 May 1813 and died on 11 November 1955. Although he died at the relatively young age of 42, Kierkegaard left behind a vast production of literary works running to about 25 books[1] and 20 volumes of Journals and Papers in which he made diary notes, experimented with drafts of his published work, and recorded his thoughts on all manner of subjects. Among the writings left unpublished in his own lifetime was an account of his authorship titled, *The Point of View for My Work as an Author*. In recent biographies of Kierkegaard, Alistair Hannay and Joakim Garff have argued that the numerous autobiographical notes in Kierkegaard's Journals and Papers were carefully crafted by Kierkegaard to convey a particular impression to those who, in years to come, would pore over his literary work in order to construct a portrait of the author himself. Be that as it may, Kierkegaard seems to have been genuinely convinced that his authorship, and indeed his whole life, was directed by 'Governance', that it was, in other words, God's purpose for him that his life should unfold as it did and that he should utilize the gifts of intellect and imagination that God had bestowed upon him, to present an account of what Christianity really is. 'To this', Kierkegaard wrote in his Journal, 'every hour of my day has been and is directed'.[2] It is clear that, in retrospect, Kierkegaard saw himself as having been shaped and moulded by God, even from childhood, to undertake this task. It is Kierkegaard who made the point that life can only be understood backwards, but it must be lived forward.[3] Retrospectively then, Kierkegaard claims to have seen the hand of 'Governance' over the whole of his life and confesses also that he could fulfil the task assigned to him by Governance only with God's help.

Kierkegaard thus regarded himself as one who stood in precisely the same position as that he sought for his readers, as one, that is, who stood in need of Christian formation.[4] Reflecting on his authorship in *The Point of View*, Kierkegaard insists that,

> Governance took the liberty of arranging the rest of my life [the period of his authorship] in such a way that there could be no misunderstanding – which indeed there never was from the beginning – as to whether it was I who needed Christianity or Christianity that needed me.[5]

Let us see then how that life was arranged in order to serve the intentions of 'Governance'.[6] Kierkegaard himself, 'in order to elucidate further the part of Governance in the authorship' offers an explanation of how he 'happened to become an author'.[7] The story does not begin happily, for Kierkegaard tells us that '[f]rom childhood on I have been in the grip of an enormous depression, the depth of which finds its only true manifestation in the equally enormous proficiency granted me to hide it under a seeming cheerfulness and zest for life'.[8] We will say more of this in a moment but first let us note Kierkegaard's own interpretation of 'the equally great magnitude of [his] depression and of [his] dissimulative art'. It signifies, he says, that 'I was assigned to myself and the God-relationship'. By temperament, personal circumstances[9] and, we are told, the direction of Governance, Kierkegaard was disposed to lead a solitary life in which the inward struggles of the self before God were to be played out with profound intensity. His solitude was accentuated by the concealment of his suffering from the public's gaze. Kierkegaard took great care over this concealment. He cultivated the appearance of a man about town, appearing regularly among the crowd at the theatre, for example, but returning home to write while the crowd took their seats before the play. He found it no effort to assume the role of 'life of the party', his wonderful wit providing easy entertainment for the crowd. But he knew the superficiality of that existence and confessed after one such occasion that he left and,

> . . . yes the dash ought to be as long as the radii of the earth's orbit———————————————————————————
> ————————————————————————————————
> ——————————and wanted to shoot myself.[10]

So great was the distance between the shallow superficiality of party-life and the intensity of his inner struggles.

Continuing the account of how he happened to become an author, Kierkegaard tells us that,

> As a child, I was rigorously and earnestly brought up in Christianity, insanely brought up, humanly speaking – already in earliest childhood I had overstrained myself under the impression that the depressed old man, who had laid it upon me, was himself sinking under – a child attired, how insane, as a depressed old man.[11]

The first 'depressed old man' mentioned in this passage was Søren's father, Michael Pedersen Kierkegaard (1756–1838), but the second is Søren himself, attired as a child with the melancholic disposition of his father. Michael Kierkegaard had begun life in humble surroundings, one of nine children of poor, serf-tenant farmers in the Danish province of Jutland. At the age of 12, Michael left home to work as a shepherd boy for a relative in a neighbouring parish. The bleak and inhospitable heaths of the Jutland peninsula made for a miserable existence for the young lad left alone for long hours to tend the sheep. One day the boy gave vent to his misery by cursing God for having dealt him such a cruel hand. It was a moment that would never be forgotten. Many years later, when the boy had grown to be an old man, the horror of the incident still weighed upon his family and Søren, the man's youngest son wrote in his Journal, 'How appalling for the man who, as a lad watching sheep on the Jutland heath, suffering painfully, hungry and exhausted, once stood on a hill and cursed God – and the man was unable to forget it when he was eighty-two years old'.[12]

Although Michael Kierkegaard lived a long life of austere piety and deep devotion to God, he felt himself unable to escape from the guilt and divine wrath incurred by that moment of sin against the Holy Spirit. Even his later prosperity was interpreted as a mark of God's judgement, for God, Michael believed, had loaded him up with material wealth, only to take away all that could have led to happiness. Michael's first wife and then, one by one, his children from a second marriage began to pre-decease him so that he became convinced that he would see the deaths of all those he loved and be left a lonely old man. As it was, five of his seven children died before him, leaving only Søren and another son, Peter, to escape the effects of the 'curse'. But did they? Søren tells us that he was afflicted by his father's depression even as a child, and he too, it seems, felt that the burden of guilt rested upon the whole family. In 1838, at about the time of his 25th birthday, and shortly before his father's death, Kierkegaard records the moment when he learned of his father's dark secret.

> Then it was that the great earthquake occurred, the frightful upheaval which suddenly drove me to a new infallible principle for interpreting all the phenomena. Then I surmised that my father's old-age was not a divine blessing, but rather a curse, that our family's exceptional intellectual capacities were only for mutual harrowing one another; then I felt the stillness of death deepen around me, when I saw in my father an unhappy man who would survive us all, a memorial cross on the grave of all his personal hopes. A guilt must rest upon the entire family, a punishment from God must be upon it: it was supposed to disappear, obliterated by the mighty hand of God, erased like a mistake, and only at times did I find a little relief in the thought that my father had been given the heavy duty of reassuring us all with the consolation of religion, telling us that a better world stands open for us even if we lost this one . . .[13]

Søren's religious upbringing was, undoubtedly, a strict one. It was a working out, perhaps, of the father's penance. The children were reared within the rigorous piety of the Moravian Brethren which, on account of its revival under Count Zinzendorf in Germany in the eighteenth century, had spread north to Scandinavia where it reached Copenhagen. While maintaining his allegiance to the State Lutheran church, Michael Kierkegaard was attracted by the energetic piety of the Moravians and by their well-considered opposition to the corrosive acids of Enlightenment rationalism. Michael had by this time made his way to Copenhagen to work as an apprentice in his uncle's clothing business. Before long he had advanced in the business and at the age of 24 he struck out on his own as a trader of cloth and textiles. His natural intelligence, business acumen and probable inheritance from his uncle, led to considerable success in business and to the amassing of sufficient wealth to retire in 1796 at only 40 years old. It has also been suggested, based on the testimony of Frederik Sibbern, a professor of philosophy in Copenhagen from 1813 to 1870, that Søren's father retired early under the belief, quite possibly brought on by his melancholia, that he would soon die.[14]

That grim outlook received nourishment, no doubt, from the death of his first wife, Kirstine Nielsdatter Røyen, who died childless in 1796 after only two years of marriage. Michael married again in 1797 but under circumstances that could well have inflicted further torment upon a guilt-ridden conscience. His second wife, Anne Sørensdatter Lund (1768–1834) had been a servant in the household and gave birth to a child only five months after the marriage. Despite the evident obligation to marry, there is evidence to suggest that Michael held Anne in great affection and that it was a happy and loving marriage. The epitaph on her gravestone records that she was 'loved and missed by her surviving children and friends, but especially by her old husband'.[15]

It was to Anne in 1913 that Søren was born, the last of seven children (three girls and four boys). Although his writings reveal little of his relationship with his mother, there appears to have been a warm and loving bond between them, and his mother's death in 1834 certainly caused him great distress.[16] At the time of Søren's birth, his father was 56 and would certainly have appeared as an 'old man' to the child during the course of Søren's upbringing. And yet the great difference in age between the father and his youngest son was no barrier to the formation of deep bonds of affection and respect between the two. Both, it appears, were highly intelligent, both shared extraordinary powers of imagination, and both possessed an acuity in philosophical and theological inquiry that became well honed through conversation with one another and with guests who Michael regularly invited to the home.

The younger Kierkegaard was introduced very early to the earnest piety and severe Christian sensibility of his father, to

the philosophical and theological debate that Michael cultivated among his friends, and sadly, as we have seen, to the
melancholic disposition of the older man. Kierkegaard reflects
a number of times in his Journals that he never had a childhood.[17] Set apart from his peers by the oddities of his dress
and frail appearance,[18] still more by his intellectual prowess, he
appears not to have established the usual friendships of childhood but was socialized into the world of his father. The one
notable exception was the friendship Kierkegaard established
with Emil Boesen who later became a pastor and who was
the only representative of the church with whom Kierkegaard
would talk in the final days of his life. Of his lost childhood,
however, Kierkegaard writes, 'I had not really lived except in
the category of mind and spirit; a human being I had not been,
child and youth least of all'.[19]

Although Søren describes his upbringing as 'insane' and while
he holds his father responsible for making him 'as unhappy as
possible', he also remembers fondly that he was 'the most affec-
tionate of fathers'.[20] His father's death, which came as a shock
to Søren who had inherited Michael Kierkegaard's gloomy
expectation that the father would outlive all his children, was
interpreted by Kierkegaard as a sacrificial death '*for* me, in order
that something, if possible, might still come of me'.[21] Devotion to
his father's memory is therefore not least among the motivating
factors undergirding the authorship. 'I am indebted to my father
for everything from the very beginning', Kierkegaard writes in
1848; 'Melancholy as he was, when he saw me melancholy, he
appealed to me: Be sure that you really love Jesus Christ'.[22] That
advice became the passion of Kierkegaard's life.

There is a passage in an early work, *De omnibus dubitandum
est*, in which Kierkegaard describes the childhood memories of
a character 'Johannes Climacus' whose requests to go out from
the house as a child were often refused but whose father occasionally compensated for the prohibition by taking the child in
hand and strolling up and down the floor. This appeared at first
to be little compensation but the father would take him on a
journey of the imagination, describing in vivid detail all that
would be seen along the way, just as if they had been out walking in the town.

[H]is father's omnipotent imagination was able to fashion everything, to use every childish wish as an ingredient in the drama that was taking place. For Johannes, it was as if the world came into existence during the conversation, as if his father were our Lord and he himself was the favored one who had permission to insert his own foolish whims as hilariously as he wished . . .[23]

Although it is not known to be the case for sure, there is strong evidence in the surrounding narrative to suggest that Kierkegaard here tells of his own childhood.[24] In any event Kierkegaard elsewhere comments on the extraordinary power of his father's imagination and indicates that his father's accounts of the biblical stories were just as vivid as those referred to in fictional guise. Paramount among the biblical stories that left a deep and lasting impression on Kierkegaard was the story of the crucifixion of Christ. What impressed the young child most of all in that story was the way in which the fickle crowd had turned against 'the most compassionate man who ever lived'.[25] The inexplicability of that would trouble Kierkegaard throughout his life, and accounts, in part, for the bitterness with which he denounced those in his own age who simply went along with the crowd.

Kierkegaard, as a child, is likely to have encountered similarly vivid accounts of Christ's suffering at meetings of the Moravian Brethren that the Kierkegaard family attended on Sunday afternoons. A sermon by curate Peter Saxtorp who was closely associated with the Moravian congregation gives an impression of the sombre Moravian piety in which Kierkegaard was raised.[26]

They spat in Christ's face, o, a frightful insult! We wretched earthworms view it as a great injury and as ill-treatment if someone merely spits *at* us. And here they are not merely spitting at Jesus or on His clothing but they spat right in His face. O, how great this insult was!

Much later Kierkegaard wrote in his Journal, '. . . already as a small child I was told – and as solemnly as possible – that "the crowds" spit upon Christ, who was in fact the truth. This I have hid deep in my heart . . . This thought is my life . . .'[27]

Solemn and strict though it may have been, Moravian piety provided, nevertheless, a counter to the rationalist Christianity of the Enlightenment, and encouraged a personal and heartfelt appropriation of the Christian faith. Involvement in the Moravian congregation was a departure too from the merely conventional religion often associated with an established church, according to which, as Kierkegaard would put it, one becomes a Christian simply by being born in Denmark. Danish citizenship was, at the time, restricted to those who were baptized members of the Danish Lutheran Church. Both distinguishing marks of the Moravian fellowship, its opposition to enlightenment rationalism and its departure from merely conventional religion, would be enduring themes of Kierkegaard's passionate and sometimes bitter critique of the church of his own day.

Despite their participation in the Moravian fellowship and their deep discomfort with conventional religion in Denmark, the Kierkegaard family retained their membership of the Lutheran Church and found cause to remain loyal to it through the influence of two men in particular, Nikolai F. S. Grundtvig (1783–1872) and Jakob Peter Mynster (1775–1854). Grundtvig was from 1822 the pastor at the Church of our Saviour in Copenhagen, but he had by that time gained fame – or notoriety, depending on one's point of view – for an attack upon the rationalist theology of Henrik Nicolaj Clausen (1793–1892), a professor of theology in Copenhagen. In contrast with a theology he thought to be detached, overly intellectual and elitist, Grundtvig emphasized the existential experience of God in Christ as the living Word who was present with the gathered congregation through Word and Sacrament. The authenticity of the divine Word was preserved for Grundtvig primarily in the living faith of the baptized community rather than in the text of Scripture considered accessible only through the work of modern historical-critical scholarship. Søren's older brother Peter Christian (1805–88), himself destined to become a pastor and eventually Lutheran bishop of Aalborg, became a 'moderate partisan' of Grundtvig's movement but, as Jørgen Bukdahl reports, Søren 'could never get past the bombastic, theatrical side of Grundtvig, which he viewed as self-indulgence, or worse'.[28] Joakim Garff likewise describes Kierkegaard's impatience with

Grundtvig's pomposity and sarcastic critique of Grundtvig's literary style, but he also notes a number of similarities between the two men.

> Both were critical of theological rationalism and of the speculative philosophy of one or another German vintage; both had advanced pedagogical views relative to their times, understanding that the truth is always dialogical and is not a disembodied, monological abstraction; both opposed their times' easygoing mixture of bourgeois virtues, spiritual humanism, and romantic sensitivity; both bound themselves — if in very different fashion — to the common man, the people; both knew that man is not (in Grundtvig's words) a 'sausage endowed with reason' but rather (in Kierkegaard's words) 'passion'; and both came to be in an increasingly strained relationship with the State Church and its representatives . . .[29]

Despite the similarities, however, and despite the alliance with Grundtvig maintained by his brother Peter, Kierkegaard's own loyalties, though increasingly strained, would remain with Jakob Mynster, the second of two influential Lutheran pastors who made regular visits to Kierkegaard's childhood home. From 1820 Mynster was the Kierkegaard family's own pastor. He too opposed the rationalism of much post-Enlightenment theology and emphasized the importance of a personal piety. He differed from Grundtvig, however, especially in his conviction that the State Church remained the proper and sufficient instrument for the nurturing of such piety. In 1826 Mynster became the royal chaplain and then in 1834 he was installed Primate of the Danish Church. Both positions confirmed Mynster's identification with the establishment. That such positions were occupied by an old family friend and his father's former pastor undoubtedly contributed to the allegiance Kierkegaard himself retained to the state church, but Kierkegaard's vehement attacks on the church placed the relationship with Mynster under considerable strain. Despite his view that Mynster was complicit in the faults of the established church, Kierkegaard never attacked Mynster personally. His problem was not with the theology that Mynster preached – that was doctrinally orthodox – but Mynster's cosy relation with the establishment and sanctioning of a comfortable, bourgeois religion stood in conflict with Kierkegaard's growing conviction that Christianity involved the renunciation of worldly comforts and an identification with Christ in his suffering. Above all, and in contrast to the pretence that being a Christian involved little more than being a good citizen in Christendom, Christianity, in Kierkegaard's view, involved an honest admission of the extent to which one fell short of the ideal of discipleship. Kierkegaard's complaint against the Church in Christendom was not that its members fall short of the ideal. His complaint, rather, was that the established Church provided absolution by redefining the ideal, by turning Christianity into something that everyone could manage without any alteration to their middle-class lives.

The gulf between that conception of things and Mynster's own view would be readily apparent to Mynster through his reading of Kierkegaard's published works, not least *Practice in Christianity* in which Kierkegaard, through the pseudonym Anti-Climacus, sets out the requirement for being a Christian. Kierkegaard expected Mynster to read it and to comment on it publicly, either to agree with Kierkegaard's account or to oppose it. But Mynster remained silent. Out of respect for his father, perhaps, and an unwillingness to offend the family friend, Kierkegaard too held his fire. But when Mynster died in 1854 and the then professor of theology in Copenhagen, Hans Lassen Martensen (1808–84), proclaimed in his funeral eulogy that Mynster had been a 'witness for the truth', Kierkegaard's fury was unleashed. A witness for the truth is one who follows Christ in his lowliness and suffering and even to his death, Kierkegaard believed. Mynster was not that, and the pretence that a life such as Mynster's constituted the ideal of discipleship was for Kierkegaard an intolerable betrayal of what Christ intends when he invites people to take up their cross and follow him. The attacks upon the Danish Church which had thus far been merely implicit in his published work or that lay concealed in his unpublished papers were now launched into the public arena with a bitterness that became obsessive. For the remaining months of his life, which were not many following Mynster's death, Kierkegaard kept up his attack on the official church and renounced his association with it.

> But one thing I will not do. No, not at any price will I do it; one thing I will not do; I will not participate, even if it were merely with the last fourth of the last joint of my little finger, in what is called official Christianity, which by suppression or artifice gives the appearance of being the Christianity of the New Testament, and on bended knee I thank my God that he mercifully has kept me from entering into it too far.[30]

That is what Kierkegaard's relationship with the state church came to in the end, but for most of his life Kierkegaard attended church regularly and several times he contemplated ordination and retreat to a quiet rural pastorate. At university Kierkegaard had undertaken the necessary studies in theology and had completed the preparations for ordination within the state church. That pattern of church attendance and his intermittent resolve to become a pastor suggests a more complex relationship with the church than the vehement attacks of his last year of life reveal. Many have read Kierkegaard's works, especially the *Attack Upon Christendom*, and have concluded that Kierkegaard was an inveterate opponent of the Church, but the matter is not so simple. Kierkegaard opposed the particular form the Church had taken in Christendom, most especially its alliance with the state,[31] but the Church conceived theologically as the communion of saints gathered to hear the Word preached and to receive the sacrament is approved by Kierkegaard, so long as 'the qualification in the direction of the existential' provided by the phrase 'communion of saints' is not overlooked.[32]

It must be acknowledged that Kierkegaard's studies in theology at the University of Copenhagen were undertaken somewhat as a matter of course rather than out of a strong personal interest in the subject. He remarks in a Journal entry, 'I am embarked on studies for the theological degree, an occupation that does not interest me in the least and which therefore is not going particularly quickly'.[33] It was his father's intention for him that Kierkegaard should follow his older brother Peter into the priesthood of the

Lutheran Church and, perhaps because he had no strong inclination to any other vocation, Kierkegaard embarked upon the necessary course of preparation. He demonstrated at university, however, little enthusiasm for the prospect of ordination and a lack of commitment to his studies that disturbed both his father and his older brother. Relations with his father deteriorated and Kierkegaard's life, now lived in lodgings of his own, became, to all-outward appearances, self-indulgent and rather aimless. Lack of enthusiasm for his theological studies did not, however, diminish the sharpness of his intellect nor the critical engagement with what was being taught by the largely undistinguished theological faculty at the university. As Kierkegaard listened to N. H. Clausen expound his rationalist theology and to the biblical scholars' dry expositions of the New Testament, he wondered whether 'the enormous mass of interpreters has on the whole done more harm than good to the understanding of the New Testament'.[34] The posing of the question by the 22-year-old student indicates that the lack of enthusiasm for the products of theological scholarship then being delivered in Copenhagen was not matched by a lack of interest in Christianity itself. We see in the citation above the beginnings of what would in fact become a principal concern of Kierkegaard's whole authorship, namely the yawning gulf between the Christianity presented to us in the Bible and the culturally domesticated form 'Christianity' had taken in Christendom.

Further indication of the young student's wrestling with the existential challenge of Christian faith comes from an oft-quoted passage written in his Journal during a period of study in Gilleleje in North Zealand. Kierkegaard writes:

> What I really need is to be clear about *what I am to do*, not what I must know, except in the way knowledge must precede all action. It is a question of understanding my own destiny, of seeing what the Deity really wants *me* to do; the thing is to find a truth which is truth *for me*, to find *the idea for which I am willing to live and die* . . . What use would it be to be able to propound the meaning of Christianity, to explain many separate facts, if it had no deeper meaning for *myself* and *my life*? . . . What use

would it be if truth were to stand there before me, cold and naked, not caring whether I acknowledged it or not, inducing an anxious shiver rather than trusting devotion? Certainly I won't deny that I still accept an *imperative of knowledge*, and that through it one can also influence people, but *then it must be taken up alive in me*, and *this* is what I now see as the main point. It is this my soul thirsts for as the African deserts thirst for water.[35]

The passage reveals the autobiographical detail of Kierkegaard's own restlessness as a young man and his longing for 'the idea for which I am willing to live and die', but it reveals also a further dominant theme in his subsequent authorship: it is not enough simply to accumulate knowledge and ideas; one must act. One's life must express the truth. Otherwise, what use would the truth be? Whatever the intellectual frustrations Kierkegaard may have had with the theological lectures heard at the University of Copenhagen, the greater frustration still was the failure to recognize that the main thing was to *be* a disciple. Jesus did not seek admirers who would merely contemplate what his life amounted to and write it up in learned books inaccessible to the 'common man'. Nor did he contemplate a church in cahoots with Caesar that offered priests a comfortable career as Christ's brocaded representatives. Jesus sought disciples who would take up the cross and follow him, whose lives conformed to the gospel that was preached. What use is it, Kierkegaard asked, to propound the meaning of Christianity if it has no deeper meaning for *me* and *my life*?

It was not just the theology professors, nor only the clergy who were guilty of this disjunction between the profession of Christian faith and a truly Christian life; the whole of Christendom was distinguished for Kierkegaard by the monstrous accommodation of the gospel to a comfortable, bourgeois existence. '. . . official Christianity', Kierkegaard would write towards the end of his life, 'the proclamation of official Christianity, is not in any sense the Christianity of the New Testament'.[36]

As a student, this critique of official Christianity and of its proclamation was still germinating in Kierkegaard's formidable intellect, but it was confined to his private journals and notebooks.

In public, for the meantime, Kierkegaard's polemical tempera-ment was turned to an altogether different and more frivolous purpose. In 1834, following a royal edict designed to stamp out 'impudent writing' a considerable controversy had erupted in Denmark concerning the freedom of the press. Kierkegaard's first venture into the debate took the form of a public response, presented at the Student Association, to an article by Johannes Ostermann which defended freedom of the press on the grounds that the press provided a voice for the marginalized and an advoc-ate against the government on behalf of the oppressed. This role was placed under threat, so Ostermann argued, by the king's introduction of censorship. Kierkegaard's response centred on the claim that the liberal press in Denmark had done precious little for the marginalized. Joakim Garff suggests that, 'reading between the lines' one may also detect an inference that it was the king himself who was to be thanked for any improvements in the lives of those disadvantaged in society. Kierkegaard mounted his offensive, it seems, not because of any particular loyalty to the king, nor because of an ideological objection to freedom of the press, but rather because he saw an opportunity to exercise his considerable wit in public debate and to receive the accolades of an appreciative audience. At least, that was the judgement of Ostermann himself who explained that Kierkegaard's lively intellect 'took hold of any issue in those days, and he exercised his brilliant dialectical skill and wit upon it. The fact that my defence [of freedom of the press] had met with a favourable reception pushed him into the opposite camp, where he allied himself more or less as a matter of indifference'.[37] The debate moved on into the printed media where Kierkegaard's con-tributions, published pseudonymously to begin with, attracted outrage and acclaim in more or less equal measure. One of those who delighted in Kierkegaard's contributions was J. L. Heiberg, the editor of the *Flyveposten*, 'the most elegant aesthetic jour-nal of the day'.[38] Heiberg was a man of culture, a poet, literary critic, aesthetician, playwright, director of the Royal Theatre and a key figure in the introduction of Hegel's philosophy to Denmark. The winning of Heiberg's approval and introduction to Heiberg's circle was a flattering development for the 23-year-old student, but Kierkegaard's delight in his association with

Heiberg would not endure long. He would later express disillusionment with a life devoted only to aesthetic ends and in time became a trenchant critic of Hegelian philosophy.

One further aspect of Kierkegaard's first ventures into publication requires mention here. Towards the conclusion of the debate over freedom of the press a new, anonymous writer entered the fray and mercilessly attacked Kierkegaard's character and appearance. While Kierkegaard emerged as the victor in the debate, the attacks *ad hominem* caused him some consternation, and, added to the teasing he received as a child at school, helped to establish a pattern of public ridicule that would recur several times in his life.

Alongside J. L. Heiberg, Prof. Martenson was another whose enthusiasm for the philosophy of Hegel profoundly influenced the Danish intellectual environment. Martenson was an ambitious man who cultivated his associations with any who might help to further his career. He was appointed Professor of Theology in Copenhagen in 1840, became Court Preacher in 1845 and succeeded Mynster as Bishop of Seeland in 1854. Martenson epitomized what Kierkegaard believed to be the faults of the church and of theology in Danish Christendom. He was thoroughly ensconced in the establishment, cultivated his relationships with the cultural elite, and propounded a theology that owed far too much, in Kierkegaard's view, to the speculative philosophy of the age. We find Kierkegaard asking, 'But Martensen's own existence – what does this express? It expresses that he wants to be a success in the world, have great honour and regard, be in high office, etc. – is this the actualisation of Christianity?'[39]

Kierkegaard found few allies in his opposition to Hegelian philosophy, but among them was Poul Martin Møller an eccentric poet and scholar who was professor of philosophy at the University of Copenhagen from 1830 to 1838. Møller too had been part of J. L. Heiberg's circle of cultural and intellectual elite but soon went his own way and rejected Heiberg's enthusiasm for Hegel. Both Møller's rejection of Hegel and his poetic sensibility were attractive to Kierkegaard as were also Møller's admiration for Socrates, his impatience with 'unfeeling thinking' and his emphasis upon 'personal interest' and subjectivity.[40] Møller's philosophy was not the stuff of abstract speculation but was lived out in conversations in the market square and with ordinary people. Møller appears to have been something of a mentor to Kierkegaard during the latter's student years and his influence probably contributed significantly to Kierkegaard's decision to take an advanced degree in philosophy, rather than in theology, and to write his dissertation on 'The Concept of Irony, with Continual Reference to Socrates'. In a Journal entry dated April 1838, the 24-year-old student indicates a new resolve, apparently prompted by Møller's death the previous month: 'Such a long period has elapsed in which I have been unable to concentrate on the least little thing – now I must make another attempt. Paul Møller is dead'.[41]

There were other events that same year that mark 1838 as a decisive turning point in Kierkegaard's life. We have learned already that in the months beginning the new year Kierkegaard had been 'unable to concentrate on the least little thing'. Estrangement from his father is one possible cause of his listlessness. Michael Kierkegaard would not have been impressed with his son's casual attitude to his university studies or by his lack of enthusiasm for the path toward ordination mapped out for him by his father. Søren, meanwhile, had moved out of the family home into lodgings of his own, thus giving very concrete expression to the growing rift between father and son. Never a well man, Kierkegaard was especially ill during the winter months and the physical weakness seems to have contributed further to his depressed spirit. In February his brother Peter Christian reported that 'Søren has recently become more and more sickly, vacillating and dejected. And my conversations with him, which I generally have to initiate, do not produce any perceptible difference'.[42] Kierkegaard appears to have found little solace in Christian faith at the time. In April he wrote, 'If Christ is to come and live in me, it will have to be according to the Gospel for the day given in the almanac: Christ enters through closed doors'.[43] But then there comes a sudden change. On May 19 an entry appears in the Journal in stark contrast with the dejected tone of the preceding entries:

There is an *indescribable joy* that glows all through us
just as inexplicably as the apostle's exclamation breaks

forth for no apparent reason: 'Rejoice, and again I say, Rejoice'. – Not a joy over this or that, but the soul's full outcry 'with tongue and mouth and from the bottom of the heart': 'I rejoice for my joy, by, in, with, about, over, for and with my joy' – a heavenly refrain which, as it were, suddenly interrupts our other singing, a joy which cools and refreshes like a breath of air, a breeze from the trade winds which blow across the plains of Mamre to the everlasting mansions.[44]

We do not know exactly what prompted this outburst of joy, but a Journal entry just a few weeks later on July 9 suggests an experience of Christian conversion.

I am going to work toward a far more inward relation to Christianity, for up until now I have in a way been standing completely outside of it while fighting for its truth; like Simon of Cyrene (Lk. 23.26), I have carried Christ's cross in a purely external way.[45]

That Kierkegaard returned with new conviction to the faith in which he had been raised must have brought great joy to his aging father and it became the occasion of a reconciliation between the two. It is doubtful whether Kierkegaard, even as a student about town, was ever a prolific sower of wild oats,[46] but there are overtones of the biblical story of the prodigal son when on July 10 he wrote:

I hope that my contentment with my life *here at home* will turn out to be like that of a man I once read about. He, too, was fed up with home and wanted to ride away from it. When he had gone a little way, his horse stumbled and he fell off, and as he got up on his feet he happened to see his home, which now looked so beautiful to him that he promptly mounted his horse, rode home, and stayed home. It depends on getting the right perspective.[47]

The talk of returning 'home' could refer equally to the family home and to the Christian faith that Kierkegaard had learned under his father's tutelage. A day earlier he had written, 'How I thank you, Father in heaven, for having kept an earthly father present for a time on earth, where I so greatly need him; with your help I hope that he will have greater joy in being my father the second time than he had the first time'.[48]

As it turned out, Michael Kierkegaard had only one further month to enjoy being a father to his son. He died on 9 August 1838 aged 81 years, grateful at last to embark upon his 'home-ward journey'.[49] Søren's Journal entry marking his father's death reveals both the affection which he felt for his father and the religious terms in which he understood the bond between them. Under a cross sketched into the Journal, Kierkegaard wrote:

> My father died on Wednesday (the 8th) [sic] at 2.00 A.M I so deeply desired that he might have lived a few years more, and I regard his death as the last sacrifice of his love for me, because in dying he did not depart *from* me but he died *for* me, in order that something, if possible, might still come of me. Most precious of all that I have inherited from him is his memory, his transfigured image, transfigured by many little single episodes I am now learning about, and this memory I will try to keep most secret from the world. Right now I feel there *is* only *one* person (E. Boesen) with whom I can really talk about him. He was a 'faithful friend'.[50]

Kierkegaard recognized the high hopes his father had for him and the extensive nurture and support his father had offered him in service of those hopes. With his new found determination to complete his studies and, more importantly still, the discovery of a heartfelt Christian faith, Kierkegaard felt that it was possible after all 'that something might still come of me'. Indeed the strange conclusion that his father had died 'for him', appears a little less strange when set in the context of the family's expectation that on account of the curse, the father would outlive his children. By dying first, Søren surmised, his father had given him a reprieve. The onus was upon him now to make something of his life. By dying when he did, Michael Kierkegaard bestowed a further gift upon his son, a financial inheritance that enabled

Søren to devote himself to his writing without ever having to take paid employment. There were times when Søren contemplated taking a pastorate, in part out of concern that his money might run out, but that never proved necessary. Although his Journals record some anxiety about his finances from time to time, the inherited money lasted until the time of his death in 1855 thereby enabling the completion of his studies at the university and, thereafter, a full-time devotion to his authorship. The hand of Governance, it may be argued, had provided all that was necessary in order that Kierkegaard should fulfil the task to which he felt himself called.

The deaths of Møller and then of his father concentrated Kierkegaard's mind upon his studies. It was surely through the exercise of his intellectual gifts that the memory of the two men and the encouragement they gave to him might best be honoured. He enrolled for the examination in theology, which he completed with the grade *laudabilis* in 1840, enrolled in the pastoral seminary in November of that year, and at the same time commenced work on *The Concept of Irony* in fulfilment of the requirements of a Magister degree in philosophy. Kierkegaard defended his dissertation in 1841 having gained special permission from the King to present it in Danish rather than in the customary Latin. The King stipulated, however, that the oral examination should be conducted in Latin. That presented no difficulty for Kierkegaard who excelled in linguistic examinations throughout his career at school and then at university.

The three years following his father's death thus proved to be the most productive of Kierkegaard's life thus far. He completed both his theology degree and the dissertation in philosophy, but in addition he published his first major work, *From the Papers of One Still Living, Published Against His Will by S. Kjerkegaard*,[51] a small book in which he offered an analysis of a recently published novel by Hans Christian Andersen. The analysis was not complimentary. Foreshadowing a recurring theme of his later authorship, Kierkegaard complained that Andersen 'totally lacks a life-view'. A life-view, Kierkegaard explains, is

'more than a quintessence or a sum of propositions maintained in its abstract neutrality; it is more than

23

experience [*Erfaring*], which is as such always fragmentary. It is, namely, the transubstantiation of experience; it is an unshakeable certainty in oneself won from all experience [*Empirie*], whether this has oriented itself only in all worldly relationships (a purely human standpoint, Stoicism, for example, by which means it keeps itself from contact with a deeper experience – or whether in its heavenward direction (the religious) it has found therein the centre as much for its heavenly as its earthly existence, has won the true Christian conviction that neither death, nor life, nor angels, nor principalities, nor powers, nor the present, nor the future, nor height, nor depth, nor any other creation will be able to separate us from the love of God in Christ Jesus our Lord'.[52]

What Kierkegaard here says about the necessity of a life-view recalls his own desire, expressed in his Journal two years earlier, 'to find a truth which is truth *for me*, to find *the idea for which I am willing to live and die . . .*'. To live requires commitment and passion, it requires that we hold fast to an idea 'with the passion of inwardness', even when all worldly appearances may seem to contradict the idea. It mattered, above all, for Kierkegaard, that one should live and die for 'the love of God in Jesus Christ our Lord', but in the first instance it matters simply that one makes a commitment to some view of life, even, for example, to Stoicism. What is intolerable, especially in an author, is an absence of passion, and the readiness to go along unthinkingly with the crowd. To live with the infinite passion of inwardness, on the other hand, was to die to the world, and to have one's life be formed under the governance of something other and less fickle than the spirit of the age. Perhaps, as Joakim Garff suggests, the title of his treatise on Andersen, *From the Papers of One Still Living,* constitutes an admission by Kierkegaard that he too stood in need of this dying to the world.[53] For all that Kierkegaard strove to make clear what a truly human life consisted in, it remained a constant of his authorship that he never set himself up as the ideal.

There was another, however, who Kierkegaard did idealize, a young girl, Regine Olsen, who Kierkegaard first met in 1837 when she was 15 years old and he 23. Most biographers report that Kierkegaard was immediately entranced by the young girl but the evidence for that claim is slim, consisting in two journal entries recounting a visit to the Rørdam family on which occasion Regine was present. The Journal entries do not mention Regine by name but speak fretfully of 'the devil of my wit . . . who places himself between me and every innocent girlish heart', and, in the second entry, of an 'inclination that begins to stir'.[54] There is no doubt that the inclination disturbed him greatly but that Regine was the cause of his disturbance is by no means clear. It is a much later Journal entry that confirms that Kierkegaard's affections for Regine had developed, if not at their first meeting, then within the following year. In 1849, long after an engagement had been entered into and then broken, and two years after Regine herself had become married to Frederik Schlegel, Kierkegaard gives a lengthy account of the relationship between the two. He confirms that it was at the Rørdam household that he first met Regina but says nothing to suggest that he was instantly infatuated. He does tell us, however, that, 'Even before my father died my mind was made up about her. He died. I studied for the examination. During all that time I let her life become entwined in mine'.[55] A confession of his love committed to his Journal on 2 February 1839 reveals both the gift of literary expression with which Kierkegaard had been endowed and the extent to which he had idealized Regine.

You, sovereign queen of my heart, 'Regina', hidden in the deepest secrecy of my breast, in the fullness of my life-idea. There where it is just as far to heaven as to hell – unknown divinity! O, can I really believe the poets when they say that the first time one sees the beloved object he thinks he has seen her long before . . . Everywhere, in the face of every girl, I see features of your beauty, but I think I would have to possess the beauty of all the girls in the world to extract your beauty, that I would have to sail around the world to find the portion of the world I want and toward which the deepest secret of my self polarically points – and in the next moment you are so close to me, so present, so overwhelmingly filling my spirit that I am transfigured to myself and feel that here it is good to be.[56]

It was a full 18 months later, however, on 8 August 1840 that Kierkegaard first declared his love to Regina herself. While listening to her play the piano he threw the music aside and said, 'O, what do I care about music; it is you I seek, for two years I have been seeking you'.[57] Regine remained silent, but after her father had given his blessing, Regine accepted Kierkegaard's proposal of marriage.

'The next day', writes Kierkegaard, 'I saw that I had made a mistake'.[58] Why he considered it to be a mistake and why, a year later, he would break off the engagement remains the subject of speculation but two factors seem the most likely cause. Immediately after confessing the engagement to be a mistake, Kierkegaard continues with his Journal account: 'Penitent that I was, my *vita ante acta,* [life before the act] my melancholy – that was sufficient'. Kierkegaard knew his vulnerability to depression, he knew the deep troughs of anguish into which he would sometimes descend and, out of love, he felt unable to yoke Regina to the burden of his melancholy.

> If I had not found my melancholy and depression to be
> nothing but a blessing, it would have been impossible
> to live without her. The few scattered days I have been,
> humanly speaking, really happy, I always have longed
> indescribably for her, her whom I have loved so dearly
> and who also with her pleading moved me so deeply. But
> my melancholy and spiritual suffering have made me,
> humanly speaking, continually unhappy – and thus I had
> no joy to share with her.[59]

The shadow of melancholy that lay over Kierkegaard's life is cited again in the following entry as a reason for preventing the marriage. But we learn also here of Kierkegaard's belief that God had called him away.

> What was my thought when I left her? It was: I am a
> penitent; marriage is an impossibility; there will always
> be a shadow to make it unhappy and that also protests the
> wedding. On the other hand – and God knows I thought
> of this too, even though I wanted to forget it or pretended

to have forgotten it – on the other hand, the decisively religious life, for which I feel a need and for which I as a penitent must have the possibility if I want to be honest with God, cannot be combined with marriage.[60]

The 'idea for which I am willing to live and die' is here seen to be taking a stronger hold on the young man. That idea was Christianity and it demanded of him here that he give up his intended marriage so that he could devote himself to his authorship, an authorship dedicated to the clarification of what Christianity really is.[61] 'It was a frightfully painful time', Kierkegaard further confesses, '– to have to be so cruel and to love as I did. She fought like a lioness; if I had not believed there was divine opposition, she would have won'.[62] To give up everything for God's sake would become a recurring theme of the authorship. Although Kierkegaard denies that his published works were in any sense autobiographical, it is clear to see that his particular conception of the nature of Christian faith was wrought upon the anvil of his own life experience.

Regine did fight hard against the split, but for Kierkegaard, there was no turning back. In order to repulse her, and in an effort to preserve her reputation, Kierkegaard made himself out to be a scoundrel, a man about town who had other women to pursue. The gossips in Copenhagen took the bait, but Regine herself was not deceived. She maintained her affection for him, as did he for her. She became 'my reader' to whom Kierkegaard's writings, in particular the religious discourses, were dedicated, and he, in pursuing his divine calling, remained one in whom she had 'unshakeable faith'.[63] Two weeks after breaking off his engagement, Kierkegaard left Copenhagen for Berlin. 'I suffered exceedingly', he wrote. 'I was reminded of her every day. Up to this day [now in 1849] I have unconditionally kept my resolve to pray for her at least once every day, often twice, besides thinking about her as usual'.[64] In the year of his death Kierkegaard named,

. . . the two people whom I love most, to whom I owe whatever I have become as an author; an old man – the errors of his melancholy love; a very young girl, almost a mere child – the lovable tears of her misunderstanding.[65]

The Journals leave no indication of his purpose in going to Berlin except for their disclosure that he attended lectures in Berlin at the University. After initially appreciating Friedrich Schelling's lectures on the 'Philosophy of Revelation', he eventually tired of them and reported in a letter to Emil Boesen that 'Schelling talks endless nonsense both in an extensive and an intensive sense'.[66] The letters to Boesen were dominated, however, by repeated enquiries about Regine's well-being, in every case accompanied by the strict instruction to Boesen that on no account should she or anyone else learn of Kierkegaard's continuing devotion to her. The period in Berlin is notable too for the habit of prolific industry that Kierkegaard established there. In a little over four months he completed a substantial portion of *Either/Or*, eventually published in two volumes running to 864 pages. *Either/Or* caused a sensation in Copenhagen, principally because of 'A Seducer's Diary', a segment of the book offering an intricate portrayal of the seducer's art. In part one of *Either/Or* Kierkegaard reveals the mind of one who lives the life of an aesthete devoted to the pursuit of pleasure and novelty. Then, in part two, a stern Judge William writes letters to the young man of part one, admonishes him for his wanton lifestyle and urges him to adopt an ethical view. The whole thing ends with a sermon in which is introduced the religious notion that 'in relation to God we are always in the wrong'. The book thus presents an array of life-views, the aesthetic, the ethical, and, briefly, the religious, all published under the name of a pseudonymous editor, Victor Eremita, who claims to have found the papers comprising the book in a writing desk he had purchased at a second-hand store.[67] Thus begins Kierkegaard's authorship proper. Life is a serious business; we may take up one of several stances in relation to it, aesthetic, ethical or religious, but whatever our choice, we are to take responsibility, and for that we must understand clearly what each position involves. Kierkegaard's authorship consists in a striving for clarity, and especially for clarity about what Christianity involves.

*Either/Or* was published in February 1843 and gave rise to speculation about who its true author was. Kierkegaard did little, apparently, to conceal his identity as the author, even noting in his Journal that the Seducer's Diary was 'intended to repulse' to cement in Regine's mind, as also in the mind of the public, the thought that Kierkegaard himself was a scoundrel whom Regine was best rid of.[68] In May that same year, Kierkegaard published under his own name *Two Upbuilding Discourses*, the first on Gal. 3.23–29 and the second on Jas 1.17–22.[69] These were the first two of eighteen discourses that would be published by Kierkegaard in six collections between May 1843 and August 1844, proof, he would later claim, that he was a religious author from first to last.[70] Kierkegaard was concerned that if the Discourses were discounted it might be said that his authorship indicated that he, as author, had changed over the years,[71] but the Discourses, from the beginning, serve directly the purpose undertaken indirectly by means of the pseudonymous works: 'to *make men aware* of the essentially Christian'.[72] Kierkegaard insists that the two strands of his authorship, the aesthetic and the religious, in fact serve a single *religious* purpose.

> . . . the duplexity is there from the very beginning. *Two Upbuilding Discourses* is concurrent with *Either/Or*. The duplexity in the deeper sense, that is, in the sense of the whole authorship, was certainly not what there was to talk about at the time: the first and second parts of *Either/Or*. No, the duplexity was: *Either/Or* – and *Two Upbuilding Discourses*.[73]

The central distinction with which Kierkegaard is concerned is not between the aesthetic life and the ethical, as might be supposed on the basis of *Either/Or*, but between Christianity and the non-Christian. That is the distinction, Kierkegaard believed, that had been entirely clouded over in his own time.

The pattern thus established of publishing discourses under his own name alongside the pseudonymous works continued throughout Kierkegaard's authorship. In the preface to *The Lily in the Field and the Bird of the Air*, published in 1849, Kierkegaard expresses the hope that his reader will be 'reminded of the preface to the two upbuilding discourses of 1844: "It is offered with the right hand" – in contrast to the pseudonyms, which were held out and are held out with the left hand'.[74] What is the difference indicated here? It is that the discourses are addressed to the reader who knows what it is to be a Christian. Kierkegaard may speak directly to such a reader. In works given with the left hand, however, he addresses those who mistakenly believe themselves to be Christian, who do not in fact know what it is to be Christian, and to whom, therefore, he must speak indirectly. 'My task is to get men deceived – within the meaning of truth – into religious commitment, which they have cast off . . .'[75] The strategy of indirect communication, of deception, will be demonstrated in subsequent chapters when we consider the pseudonymous works in more detail, but an outline of the strategy is ventured here. To communicate effectively with those who are deceived requires, Kierkegaard suggests, that we play along with the deception, at least to begin with. In a culture committed to rationalism and objectivity and which insists that truth is accessible only through such means, Kierkegaard, through the pseudonym Johannes Climacus, for instance, opts to play along, to undertake in *Philosophical Fragments* a little philosophy of his own designed to captivate those who suppose that everything will be revealed through rational thought. But the 'thought experiment' is a deception. As it turns out, the reader is caught in a trap. She is confronted in the end with an account of Christianity that accords completely with that of the New Testament – and so must be admitted to be true by one who understands herself to be a Christian – and yet is radically at odds with the prevailing, rational account of what Christianity is. The reader has been taken unawares, has been enticed upon a journey of rational deliberation, only to discover that revelation rather than reason provides the most compelling claim to truth.

There is a further, equally important, reason for the strategy of indirect communication: in the matter of what it means to exist, readers must be engaged existentially. They must be brought to the position where a subjective appropriation of the truth becomes possible. Only in that way can they be said to be 'in the truth'. This is not achieved merely by presenting someone with the facts. Direct communication may do that, but it will do no good in Christendom to advise people that they are not Christian after all. 'Who are you to tell us that we are not Christian?', the cultured defenders of Christianity might say; 'We have it on good authority [the authority of reason no less], that everyone in Denmark is a Christian. Can you not see that we attend church regularly and are respected citizens in this city? How dare you claim that we are not Christian?'

The truth must be approached by some other means. Another way must be found to bring people to the recognition that their lives are lived in immediacy and do not express the essentially Christian.

> . . . one does not begin *directly* with what one wishes to communicate but begins by taking the other's delusion at face value. Thus one does not begin . . . in this way: I am a Christian, you are not a Christian – but this way: You are a Christian, I am not a Christian. Or one does not begin in this way: It is Christianity that I am proclaiming, and you are living in purely esthetic categories. No, one begins this way: Let us talk about the esthetic. The deception consists in one's speaking this way precisely in order to arrive at the religious. But according to the assumption the other person is in fact under the delusion that the esthetic is the essentially Christian, since he thinks he is a Christian and yet he is living in esthetic categories.[76]

The strategy is to allow deluded readers to discover for themselves, under the maieutic guidance offered by the pseudonymous authors, that their lives express something utterly at odds with authentic Christian faith.

Having embarked, then, upon this strategy, Kierkegaard pursues it with astonishing industry. The publication of *Either/ Or* in February 1843 was followed by *Two Upbuilding Discourses* published on May 16 that same year. *Repetition, Fear and Trembling* and *Three Upbuilding Discourses*, all appeared on 16 October and before the year was out a further *Four Upbuilding Discourses* were offered for those who could keep up. 1844 saw no let up. A further *Two Upbuilding Discourses* appeared in March, *Three Upbuilding Discourses* in June and in the same month, *Philosophical Fragments*, *The Concept of Anxiety* and *Prefaces*. There were a further *Four Upbuilding Discourses* published in August. The pace slowed a little in 1845 and 1846 but among other smaller works published in those years, the two massive volumes, *Stages on Life's Way* and *Concluding Unscientific Postscript to Philosophical Fragments*, were offered to Copenhagen's reading public.

This last work is described by Kierkegaard as the midpoint of the authorship.[77] It is that work he says, 'which poses the issue, which is the issue κατ᾽ ἐξοχήν [in the eminent sense] of the whole authorship: becoming a *Christian*'.[78] Thereafter, 'the exclusively religious writing begins: *Upbuilding Discourses in Various Spirits, Works of Love Christian Discourses*'.[79] Kierkegaard does not mean here that the religious writing as such begins here, only that henceforward he confines himself to 'direct' religious writing and no longer engages in the pseudonymous, aesthetic mode of communication. That is not, however, entirely true. A little aesthetic article by 'Inter et Inter' is published in a newspaper in July 1848, *The Crisis and a Crisis in the Life of and Actress*, and in 1849 he again adopts the pseudonymous strategy in publishing *Two Ethical Religious Essays* by H. H and *The Sickness Unto Death* by Anti-Climacus who appears again in 1850 as the author of *Practice in Christianity*. Anti-Climacus is engaged to represent the exemplarily Christian, however, a position that sets him apart from the other pseudonyms and, by his own admission, also from Kierkegaard himself.

In 1854 the authorship takes a different turn. Bishop Mynster had died in January of that year, and in April, H. L. Martenson succeeded him as primate of the Danish Church. Whereas Mynster had redeeming features that dissuaded Kierkegaard from attacking in public either Mynster himself or the church he stood for, Kierkegaard felt no such allegiance to Martenson. On 18 December, Kierkegaard published the first of a series of articles directly attacking Martenson and the Danish Church. There were no more pseudonymous works, and no more indirect communications. Kierkegaard in his final year of life writes in somewhat embittered style against the monstrous illusion that all are Christians in Christendom. No longer does he shrink from saying directly, 'you are not Christian', and, as he himself predicted when in calmer state of mind, the people of Copenhagen took umbrage and answered back with mocking derision of their own.

> Søren Kierkegaard, who shouts that the Church of Christ
> has perished, is for me like a bogey who screeches to

terrify the unbelieving and superstitious children of
this world. But a Christian laughs at him. If he went to
the ends of the earth like the Shoemaker of Jerusalem,
shouting that the Church of Christ has perished, I would
ask that I might be permitted to walk behind him and
say: 'You are lying, Søren! According to the testimony of
Christ and the Spirit of God, you are a great liar!'[80]

Such was the response of Pastor Hans Rørdam during the
height of the controversy. The battle and the derision took its
toll and left Kierkegaard with little energy to fight the ravages
that recurring illness had imposed upon his fragile frame. On 2
October 1855 Kierkegaard was admitted to Frederiks Hospital
and on 11 November he died.

Even on his deathbed, however, with little strength and only a few
days left to him, Kierkegaard's battle against 'the play–Christianity
of the pastors'[81] continued. Emil Boesen, who was the most regular
visitor to his hospital bedside, reports that Kierkegaard refused to see
any pastors, including his own brother.

He had slept a couple of hours the evening before and
was in good spirits. His brother had been there but
had not been permitted to come in. S. K. said that he
[Kierkegaard's brother, Peter Christian] could be stopped
not by debate but by action, and in this manner he had
taken action and stopped him.

Won't you take Holy Communion?
'Yes, but not from a pastor, from a layman'
That would be quite difficult to arrange.
'Then I will die without it'.
That's not right!
'We cannot debate it. I have made my choice. I have
chosen. The pastors are civil servants of the Crown and
have nothing to do with Christianity'.[82]

His argument was with 'official Christianity'. So far was it
from the Christianity of the New Testament that Kierkegaard
could make no peace with it, or with the pastors who defended

it. But he did find peace with God. When Boesen observes that Kierkegaard 'believes in Christ and takes refuge in him in God's name', the response comes, 'Yes, of course, what else?'[83] In a Journal entry from 1848, Kierkegaard's gratitude to God is expressed at more length.

> I almost feel an urge to say not one single word more except: Amen, for I am overwhelmed with gratitude for what Governance has done for me. That everything actually can turn out for a man this way – I know of nothing that has happened to me of which I poetically might not say it is the only thing which is appropriate to my nature and it is impossible for me to conceive that I could be happy without having to become someone else. My unhappiness became my blessing. I am saved, humanly speaking, by one who is dead and gone, my father, but it is impossible for me to conceive of any living person's being able to save me. Then I became an author, precisely according to my potentialities; then I was persecuted – but without it my life would not have been my own. Melancholy shadows everything in my life, but that, too, is an indescribable blessing. That is precisely how I became myself by the indescribable grace and help of God; I could almost be tempted to say by his partiality, if this were not less to me than the blessed thought which I believe and which puts my mind at rest; that he loves every man in the same way.
>
> In all literalness I have lived with God as one lives with a father. Amen.[84]

# Chapter 3

# What it Means to Become a Christian

*. . . my whole authorship pertains to Christianity, to the issue: becoming a Christian, with direct and indirect polemical aim at that enormous illusion, Christendom . . .*[1]

We will begin with Johannes Climacus and with his question: 'How can I, Johannes Climacus, share in the happiness that Christianity promises?'[2] There are important things to notice about this question, among which are, first, that Climacus asks, 'how', implying that in the matter of Christianity there is something to be done, and second, that the question concerns the individual – we cannot become Christian just by going along with the crowd. The question recalls the query of the young man who came to Jesus asking, 'what must I do to inherit eternal life?' (Lk. 18.18–25), to which Jesus offered no universal formula but a challenge addressed to the young man's point of greatest resistance: 'Sell all that you own and distribute the money to the poor, and you will have treasure in heaven; then come follow me'. The 'following me' is, of course, crucial, and we will return to the point in due course, but the first problem to deal with is the obstacle in the way of following Christ. That is also the problem for Climacus who has two obstacles, not one, in the way of becoming a Christian. The first problem, he is well on the way to dealing with; it is the problem of Christendom, that cultural landscape in which it is supposed that everyone is Christian without having to do anything at all. Climacus, however, has discovered that Christianity requires something more of him. But what? Here the second obstacle proves much more difficult to overcome. It is the obstacle posed by the supposition in Modernity that everything must be reasonable, that we cannot commit ourselves to anything about which there is the least bit of reasonable doubt. The difficulty is, in Modernity, that setting aside one's reason is every bit as scandalous as selling all one's possessions and distributing the money to the poor.

In light of that obstacle, Climacus sets out in *Concluding Unscientific Postscript* to deal first with the objective issue through which it will be made clear that human reason cannot master the subject matter of Christian faith, and then with the subjective issue in which Climacus will explore what is involved in following Christ without the benefit of reason's guiding light. 'The objective issue, then, would be about the truth of Christianity. The subjective issue is about the individual's relation to Christianity'.[3] Before we explore the matter further, however, let us pause to consider who this enquirer is and why it is that Kierkegaard adopts a pseudonym for his enquiries. Johannes Climacus, the pseudonymous author of *Philosophical Fragments* and *Concluding Unscientific Postscript to Philosophical Fragments,* takes his name from Saint John Climacus, a sixth century Christian monk from the monastery of Mt Sinai who wrote a celebrated work, the *Climax* (Scala in Latin) or *Ladder of Divine Ascent.* The book describes how one may ascend to God, thus addressing the very problem that Kierkegaard's Climacus has in view. Kierkegaard positions Climacus at the foot of the ladder, willing and eager to make the ascent, as yet unsure of all the steps to be undertaken, but well-armed, he thinks, with the considerable resources of human reason. This is the position in which we find him at the beginning of *Philosophical Fragments* and from there he embarks upon a thought experiment, determined to learn the truth.

This is not Kierkegaard's own position. Kierkegaard himself has committed himself to the truth of Christianity and to the way of Christian discipleship, although he studiously avoids portraying himself as a model for others. Nor does Kierkegaard believe, as Climacus does at the outset, that human reason is a sufficient resource for the understanding of truth. Climacus is a philosopher, but humble with it. He has no 'system' but only a few fragments or scraps to offer.[4] He recognizes, furthermore, that he has much to learn, and he sets out to learn it armed with the tools commended by his speculative philosophical age. Those willing to accompany him, who are attracted by the invitation to engage in a 'thought experiment', will find, however, that the presumed competence of speculative reason is more and more called into question by the truth that is encountered in Christ.

## a. Can the Truth be Learned?

*Philosophical Fragments* begins with the question, 'Can the truth be learned?' It soon becomes apparent that the particular truth in question is the truth embodied in 'the God-man', the truth, that is, of Jesus Christ. The Age of Reason was not antagonistic to the claim that the truth was made known in Jesus, but the truth revealed in him ought to conform, it was believed, to the dictates of human reason. Post Enlightenment reflection on the truth claims of Christianity had yielded several strategies for ensuring such conformity. The first, chronologically speaking, was that of G. E. Lessing who, despairing of the possibility of deriving from the record of Jesus' history the theological claims about his being the Son of God, concluded that the enduring and rationally ascertainable truth conveyed through Jesus was the truth of his ethical teaching, summarized, above all, in the command to 'love one another'.[5] Alerted by Lessing to the impossibility of deriving from history the theological affirmations about Jesus contained in the Christian creeds, D. F. Strauss, and many after him, set aside the traditional affirmations of faith and attempted to discern instead which if any of the customary claims about Jesus could be supported by rational, historical enquiry. That industry has continued through successive waves of the quest for the historical Jesus, each of which confirms once more that historical enquiry cannot confirm what Christian faith proclaims to be true.[6] Those determined to reject all claims that do not conform to the canons of historical method then set about constructing a picture of Jesus in which they can believe. Kierkegaard examines and critiques both these approaches at numerous points in his corpus, but there is a third approach to Jesus favoured in the Age of Reason which is the principal concern of the thought experiment in *Philosophical Fragments*. This is the approach of Hegel who recasts the truths primitively expressed in the New Testament into a grand philosophical scheme within which the incarnation is construed as an expression of the true identity of all humanity as a synthesis of matter and spirit, and the unfolding of the divine being itself. This pantheistic vision entails that the spark of divine truth rests within us all and can be brought to consciousness through the determined application of reason. Jesus Christ, at once both divine and human, instantiates and reveals the true identity of humanity as a whole.

An Hegelian response to the question, 'Can the truth be learned', is that it may be learned by virtue of the fact that it already lies within the human mind or soul. Knowledge of all truth is latent within the soul and requires only to be brought to birth. Hegel offers himself as mid-wife but the truth itself, and the condition for attaining it – human reason, is native to every human spirit. This account of the matter, Climacus points out, is precisely that of Socrates to whom the question of whether the truth may be learned was first put. Socrates offered in response his doctrine of *anamnesis* (recollection) in which the truth lay within the individual soul and required only to be recollected. Reason is the condition or the instrument through which this recollection may take place. If a teacher is required, then it is only in the role of a mid-wife. Such a teacher imparts nothing to the learner and their historical encounter is of no enduring significance. Indeed nothing in history is decisive here. The occasion in which a learner recollects the truth is entirely incidental, for the exercise of pure reason was thought to be, in the Age of Reason, wholly transcendent of circumstantial concerns. Historical circumstance, it is said, has no bearing on whether $2 + 2 = 4$. Reason discerns the truth of the matter by deliberations that are totally independent of history. History, for Hegel, is merely the outworking of rational truths discernible by ahistorical means. The incarnation of the Logos in Jesus of Nazareth, accordingly, is simply the historical unfolding of a logic discerned by rational means. That logic is the logic of humanity's identity with the divine, or, to use Hegel's own terms, it is the synthesis through human consciousness of the absolute Spirit and the finite spirit.

That is Hegel's story, a more sophisticated but essentially identical version, he believes, of the story told in the New Testament of the Word made flesh. Given the popularity of Hegel's story in Denmark in the early nineteenth century, at least among the intelligentsia, Climacus is eager to consider it further. For the purposes of his thought experiment Climacus continues to refer to it as the 'Socratic' story rather than the Hegelian story, perhaps because he does not want to pre-judge, nor let his readers too hastily assume, that this account of how the truth may be learned is indeed identical with the New Testament story as Hegel claims. Slowly and deliberately in chapter one of *Philosophical Fragments,* Climacus sets down in print the essential elements of the Socratic doctrine. 'Viewed Socratically', Climacus writes, 'any point of departure in time is *eo ipso* something accidental, a vanishing point, an occasion. Nor is the teacher anything more . . . In the Socratic view, every human being is himself the midpoint, and the whole world focuses only on him because his self-knowledge is God-knowledge'.[7] The point of departure in time, to which Climacus here refers, is elsewhere called the 'moment'. Within the Socratic account, as we have seen, no historical moment can be decisive. Circumstances have no bearing on reason's access to the truth. Nor can any teacher be regarded as indispensable. A teacher may prompt and coax the learner through the process of recollection[8] but the teacher, like the historical moment, has no essential relation to the truth that is recollected. The truth learned may be retained and appropriated by the learner without any further recourse to the teacher and long after the teacher has been forgotten. The teacher, too, may vanish into the past. Climacus observes:

> If this is the case with regard to learning the truth,
> then the fact that I have learned from Socrates or from
> Prodicus or from a maidservant can concern me only
> historically . . . My relation to Socrates and Prodicus
> cannot concern me with regard to my eternal happiness,
> for this is given retrogressively in the possession of the
> truth that I had from the beginning without knowing it.[9]

The mention of 'eternal happiness' here alerts us to the fact that Climacus is concerned above all with the truth that concerns us ultimately, the truth of one's existence and of one's relation to God. Although he has posed the question in general, 'can the truth be learned?', we are reminded here of the larger project expressed in the question, 'How can I, Johannes Climacus, share in the happiness that Christianity promises?'

Having identified the central features of the Socratic account, Climacus then muses about an alternate view.[10] What might be the case, he wonders, if Socrates were wrong? Suppose we do not possess the truth within ourselves, nor the condition for attaining it; suppose the moment is decisive; suppose that the teacher is not merely incidental to our learning but essential to it? If all this were true, then the situation of the learner would be quite different than Socrates (and Hegel) imagined it to be. We should have to say that the learner exists in untruth, and because the learner does not possess the condition for learning the truth, we should have to say also that this existence in untruth is a kind of bondage. The learner has no capacity to free herself from existence in untruth for she is bereft of the condition. Something more than a mid-wife would then be required, for it is no longer a question of bringing to birth that which lies within the learner, but rather of imparting something new to the learner, both the condition and the truth. What would be needed is a radical transformation of the learner, something akin to a new birth. Here the problem becomes even more difficult. What kind of teacher would be capable of such a feat? '[N]o human being is capable of doing this;' Climacus writes, 'if it is to take place, it must be done by the god himself'.[11]

Climacus muses further on this scenario, and begins to specify more precisely its various features. He supposes that the learner must exist in untruth through his or her own fault. It would be a contradiction, he explains, for God to have created the learner without the condition for understanding the truth. Admittedly this logic works best within a biblical conception of humanity's creation by God to live in covenant relationship with himself, but the biblical resonances are now becoming more and more apparent. On account of the learner's culpability, Climacus proposes that the state of existence in untruth be called *sin*.[12] As for the teacher,

> Let us call him a *savior*, for he does indeed save the
> learner from unfreedom, saves him from himself. Let us
> call him a *deliverer*, for he does indeed deliver the person
> who had imprisoned himself, and no one is so dreadfully

imprisoned, and no captivity is so impossible to break out of as that in which the individual holds himself captive! And yet, even this does not say enough, for by his unfreedom he had indeed become guilty of something, and if that teacher gives him the condition and the Truth, then he is, of course, a *reconciler* who takes away the wrath that lay over the incurred guilt.[13]

Such a teacher is no mere mid-wife. The teacher gives both the truth and the condition for understanding it. Such a teacher re-creates the learner, makes a new person of her, brings about a new birth. The train of Climacus' thought experiment follows here the pattern of Jesus' conversation with Nicodemus. Nicodemus came to Jesus seeking understanding and received the news that he must be born again. After expressing his puzzlement at this news, it is explained to Nicodemus that it is on account of what God has done in sending his Son that the world may have life, may be reconciled, that is, with the truth. Finally, towards the end of Climacus' musings, we learn that the condition making all this possible is faith.[14] Faith is to be understood here, not primarily in epistemological terms, but rather as the divinely bestowed gift of a new life lived in reconciled relation with God. There is an epistemological result of all this – the learner understands the truth, the objective truth of Christian faith, but attention is given first to the subjective matter, to the being of the learner who stands in radical need of forgiveness, of transformation, and of new life.

What has been Climacus' purpose in conducting such a thought experiment as this? Ostensibly it is mere sport, a little rational game for the amusement of a speculative age. But the underlying intent is to draw into sharp relief the radical distinction between the Christian account of how we may learn the truth and the optimistic nineteenth century account that was founded upon human prowess and supposed that the speculative philosophy of the age not only encompassed all that Christian faith had to offer, but surpassed it in explanatory power. Climacus offers his fragments of philosophy to unmask the error of that supposition. Let us note, however, Climacus does not argue that the speculative philosophers are wrong. It may be that humanity on account of its rational power does indeed have the capacity to learn all truth and thus to save and perfect itself. Climacus leaves that possibility open. Kierkegaard, through Climacus, wants his contemporaries to recognize, however, that the Socratic/Hegelian account contradicts in every significant particular the biblical account of how we may learn the truth. In contrast with Hegel's own estimation of the matter, speculative philosophy and the Bible do not say the same thing. The thought experiment of the *Fragments* was designed to relieve both Kierkegaard's contemporaries, and us, of that widespread misconception. Our own age, to be sure, is less inclined to articulate the matter in explicitly Hegelian terms, but we remain convinced, for the most part, that the truth to be found in Jesus must be accommodated to the presuppositions of our age, and, concomitantly, that the truth may be learned without any transformation of the self.

Climacus' thought experiment sets before the reader two contrasting epistemologies. The first presumes that the learner begins from a position of strength. The learner has the truth already within; she exists in truth in such a way that all new claims to truth must prove themselves to be true by their conformity to the learner's self-knowledge. The individual, equipped already with an utterly reliable epistemic capacity (the 'condition'), becomes the touchstone and arbiter of all truth. The second epistemology developed by Climacus contrasts sharply with the first. In the second case the learner does not possess all truth. She is radically estranged from the truth. Indeed, she exists in untruth. Such a learner, moreover, lacks the capacity to learn the truth. She is bereft of the condition and stands in need of personal transformation, a transformation in which she is made a new person and is brought into relationship with the truth. Put simply, the first epistemology proposes that the truth be accommodated to the learner; the second proposes that the learner be accommodated to the truth.

Climacus, we have noted, is not a proponent of either view. His concern, so far in *Philosophical Fragments*, is simply to distinguish clearly between the two possibilities, although he has let it be known that it is the second view that conforms precisely to the New Testament. That observation will be crucial in his quest to discover how one may attain the blessedness promised by Christianity. Kierkegaard himself, however, has made it clear elsewhere that the second epistemological proposal rather than the first describes the true situation of human beings. Alongside the pseudonymous works, Kierkegaard published under his own name a steady stream of discourses that reveal his own view. During the course of 1843 and 1844, at which time the themes emerged and the writing of Philosophical Fragments took place, Kierkegaard published eighteen signed discourses three of which are reflections on the biblical text, 'Every good and every perfect gift is from above' (James 1:17). Another is titled 'The Expectancy of Faith' and yet another, published ten weeks after *Philosophical Fragments*, bears the title 'To Need God Is a Human Being's Highest Perfection'.[15] The titles indicate, and the discourses themselves confirm, Kierkegaard's own view that in all things human beings stand in need of God. That applies especially to the individual's understanding of the truth. Understanding is given through God's transforming and reconciling work. Kierkegaard puts it thus:

> Just as knowing oneself in one's own nothingness is
> the condition for knowing God, so knowing God is
> the condition for the sanctification of the human being
> by God's assistance and according to God's intention.
> Wherever God is in truth, there he is always creating.
> He does not want a person to be spiritually soft and to
> bathe in the contemplation of his glory, but in becoming
> known by a person he wants to create in him a new
> human being.[16]

## b. The Objective Inquirer

The two epistemological proposals set forth by Climacus correspond to two kinds of learner. The inquiring subject in the first case asks about the truth, but she asks objectively. She asks in a disinterested fashion without being so vain as to suppose that her own person might be put under the spotlight, or that she as an individual might be the subject, or have need, of God's redemptive and sanctifying attention. The objective inquirer keeps the whole matter at arm's length and sets out to determine the truth in a wholly dispassionate way.[17] The subjective inquirer, by contrast, is concerned above all with her relation to the truth, with appropriation, and with what may be required in terms of personal transformation for her to exist in the truth. We will follow Climacus' lead in *Concluding Unscientific Postscript* in considering first the concerns of the objective inquirer particularly in respect of Christianity.

'Objectively understood', Climacus notes, 'truth can signify: (1) historical truth, (2) philosophical truth'.[18] These correspond to the traditional categories, formulated by Leibniz,[19] of synthetic truth or the contingent truths of history, and analytical truth or the necessary truths of reason. Climacus continues,

> Viewed as historical truth, the truth must be established
> by a critical consideration of the various reports etc., in
> short, in the same way as historical truth is ordinarily
> established. In the case of philosophical truth, the inquiry
> turns on the relation of doctrine, historically given and
> verified, to the eternal truth.[20]

Climacus turns his attention first to 'the historical point of view'. 'If Christianity is viewed as a historical document, the important thing is to obtain a completely reliable report of what the Christian doctrine really is'.[21] But here the difficulties begin, at least for the subjective inquirer who wants to commit her life to, and exist within, the truth Christianity proclaims. For it soon becomes apparent that historical inquiry can yield no certainty. 'With regard to the historical the greatest certainty is only an *approximation*'.[22] This is the dilemma identified by G. E. Lessing who, recognizing that historical truths can never be proven absolutely, famously concluded that 'accidental truths of history can never become the proof of necessary truths of reason'.[23] The observation strikes a blow to the person who, like Lessing, wants to commit himself absolutely to the truth of Christianity but finds that the truth in question cannot be absolutely confirmed. But there is a further problem: even if one had no objection to the claim of the gospels that, for instance, Christ rose from the dead, that does not confirm that Christ was the Son of God. These are two different classes of truth, Lessing thinks. The resurrection, if true, is an historical truth, but the claim that Christ was the Son of God, is a metaphysical truth, a truth about the nature of God's being. An historical premise, Lessing further explains, cannot provide proof of a metaphysical conclusion.[24] 'That, then', he says, 'is the ugly, broad ditch which I cannot get across, however often and however earnestly I have tried to make the leap'.[25]

Lessing's strategy, in face of this dilemma, is to reform Christian truth claims into something that can be believed. Christianity is adapted precisely so that his own epistemic principles may be preserved intact. What Christianity amounts to in Lessing's adaptation is the 'Testament of John', 'little children, love one another'.[26] This ethical injunction, it is supposed, is something that all reasonable people can believe in without the inconvenience of having to be transformed. There is a further advantage for the objective inquirer. It matters not whether the testament originated with John or with Jesus or with any teacher in particular. The worthiness of the testament is confirmed by one's own reason, and so might just as well have originated there. We have returned to the Socratic point of view! But, as Climacus reminds us, that is quite a different thing from the position of the New Testament. Climacus reminds us also of another truth: it is Scripture [rather than Lessing] that is 'the secure stronghold that decides what is Christian and what is not'.[27]

For the moment, however, Climacus is concerned with the objective approach to Christian truth. Recognizing that Scripture is crucial here, the objective inquirer sets about securing the authority of Scripture. 'The important thing is to secure Scripture historically-critically. Here the canonicity of particular books is dealt with, their authenticity and integrity, the author's axiopisty [trustworthiness], and a dogmatic guarantee is posited: inspiration'.[28] In other words, the industry of theological scholarship gets underway in an effort to make it objectively certain that Scripture can be trusted. This is a fascinating passage, for as we know, and as Kierkegaard knew, the historical-critical approach and the dogmatic approach to Scripture are generally thought to be poles apart. Historical-critical method, allegedly, eschews all dogmatic considerations in delivering an account of what Scripture says, while the dogmatic approach makes dogmatic considerations foundational to the proper reading of Scripture.[29] Kierkegaard detects a fundamental similarity in the two approaches however. Both seek an objectively certain basis for whatever it is the Bible has to say. Historical–critical scholarship seeks objective certainty through the scientific character of its method, while, on the dogmatic, side the objective certainty of the Bible is secured through a particular construal of the doctrine of inspiration, a construal that renders the Bible infallible and hermeneutically straightforward. We have only to read the text to know the will of God. Different though they may be in some respects, the historical–critical approach and the dogmatic approach, as outlined here, have both capitulated to the Modernist insistence that in order to count as knowledge, our truth claims must be objectively certain. The interesting result is that one's relation to the biblical witness, and more particularly to Jesus, is no longer a matter of faith, but is determined by the outcomes of scholarly inquiry. Becoming a Christian depends crucially on assent to the deliverances of modern scholarship, whether that scholarship, through historical inquiry, reveals who Jesus really was and what he really said and did, or whether, through some other scholarly procedure, it succeeds in establishing that the Bible really is the inspired and infallible word of God. The ridiculousness of this situation, which Kierkegaard sought to expose, is demonstrated by imagining that in response to Jesus' invitation to leave their nets and follow him, the disciples responded that they needed time to go and check with the scholars who would be able to determine whether the Word of Jesus could be believed. Becoming a Christian, as we saw with Lessing, is reduced to a calculation about the degree of rational certainty attending the claims of Jesus Christ.

A further difficulty attending this quest for objective certainty is that it is infinitely prolonged. There is always room for doubt. 'And yet', says Climacus, 'that is how things have gone on'.

> One generation after the other has died; new difficulties have arisen, have been conquered, and new difficulties have arisen. As an inheritance from generation to generation, the illusion has persisted that the method is

the correct one, but the learned theological scholars have
not yet succeeded . . . The subject's personal, infinite,
impassioned interestedness (which is the possibility
of faith, and then faith, the form of eternal happiness
and then eternal happiness) fades away more and more
because the decision is postponed, and is postponed as a
direct result of the results of the learned research scholar.[30]

The subject's 'personal, infinite, impassioned interest' is a
matter of vital importance, not just to Climacus, but also to
Kierkegaard. The matter of becoming a Christian is personal.
That's the first point. We cannot entrust the decision of faith to
the scholars, to the clergy, to the so called Christian society in
which we live, or, indeed, to anyone else. Jesus' question, 'Who
do you say that I am' (Mt. 16.15: cf. Mk 8.29), is addressed personally and can be answered in truth only by those who are willing
to trust themselves to that transformative encounter with Christ
in which disciples are made. As Matthew's gospel makes clear,
it is the 'Father in heaven' who reveals who Jesus truly is rather
than the deliberations of 'flesh and blood' (Mt. 16.17). A reading
of Mt. 16.13–17 also reveals the point of Kierkegaard's repeated
emphasis on the individual. Prior to the question, 'Who do you
say that I am', Jesus asks, 'Who do people say that the Son of
Man is?' (vs.13) to which the answer is given, 'Some say John the
Baptist, but others Elijah, and still others Jeremiah or one of the
prophets'. Then follows Jesus' more probing question: 'But who
do *you* say that I am'. The individual is called upon to respond.
Genuine faith is not a matter of going along with public opinion;
it is matter of personal response, and personal commitment. If
this is not understood, then Christianity is not understood.[31]

The subject's interest is also 'infinite', which is to say that one
is invited to stake one's life on the truth revealed in Christ. This
is not a matter for half-hearted or merely professional interest, as
may be the case with those scholars whose work in the academy
bears little relation to their own existential commitments. The
question, 'Who do you say that I am', cannot be put off with
the protest, 'I'll let you know just as soon as I have finished my
latest book'. The question is of infinite importance, which is to
say that no other claim upon us can be allowed to take priority.

Finally, the interest of the subject is 'impassioned' which means that it is a matter of absolute, existential importance. The question of who Jesus is, is not answered truly merely by offering some proposition or other about his identity. If it is true that Jesus is Lord and Saviour, for instance, then the question of his identity is truly answered only by the person whose whole life is obedience and whose whole life is an expression of repentance, of gratitude and of praise. Passion thus entails existential engagement, a commitment of one's life in discipleship that is unreserved and unconditional. 'Christianly, the only question is that of obedience'.[32] That is the Christian requirement. We will say more in due course about Kierkegaard's recognition that we constantly fall short of this ideal, but for the moment the point is simply to recognize the vast difference between the person who studies the matter objectively, thereby keeping the whole thing, and God himself, at arm's length, and the person who, in faith, gives her whole life to the service of God.

## c. The Subjective Inquirer

The subjective thinker, Climacus explains,

> . . . has another kind of reflection, specifically that of inwardness, of possession, whereby it belongs to the subject and to no one else. Whereas objective thinking invests everything in the result and assists all humankind to cheat by copying and reeling off the results and answers, subjective thinking invests everything in the process of becoming and omits the result, partly because this belongs to him, since he possesses the way, partly because he as existing is continually in the process of becoming . . .[33]

Here again we see that Christianity does not consist in assent to some proposition or other delivered up as the assured result of objective scholarship. It consists rather in a form of life, a way to be travelled, a long obedience and process of becoming. That is true not only of Christianity but of any life-view. Human beings are finite creatures, and their capacity for knowledge, impressive though it may be, is not an infinite capacity. It has limitations most especially in the sphere of existence. We may achieve absolute certainty about some analytical proposition or a mathematical equation, for example, but in the matter of one's life-view – in the matter of the meaning and purpose and foundation of one's being, absolute certainty is a chimera. It makes no sense, therefore, to postpone endlessly one's commitment to a life-view until certainty is attained. Life must be lived; we must engage in it without all questions having been settled; we must venture out over the seventy thousand fathoms, as Kierkegaard was fond of saying. The person who waits for objective certainty in relation to the claims of Christian faith, or, indeed, to the claims of any viable[34] form of life, renders herself impotent. She cannot act, for all actions are an expression of some life-view or other. Getting out of bed in the morning, for example, depends upon our believing that there is something worthwhile to be accomplished by doing so. It would be ludicrous to delay the decision to get out of bed until we had established beyond all doubt that something worthwhile would in fact be accomplished thereby. Instead, we must have the courage of our convictions. Granted, the decision regarding Christianity is far more momentous than getting out of bed and so more care should be taken over it, but, in that matter too, as in all existential decisions, absolute certainty is not available. We must act and we must take responsibility. We must strive for conformity between our existence and our convictions. Kierkegaard calls this 'reduplication', or sometimes 'redoubling'. Thus,

> When Christianity (precisely because it is not a doctrine)
> does not reduplicate itself in the one who presents it,
> he does not present Christianity; for Christianity is an
> existential–communication and can only be presented –
> by existing. Basically, to exist therein [*at existere deri*], to
> express it in one's existence etc. – this is what it means to
> reduplicate.[35]

But this is never something that has been accomplished; it is the task of a lifetime. In this matter, as we have seen, we cannot endlessly wait upon the outcomes of objective scholarship and defer the decisive act until the scholars have delivered objective certainty. The endeavours of scholarship will never succeed in eliminating all doubt.[36]

Under his own name, Kierkegaard writes,

> If someone wanted to be his [Christ's] follower, his approach, as seen in the Gospel, was different from lecturing. To such a person he said something like this: Venture a decisive act; then we can begin. What does this mean? It means that one does not become a Christian by hearing something about Christianity, by reading something about it, by thinking about it, or, while Christ was living, by seeing him once in a while or by going and staring at him all day long. No a *setting* (*situation*) is required – venture a decisive act; the proof does not precede but follows, is in and with the imitation that follows Christ.[37]

Venturing the decisive act in this manner is precisely what Climacus (and Kierkegaard) mean with the claim that 'truth is subjectivity'. There comes a point when we must take responsibility, and, just as we do so, we act on the basis of personal convictions over which objective doubt remains. Climacus insists that truth consists precisely in this. That does not mean, however, that the conviction expressed in our action is itself true – it may or may not be – but our acceptance of responsibility and our personal, subjective commitment to the course of action, whatever it may be, is true to the nature of our existence as finite human beings. It is in this sense that 'becoming a subjective individual is the highest task assigned to every human being'.[38] Climacus therefore admires the person whose life is an expression of her convictions, even if the convictions themselves be false. Far less admirable is the person whose convictions are true, who recites the Christian creed, for instance, and attends church on Sundays, but whose life does not express the Christian imperative – following Christ. The first is a person of faith, whereas the second is a hypocrite. Lest we be too quick to judge others, however, Climacus also warns us that 'the infinite can be at work in a human being, and no one, no one discovers it by looking at him'.[39] Another pseudonym, Johannes de Silentio, makes the same point: the 'knight of faith' may have no distinctive outward appearance but instead look 'just like a tax-collector'.[40] Authentic Christian faith, is more likely to be found, Kierkegaard suggests, in the humble person who, without fanfare or public recognition lives a life of prayer and selfless service of others, than in all the pomp and ceremony of official Christianity. It is for that reason, no doubt, that Kierkegaard found far more joy in his conversations with ordinary folk, than he did with the clergy and educated elite of his day.[41]

An oft-quoted passage from *Concluding Unscientific Postscript* highlights the distinction between objective and subjective truth:

> If someone who lives in the midst of Christianity enters, with knowledge of the true idea of God, the house of God, the house of the true God, and prays, but prays in untruth, and if someone lives in an idolatrous land but prays with all the passion of infinity, although his eyes are resting upon the image of an idol – where, then, is there more truth? The one prays in truth to God although he is worshipping an idol; the other prays in untruth to the true God and is therefore in truth worshipping an idol.[42]

It is a challenging conundrum and echoes, of course, the parable Jesus told of a Pharisee and a tax-collector who went up to the temple to pray (Lk. 18.9–14). We may take the Pharisee as a direct match for the first of Climacus's characters. The Pharisee prayed, 'God, I thank you that I am not like other people: thieves rogues, adulterers, or even like this tax-collector. I fast twice a week; I give a tenth of all my income'. He thus prayed in untruth albeit in the house of the true God. The tax-collector, by contrast, beat his breast and prayed, 'God, be merciful to me a sinner'. Climacus adapts the second character in his own story so that the man now prays, not in the house of the true God, but in an idolatrous land. His prayer, however, is approved just the same, while the first man, standing in the house of the true God, effectively addresses an idol, a god of his own making. It is a mistake to read this parable as an argument for relativism, as though it does not matter which God we worship so long as we do it honestly and sincerely. That is not the point here. Climacus wants us to learn, instead, that authentic discipleship is not attained just by adopting a set of true beliefs, by fulfilling the objective requirement. Authentic discipleship has to do, rather, with the purity of one's heart.[43] In a Discourse on the tax collector, Kierkegaard writes:

> Oh, the natural man finds greatest satisfaction in standing erect; the person who truly learned to know God, and by learning to know God learned to know himself, finds blessedness only in falling upon his knees, worshiping when he thinks about God, penitent when he thinks about himself.[44]

The subjective approach to truth is concerned not only with the object, with true propositions about God, for example, but rather, and even more importantly, with one's relation to the object, with one's relation, in this case, to God. Put otherwise, the objective approach concerns itself only with the 'what' – with what is to be believed. The subjective approach, by contrast, is concerned also and primarily with 'how' – with how one is related to the truth. '*Objectively the emphasis is on **what** is said; subjectively the emphasis is on **how** it is said*'.[45]

## d. The 'What' and the 'How'

Climacus' concern with *how* it is said 'is not to be understood as manner, modulation of voice, oral delivery, etc., but it is to be understood as the relation of the existing person, in his very existence, to what is said'.[46] Here there is a further echo of the teaching of Jesus: 'Not everyone who says to me "Lord, Lord," will enter the kingdom of heaven, but only the one who does the will of my Father in heaven' (Mt. 7.21). Something other than lip-service is required, for the words, 'Lord, Lord', become an untruth on the lips of one who serves a different master.[47] Christianity is not, first of all, a set of doctrinal propositions, but a form of life, a form of life distinguished by the *following* of Christ. A university education is not required; familiarity with the latest developments in speculative thinking is not required; expertise in the methods of historical-critical scholarship is not required. Obedience is required, and purity of heart. Kierkegaard writes in his Journal,

> In the New Testament faith is presented as having
> not an intellectual but an ethical character; it signifies
> the relationship of personality between God and
> man. Therefore faith is demanded (as an expression of
> devotedness), believing against reason, believing although
> one cannot see (wholly a qualification of personality, and
> ethical). The apostle speaks of the *obedience* of faith . . .[48]

Through the late 1840s and into the 1850s, Kierkegaard grew more and more convinced of the view that Christian faith involved suffering. Indeed, suffering was increasingly presumed to be the mark of obedience. In support of this conviction, Kierkegaard took the example of Christ.

> Christ learned *obedience* from what he suffered . . .
> Therefore his life was obedience, obedience unto death,
> unto death on the cross. He who was the Truth and the
> Way and the Life, he who needed to learn nothing, he
> still learned one thing – he learned obedience. Obedience
> is so closely related to the eternal truth that the one who
> is Truth learns obedience.[49]

Those who wish to learn the Truth, who wish to take the Way of Christian faith, and who seek the Life that Christianity promises have also, then, to learn obedience. If a central, paramount point may be distilled from Kierkegaard's rich and multi-faceted concern to 'make it clear what Christianity is',[50] this is it: Christianity is a life of obedience after the pattern of the one who is himself the Way, the Truth and the Life. It calls forth, accordingly, an infinite passion, subjectivity – that is, the personal engagement of the individual – and a willingness to obey even while objective uncertainty remains. The blessedness that Christianity offers is discovered along this road of obedience and cannot be secured in advance by detached, objective enquiry. This is a paradox, Climacus observes. 'The eternal, essential truth, that is, the truth that is related essentially to what it means to exist . . . is a paradox'.[51] We are asked to commit ourselves absolutely to the truth, and yet there is no absolute assurance that this truth, the truth of Christianity, is objectively true. '. . . the eternal, essential truth is itself not at all a paradox', Climacus continues, 'but it is a paradox by being related to an existing person'.[52] The existing person does not have the capacity to see as God does, to view the world *sub specie aeternitatis*. We are constrained by all manner of things, by our finitude, our sinfulness, by our cultural, linguistic and intellectual heritage, and so on. We see only in part, 'through a glass darkly', it might be said. And yet we are called to venture the decisive act. That is the paradox.[53] That is why subjectivity is truth. And this *definition* of truth, 'is a paraphrasing of faith'.[54]

Thus Climacus says, 'The passion of the infinite, not its content, is the deciding factor, for its content is precisely itself. In this way the subjective "how" and subjectivity are the truth'.[55] *What* then is Christianity? It is not a doctrine but an 'existence communication'.[56] The content of Christianity is precisely the way of discipleship. There are things to be said of a doctrinal nature, as we shall see, and Kierkegaard is well aware of that, but he refuses to allow doctrine, for instance, propositions *about* Christ, to be put in the place of *following* Christ. The reciting of doctrines, even though they be true, is counterfeit Christianity if in all other respects one's life remains unchanged.

## e. The Possibility of Faith

While Climacus may have clarified for us what Christian faith consists in, namely, a life lived in obedience to Christ, we have yet to learn how such a life becomes possible. Climacus has considered the possibility that 'the learner' is bereft of the condition to learn the truth, or, what amounts to the same thing in this case, to live truthfully. The lack of the condition can be amended, Climacus further supposes, only by God for God

'critical' inquiry and contends, furthermore, that all the scholarly industry, all the effort to establish by objective inquiry who Jesus really was, is but one more attempt to avoid the real issue, the issue of following Christ. Kierkegaard's relentless focus on the subjective issue, 'what is required of me?' is apparent, for instance, in a Discourse on 1 Tim. 3.16. The text reads: 'And great beyond all question is the mystery of godliness: God was revealed in the flesh, was justified in the Spirit, seen by angels, preached among the pagans, believed in the world, taken up in glory'. Taking this text as his theme, Kierkegaard simply takes for granted the truth of the doctrinal claims. 'Yet', he says, '. . . there is a very remarkable difference between the separate statements. Or rather, there is one among them, if you catch sight of it or it, as it were, catches sight of you, then everything is changed'.[4]

> See, 'God was manifested in the flesh' does not pertain to
> you; it pertains to him. Neither does 'he is justified in the
> Spirit' pertain to you; it pertains to him. It was he who
> was justified in the Spirit. Nor was it you who 'was seen
> by angels'; it was he. And it was he 'who was proclaimed
> among the pagans' and he who 'was taken up in glory'.
> But this 'He was believed in the world'! This does pertain
> to you, does it not; it pertains to you . . . It seems, then,
> as if the apostle is saying only something historical about
> Christ, and so indeed he is. But in the middle of the
> historical he has used a few words that are directed to
> you. 'He was believed in the world': that is, have you
> then, believed him?[5]

For Kierkegaard, the dogmatic claims pertaining to Christ are not at issue. Our response to them, or more particularly, our response to Christ, is the issue. Of course, it matters to Kierkegaard that the dogmatic claims are true. If it is not true, for instance, that Jesus is Saviour and Deliverer, if it is not true that in Jesus God himself has come among us in the lowly form of a servant, then it is of little consequence how we respond to the apostolic testimony presented to us in the New Testament. The individual's existential response to Christ is of eternal significance precisely because the doctrinal claims are true. Given that the doctrinal claim is true – that in Jesus we are encountered by God himself – the important thing, according to Kierkegaard, is that we get clear about the response required of us.

Kierkegaard often remarks critically about the propensity of assistant professors to devote themselves endlessly to the defence and precise articulation of doctrine, as though the truth depended on their getting the proof just right. Kierkegaard considers it foolish to suppose that God must be subjected to the limits of human conceptuality, that God must prove himself to our limited capacity to understand. In his Journal he asks, '[W]ould it not have an almost madly comical effect to portray a man deluded into thinking that he could prove that god exists – and then have an atheist accept it by virtue of the other's proof. Both situations are equally fantastic . . .'[6] 'Christianity', Kierkegaard says, 'is an *existence communication*, has entered into the world by the use of *authority. It is not to be an object of speculative thought* . . .'[7] The truth of Christianity is not established through any speculative calculus. Instead of being 'proven' it is testified to – by the one who lives it. The same principle applies in Christology; there is a 'giveness' about revelation resting upon the fact that divine authority is superior to human authority. What is given in Jesus, as testified to in the New Testament, is simply to be proclaimed. It cannot be subjected to a proof. Kierkegaard explores this point at some length in what came to be published posthumously as *The Book on Adler*. A local pastor in Denmark, Magister Adler, claimed to have received a special revelation from God, but, exploring the case, Kierkegaard finds that in defending his claim, Adler appeals to human reflection or human reason. That, for Kierkegaard, constitutes a betrayal of divine authority which, precisely by virtue of its superiority to all human authority, must be allowed to speak for itself. If others think a person a fool for proclaiming something on the authority of revelation, so be it. Such a person stands thus in the company of the apostles who proclaimed, according to Paul, a doctrine that was foolishness to the Greeks. The person who, on the other hand, appeals to human authority 'presumptuously makes himself into a genius as a substitute for his having been called by God to be an apostle'.[8] In relation to Christ, the proclamation of the apostles confronts the hearer with the challenge whether to believe or otherwise to take offence. No amount of human reasoning, philosophical speculation, historical critical inquiry, or study of the development of religions can absolve the hearer of the responsibility to take this decision for herself. When the individual is confronted with the apostolic testimony concerning Jesus,

> . . . there is very little or nothing at all for assistant professors and licentiates and paragraph swallowers to do. The assistance of these gentlemen is needed here no more than a maiden needs a barber to shave her beard and no more than a bald man needs a hairdresser to 'style' his hair. The matter is very simple: will you obey or will you not obey; will you in faith submit to [the] divine authority or will you take offence.[9]

That paragraph constitutes a rebuke to those who set out upon the task of Christology as though the authenticity of the apostolic witness to Christ stands in need of verification. Revelation must be allowed to speak for itself. The proper concern of those who attend to revelation is, 'how does it pertain to me'.

In *Practice in Christianity*, published under the pseudonym Anti-Climacus who is described as 'a Christian on an extraordinary level',[10] Kierkegaard begins:

> Lord Jesus Christ, would that we . . . might become contemporary with you . . . might see you in your true form and in the surroundings of actuality as you walked here on earth, not in the form in which an empty and meaningless or a thoughtless-romantic or a historical-talkative remembrance has distorted you, since it is not the form of abasement in which the believer sees you, and it cannot possibly be the form of glory in which no one has yet seen you. Would that we might see you as you are and were and will be until your second coming in glory, as the sign of offence and the object of faith, the lowly man, yet the Savior and Redeemer of the human race, who out of love came to earth to seek the lost, to suffer and die, and yet, alas, every step you took on earth, every time you called to the straying, every time you reached

out your hand to do signs and wonders, and every time
you defencelessly suffered the opposition of people
without raising a hand – again and again in concern you
had to repeat, 'Blessed is the one who is not offended at
me'. Would that we might see you in this way and that
we then might not be offended at you.[11]

Several features of Kierkegaard's Christology become apparent here. First, Jesus Christ is not the embodiment of an abstract
idea, of a 'christic principle' that could be generated through
human speculation and that might also be found elsewhere.
Christ is uniquely to be found in the historical actuality of Jesus
to whom the Bible bears witness. The form in which Christ
was found on earth, 'in the surroundings of actuality', is his
true form. This true form of Christ, furthermore, remains inaccessible to 'empty and meaningless', 'thoughtless-romantic', or
'historical talkative remembrance'. It is accessible only through
faith, or what Kierkegaard here calls 'contemporaneity'. We will
return below to this point. Second, Christ is known in the form
of abasement, in lowliness rather than in glory. And third, he
is the Saviour and Redeemer of the human race who, out of
love, came to seek the lost, suffered and died, performed signs
and wonders, and yet encountered both rejection and offence.
These categories provide a starting point for our exploration of
Kierkegaard's Christology.

## a. Historical Actuality

We have seen in *Philosophical Fragments*, discussed in chapter
two, Kierkegaard's enquiry into how we learn the truth. Can
the truth be learned through some rational process abstracted
from the vagaries of history and the particularities of personal
circumstance? That has been the prevailing view in Western
culture, especially since the Enlightenment. Although post-
modernity offers a sharp critique of the notion that the truth is
learned best through detached, objective and rational enquiry,
this presumption of Modernity has profoundly shaped biblical
and theological scholarship during the past two hundred years.

If the truth is learned best through rational deliberation and if human reason provides the most complete account of what is true, then the gospel accounts of the life of Jesus, along with their allegedly primitive conceptions of the structure of the universe, must be subjected to the scrutiny of human reason in order that the essential truth of Christianity may be distilled. A further corollary of the conviction that reason provides the most reliable guide to the truth is that the truth itself is eternal, necessary and universal. Mathematics provides the best model here. The equation $1 + 1 = 2$ is not true only at some times and in some places. It is eternally and universally true. What is more, it is necessarily true. It cannot be otherwise; its truth–value is utterly impervious to the contingencies of history – or so it is believed.[12]

That the contingencies of history disrupt the pure certainties of rational enquiry led in the modern world to a disparagement of history. This disparagement has conceptual roots in Plato's philosophy but was asserted with renewed vigour during the Enlightenment. Descartes, for instance, dismissed historical enquiry as a means of determining the truth precisely because such enquiry deals in the contingent and the uncertain whereas truth ought to be characterised by necessity and indubitability.

The corollary for Christology, as we have seen already in chapter two, is that the historical contingencies surrounding the person of Jesus do not form part of the essential truth upheld by Christianity. The truth, it is alleged, is eternal and universal and depends not at all upon the particularities of Jesus himself. The association of Jesus with the truth, on this view, consists in his being an embodiment of an idea, an idea discoverable, in principle, without reference to Jesus himself. Jesus becomes a vanishing point, a dispensable vehicle for the conveyance of a truth that could just as well be discovered and upheld without him.

Against this view, Kierkegaard, insists that 'the surroundings of actuality' are not incidental to but constitute the truth itself. What does he mean by this? He means, simply, that the truth Christianity is concerned with is the truth of 'the god's existence in time'. Kierkegaard's Christology is founded upon the Johannine proclamation that 'the Word became flesh and lived among us' (Jn. 1.14). The gospel is the news that the Word has become flesh. The 'teaching' of Christianity, accordingly, is not the content of Jesus' ethical teaching as Lessing, and Spinoza, and Kant, and numerous theologians of the twentieth century have assumed; the 'teaching' is the actuality of God's presence in the midst of our history. 'The presence of the god in human form – indeed, in the lowly form of a servant – is precisely the teaching . . .'[13] A great deal follows from this proclamation. It follows, for instance, that the truth is to be learned by attending to the historical actuality of the Word's incarnation. It follows that the truth is determined not by what human reason can conceive apart from 'the teacher' but by what God has done in the midst of the world's history. It follows that humanity's relation to God, and the world's salvation, is worked out through the conditions of historical existence. This created order of space and time is indeed 'good' as is proclaimed in Gen. 1.31, precisely because it is suitable terrain for the completion of God's purposes. Perhaps this is what Kierkegaard meant when he wrote, 'When God created the whole world, he looked at it and – behold, it was very *good*; when Christ died upon the cross, he said – "It is *finished*."'[14] Creation is brought to completion in the redemptive and reconciling death of Christ. Creation, and history with it, is not therefore to be disparaged. The 'moment' in time, the historical actuality of the god-man, is decisive in bringing about our reconciliation to the truth, our reconciliation, that is, to God.

## b. The Lowliness of Christ

Humanity's reasoned resistance to the appearance of God in time is compounded by the form of God's appearance. God takes the form of a servant. As Phil. 2 puts it, Christ 'emptied himself, taking the form of a slave . . . he humbled himself and became obedient to the point of death – even death on a cross' (Phil. 2.7–8). The one who addresses us when he calls us to come to him is 'the abased Jesus Christ, the lowly man, born of a despised virgin, his father a carpenter, in kinship with a few other folk of the lowest class, this lowly man who moreover claimed to be God . . .'[15] Thus, 'the form in which he appears is as different as possible from what the majority expect'.[16] Following Martin Luther here, but also John Calvin,[17] Kierkegaard's theology is a *theologia crucis* rather than a *theologia gloriae*. It is the lowly Christ, the suffering and the crucified Christ who reveals the truth of God; and it is the lowly Christ who invites followers. This has been forgotten, Kierkegaard contends. Christendom wants Christ, but without the suffering and it wants discipleship without the way of the cross.[18] But God in Christ keeps company with tax-collectors and sinners; he has made himself one with the most wretched. Upholding orthodox Christology against Docetism, Kierkegaard insists that 'the form of the servant was not something put on'.[19] The humanity of Christ was not merely a ruse but is essential to God's identification with fallen and wretched humanity. God genuinely takes our life upon himself. 'Therefore the god must suffer all things, endure all things, be tried in all things, hunger in the desert, thirst in his agonies, be forsaken in death, absolutely the equal of the lowliest of human beings – look, behold the man'.[20] The accumulation of biblical references here demonstrates Kierkegaard's resolute allegiance to the apostolic account of who Jesus is, while the particular texts chosen are themselves profoundly suggestive. The reference to 1 Cor. 13: 'the god suffers all things and endures all things' indicates that the suffering and lowliness of Christ is to be understood as an expression of love. Likewise, the following biblical citations referring to Christ's temptation in the wilderness (Lk. 4.1–4), his thirst on the cross (Jn. 19.28) and his God-forsakenness (Mt. 28.46; Mk 15.34) indicate the full depths of Christ's identification with sinners. Then there comes a typically Kierkegaardian twist: 'look, behold the man'. These are Pilate's words, uttered at the moment that Jesus is presented to the crowd for their verdict (Jn. 19.5). We are part of that crowd, so Kierkegaard suggests. And so the question is put to the reader too: will you take offence at this wretched figure who speaks (blasphemously) as if he were God – or will you believe?

This challenge is the recurring theme of *Practice in Christianity*. Kierkegaard reminds us again and again that the gospel is a scandal. Jesus himself is 'the sign of offense'[21] and those who seek Christ, who seek the blessedness promised by Christian faith, are consistently 'halted by the possibility of offense'.[22] The offence may take two forms, Kierkegaard suggests; the first is 'the offense of lowliness', and the second, 'the offense of loftiness'.

The offence of lowliness is the offence taken at the suggestion that the eternal, infinite and all-powerful God should be found in the lowly form of a servant. Docetism is the form such offence has commonly taken. Docetism proposes that the lowliness of Christ, his frail humanity and his suffering and death do not belong to the essence of who Christ is, but are a temporary and incidental accommodation of God to the human condition. Christ's apparent humanity, his humiliation, is a mere guise for the sake of making himself known in the world. It might be supposed that this Christological error is largely a thing of the past. Few people now believe that Jesus was not fully human; the Christological claim more likely to cause offence today is the claim that Jesus was divine. But Kierkegaard devotes a great deal of attention to the refutation of Docetism. He suggests, indeed, that Docetism is rife, especially among Christians! A docetic conception of Christ is entailed wherever it is supposed that the lowliness and suffering of Christ are incidental, that they were not essential to who he was.[23] That conviction expresses itself in the view that it is possible to follow him, to imitate him, and to become one with him, as the New Testament recommends, without the lowliness and without the suffering. Docetism expresses itself whenever it is supposed that one can be a follower of Christ without emptying oneself, without taking the form of a slave, without humbling oneself and without becoming obedient to the point of death – even death on a cross, to recall Phil. 2.7–8 once more. While there is good news – grace – for those who fail to follow Christ in this way, Kierkegaard is concerned that the requirement be made clear. The invitation to discipleship is the invitation to *take up one's cross* and follow Christ. It is a form of Docetism to suppose that Christ can be followed while setting his lowliness and his suffering aside. 'To follow Christ means . . . to deny oneself and means to *walk the same road* Christ walked in the lowly form of a servant . . .'[24]

## c. The Loftiness of Christ

The opposite error to Docetism, opposed by the early Church, was represented by Ebionitism and Arianism, both of which take offence at 'loftiness', at the apostolic claim that this lowly human being was fully and truly divine. Ebionitism regards Jesus as a teacher of the law, sent and inspired by God to be sure, but not himself divine. This attitude too remains common in our time. Jesus, it is commonly argued, was a great and inspired teacher of wisdom, of a revolutionary ethic, of social and political dissent; but the claim that he was divine should be understood as a primitive, mythological, and so dispensable expression of the esteem in which he was held by those who first bore witness to his significance. People of the modern age, having outgrown the 'primitive' metaphysics of the biblical authors, are encouraged to express their esteem for Jesus in far less lofty terms.[25] Jesus is accounted for entirely within anthropological categories. 'Everything is adjusted for the convenience of finitude'.[26]

Arianism, commonly described as 'the archetypal Christian heresy' also takes offence at the loftiness of the apostolic Christological claims. It cannot be true that Jesus and the Father 'are one' (Jn. 10.30), Arius appears to have argued,[27] because God the Father is, by definition, absolute unity, whereas Jesus 'the Son', by virtue of his participation in the temporal realm of flux and change, is multiplicity. Furthermore, Arius thinks, 'the essential life of one subject cannot . . . be shared by another'.[28] Although Kierkegaard does not mention Arius anywhere in his writing, he would not fault Arius's reasoning. The possibility of offence at the lofty claim that Christ is God lies precisely in the contradiction, the contradiction between what it is to be a human being, most especially a *lowly* human being, and what it is to be God.[29] For this reason Kierkegaard argues that the divinity of Christ can never be seen directly. Even the miracles do not demonstrate that Christ was divine.[30] The offence arising from the claim that this lowly human being is God can be overcome neither by direct observation nor by our own intellectual prowess. Reasoned speculation can arrive, with Arius, only at the conclusion that Christ cannot be God. The eternal cannot be found in time; the immutable cannot suffer; the infinite cannot be constrained by the limitations of human flesh . . . The confession of the incarnation offends against these certainties of human reasoning. To believe in the face of such 'certainties', requires that one pass through the possibility of offence.[31] As we have seen in chapter three above, passing through the possibility of offence involves passion, faith, the existential commitment of a life of obedience. Only in following Christ does one find the truth of the New Testament proclamation confirmed. 'What nonsense, then, that – instead of imitating Christ or the apostles and suffering as they suffered – that one becomes a professor instead'.[32]

Kierkegaard's dismissal of the presumption that speculative thought can reveal the true identity of Christ, is matched by his critique of historical method in Christology. That the true identity of Christ cannot be seen directly, entails that it cannot be seen by the historian qua historian.

## d. Historical Inquiry

In 1835, while Kierkegaard was still a student, David Friedrich Strauss published in Germany *Das Leben Jesu*, later translated into English as *The Life of Jesus Critically Examined*. In that work, Strauss employs the methods of historical enquiry to show, allegedly, that the gospel accounts of Jesus' life are not history but myth. The form of the gospels was the product of an enthusiastic religious imagination that clothed spiritual truths in the form of historical narrative. The task of the biblical interpreter, therefore, is to separate the religious message from the naïve quasi-historical terms in which the message was expressed. Strauss, like H. S. Reimarus before him, thought it possible to work through the gospels and separate out the historical from the mythical. While Strauss himself was vilified for his sweeping dismissal of the historical worth of the gospel narratives, his conviction that historical critical methodology yields the true picture of who Jesus is was taken up with considerable enthusiasm in what became known as 'the quest of the historical Jesus'. Paramount among the aims of the Quest was the determination to distinguish the *real* 'Jesus of history' from the *fantastical* 'Christ of faith'.

Kierkegaard took up the theme, most especially in *Philosophical Fragments*, in *Concluding Unscientific Postscript to Philosophical Fragments*, and in *Practice in Christianity*. The matter also crops us frequently in his *Journals*.[33] The Quest, in Kierkegaard's view, was yet another attempt to domesticate God, to confine God within the limits of what we with our critical faculties can conceive. When in *Practice in Christianity* Kierkegaard asks, through his pseudonym Anti-Climacus, 'Can one come to know something about Christ from history?',[34] the answer is an emphatic 'No!' Against the view that getting to the truth about Jesus depends, if not entirely, then to a very considerable extent, on the deliverances of historical inquiry, Anti-Climacus contends that historical inquiry or 'historical-talkative remembrance' as he pejoratively refers to it,[35] distorts and falsifies rather than aids the genuine seeker after Christ.

The 'Invocation' at the beginning of *Practice in Christianity* immediately confronts the error of supposing that we have to do with Christ merely as a past historical figure:

> It is indeed eighteen hundred years since Jesus Christ walked here on earth, but this is certainly not an event just like other events, which once they are over pass into history and then, as the distant past, pass into oblivion. No, his presence here on earth never becomes a thing of the past, thus does not become more and more distant . . .[36]

This alerts us to the first of the problems Anti-Climacus sees with the historical quest for Jesus Christ: it treats the reality with which Christology is concerned as a thing of the past. 'Christendom has taken the liberty', he later explains, 'of construing the whole thing altogether historically, of beginning with letting [Christ] be dead'.[37] The consequence of this move, as has been noted above, is laid out in *Philosophical Fragments*. The person of Christ becomes a vanishing point, a moment *without* decisive significance, a mere occasion. The central interest of Christian faith, accordingly, is no longer the person of Christ, but rather his teaching – a teaching that happily conforms, it is thought, to the best insights of human reason. It is Climacus' view, however, that such a procedure does not illumine but subverts authentic Christian faith. The historical approach to Jesus, he contends, simply muddies the waters. When Christ becomes a vanishing point, and only his teaching is left, then Christianity vanishes with him. That is a view confirmed by Anti-Climacus who writes, '. . . Christ has been abolished altogether, thrown out and his teaching taken over, and finally he is almost regarded as one regards an anonymous writer: the teaching is the principal thing, is everything'.[38] And further:

> But in our day everything is made abstract and everything personal is abolished: we take Christ's teaching – and abolish Christ. This is to abolish Christianity, for Christ is a person and is the teacher who is more important than the teaching. – Just as Christ's life, the fact that he has lived, is vastly more important than all the results of his life (as I have tried to show in another work[39]), so also is Christ infinitely more important than his teaching. It is true only of a human being that his teaching is more important than he himself; to apply this to Christ is a blasphemy, inasmuch as it makes him into only a human being.[40]

There are two theological convictions in the citations above that point to the reasons why Kierkegaard denies the competence of historical inquiry in the sphere of Christology. First is the confession that Christ is not dead but is risen and is therefore present in some manner. Second, is the contention that it is a mistake to think of Christ as 'only a human being'. The Christian gospel, in a nutshell, is the news that through the person of Jesus Christ, humanity is encountered by God himself, and through Christ's death and resurrection God accomplishes an atonement for sin, thus effecting a reconciliation between God and his wayward creatures, and restoring the creation to its intended life of communion with God. This is not simply a teaching, a form of wisdom, or an ethical injunction. The gospel describes, rather, a series of events centred on the person of Christ, in whom God himself is present. Everything depends, accordingly, not on what Christ teaches, but on who he is. If this is the truth of Christian faith, then why is it, as Kierkegaard insists, that historical inquiry cannot get at this truth? It is not that the events themselves are not historical. Kierkegaard readily admits that they are. The moment in time *is* decisive. Our eternal happiness *is* based on an historical point of departure. So why cannot the truth be told about these events within the limits of historical reason alone? To answer that question let us look at what those limits are.

Western historiography has taken many twists and turns since its beginnings in the classical writings of Herodotus and Thucydides. Of interest to our study of Kierkegaard, however, is the historiography developed after the Enlightenment. We have already considered the position of G. E. Lessing who observes, quite correctly, that history is the sphere of the contingent. The things that happen may just as well happen in another way altogether or even not at all. In other words, no necessity attaches to the events of history.[41] Just because of this, Lessing contends that historical knowledge is not subject to rational proof, and he therefore concludes that we cannot be certain of any historical truths. We are obliged then, to seek a basis for 'Christian faith' elsewhere.

The negative estimation of history that is the precursor to Lessing's problem has its roots in Platonism but re-emerges in the philosophy of Leibniz (1646–1716) and Spinoza (1632–1677), both of whose writings are counted amongst Lessing's favourite philosophical reading. Leibniz's theory of knowledge tells us that there are two kinds of truths: necessary truths, knowledge of which is attained through the exercise of pure reason, and contingent truths, attained through the senses. 'The original proof of necessary truths comes from the understanding alone, and all other truths come from experiences or from observations of the senses'.[42] Truths of reason belong to a higher order and valuation than mere truths of fact. Leibniz's explanation of this difference was that 'truths of reason are necessary and their opposite is impossible; those of fact are contingent and their opposite is possible'.[43] Spinoza likewise argues that the natural divine law,

> does not depend on the truth of any historical narrative whatsoever, for inasmuch as this natural divine law is comprehended solely by the consideration of human nature, it is plain that we can conceive it as existing as well in Adam as in any other human being . . . The truth of a historical narrative, however assured, cannot give us the knowledge nor consequently the love of God,

for love of God springs from knowledge of God, and
knowledge of God should be derived from general ideas,
in themselves certain and known, so that the truth of
a historical narrative is very far from being a necessary
requisite for our attaining our highest good.[44]

Taking up this view Lessing argues that historical truths cannot give rise to certainty for any of three reasons: (a) historical
certainty is limited because the truth claims do not arise out of
my own rational essence but are imported as the judgements and
testimonies of others; (b) as distinct from mathematical propositions or rational truths, historical certainty means approximation
and can have, at best, only the rank of probability; (c) if something is to be historically verifiable and therefore certain to me,
it must satisfy the criterion of analogy (i.e. there must be the
possibility of its occurrence elsewhere), causality (we cannot
conceive of any event without a cause) and immanence (i.e. we
must be able to recognise it as belonging to the objectifiable
realm of occurrence).

Testimony to the resurrection of Jesus Christ, according to
Lessing, does not fare well by any of these criteria. At the more
general level however, Lessing argues that if all historical truths
are uncertain then they cannot prove anything. That is, if our
premises are not indubitable our argument cannot have the status
of a proof. His position is articulated in the famous proposition
that 'accidental truths of history can never become the proof
of necessary truths of reason'.[45] There exists a broad ugly ditch
between the two types of truth such that 'it is impossible to
get across however often and however earnestly I have tried to
make the leap'.[46] Kierkegaard, it is to be remembered, is a great
admirer of Lessing. While rejecting utterly Lessing's account of
Christian faith, he nevertheless approves Lessing's recognition
that the confessions of biblical faith are not verifiable by historical inquiry. The reason is plain to see in Lessing's criteria set
out above, especially, as we shall see, in the criteria of analogy,
causality, and immanence.

Those same criteria have been asserted even more forcefully
since the time of Kierkegaard by figures such as Ernst Troeltsch (1865–1923). Troeltsch sets out three principles of historical

method: (1) Criticism: the documentary witnesses to the past must not be taken at face value, but carefully examined to assess their accuracy. Thus no witnesses are to be regarded as absolutely authoritative, and, in consequence, historical judgements may be probable but not certain in character. (Compare, Lessing's criteria a and b); (2) Analogy: the historian can do nothing other than assume that the past is like the present. Our judgements about past events must be based on analogous experiences in our own time (Lessing's criterion c): (3) Correlation: all phenomena of the past must be regarded as the products of a particular context (again, Lessing's criterion c).[47] Troeltsch's approach confirms the reasons for Kierkegaard's objection to the supposition that the truth about Jesus Christ is accessible within the limits of historical reason alone. The criteria of analogy and correlation are the principal problems, for if it is determined in advance of any historical inquiry that all historical events must have a correlate or analogy in our own time, this precludes the occurrence of anything unique. Christian faith, however, is premised on the conviction that the event of the incarnation and the person of Jesus Christ are unique. That claim is certainly contestable. One might very well take offence at it and offer reasons why one might object to it. But it makes no sense to decide the matter in advance. This is what happens, however, in the historiography of Lessing and Troeltsch.[48]

Against the supposition that Jesus is to be understood by analogy with other historical figures and happenings, Kierkegaard, or more particularly his pseudonyms, insist that the 'god-man' is a paradox. He cannot be accounted for within the canons of historical reason. He is, without analogy, the *only-begotten* son of the Father, to use the language of the Christian creeds. Or to put the matter as Anti-Climacus does: 'one cannot *know* anything at all about *Christ*; he is the paradox, the object of faith, exists only for faith'.[49] We shall consider further below this claim on behalf of faith, but let us stay with the analysis of historical inquiry for the moment. Anti-Climacus goes on to ask, 'Can it be demonstrated from history that Christ was God?'[50] Anti-Climacus contends that there is something absurd about the proposal to demonstrate according to the canons of reason something that 'conflicts with all (human) reason'. 'One can "demonstrate"', he continues, 'only that it [the claim that Christ was God] conflicts with reason'.[51] And later, 'the understanding comes to a standstill at the absolute'.[52] It is, however, 'human' reason and understanding that is in conflict with the idea that Christ was God. Anti-Climacus leaves open the possibility that there may be a higher rationality, that of the Logos himself perhaps, according to which the incarnation reveals the true order of things, and according to which the absurd is no longer absurd.[53] Thus does Kierkegaard contend that human reason has limitations that are exposed most especially by the reality with which we are confronted in Christ.

Anti-Climacus' discussion of those limitations echoes that of Johannes Climacus in *Philosophical Fragments*. In Chapter III of the *Fragments*, subtitled, 'A Metaphysical Caprice', Climacus contends that in respect to the paradox the best that reason can do is to will its own downfall. It cannot demonstrate the existence of the god. Lessing and Troeltsch would agree. To 'demonstrate' historically is to find an analogy and a correlate for the event in question, and even then one does not really demonstrate but only estimates a level of probability for the event. The error of Lessing, Troeltsch and of those who follow them, is to suppose that theology has no option but to work within these limitations, and to conclude, therefore, that we must reject (or, pace Hegel, reinterpret so as not to give offence to reason) the claim that Christ was God.

Anti-Climacus continues his argument by sharpening his polemic further:

> The demonstrations for the divinity of Christ that Scripture sets forth – his miracles, his resurrection from the dead, his ascension – are indeed only for faith, that is they are not 'demonstrations'. Neither do they want to demonstrate that all this is in complete harmony with reason; on the contrary, they want to demonstrate that it conflicts with reason and consequently is the object of faith.[54]

Miracles and the resurrection – though he does not mention the ascension – are precisely those elements of the gospel narratives that Lessing finds it impossible to accept.[55] He is unable, quite simply, to accommodate them within the framework of analogy, causality and immanence, that would give historical warrant to the gospel story. Again, Kierkegaard himself agrees; but he does not follow Lessing in supposing that the matter is therefore at an end. Kierkegaard's view, expressed through both Climacus and Anti-Climacus, is that the collision between the gospel narrative and historical reasoning reveals, not the falsity of the gospel proclamation, but rather the incapacity of historical reason to tell the truth of Christ.

One of the ways in which history judges the significance of human beings is to examine the results of their lives, to consider the impact they have had and the way the course of history itself has been shaped by their actions. Beginning with Origen, it was once a standard argument of Christian apologetics that the truth of Christian claims about Christ was confirmed by the spread of Christianity throughout the known world. Indeed, Lessing, while not himself convinced by the argument, nevertheless defends the orthodoxy of Jerome Cardan, a Milanese philosopher of the Italian Renaissance who had been accused of atheism, by adducing Cardan's employment of this argument from history.[56] Cardan may be orthodox but, in Lessing's view, he is also wrong. The identity of Jesus as the Christ is not confirmed by the passing of time. Anti-Climacus agrees:

> 'Is it not eighteen hundred years now since Christ lived, is not his name proclaimed and believed throughout the whole world, has not his teaching (Christianity) changed the shape of the world, victoriously penetrated all its relations, and therefore has not history adequately, or more than adequately, established who he was, that he was – God?' No, history has neither adequately nor more than adequately established that; never in all eternity can history establish that.[57]

Again, Anti-Climacus is ready to give his reason why not. Accepting that the influence of Christ has been widespread, that his name is proclaimed all over the world, and that Christianity has changed the shape of the world, it is nevertheless the case that this demonstrates no more than that 'Jesus Christ was a great man, perhaps the greatest of all. But that he was – God – no, stop; with the help of God that conclusion will surely miscarry'.[58] The problem here is that this procedure is guilty of a *metabasis eis allo genos*. Beginning with a man and the results of his life such a procedure will 'suddenly by way of a conclusion obtain the new quality, God'.[59] To judge the god-man on the results of his life is to make a category mistake, judging him as a mere man without the qualification 'God'.

Anti-Climacus speaks, of course, from the position of faith. He employs an argument that non-believers may regard as circular and thus as completely unconvincing, but we must not dismiss the argument too hastily. Those who would judge Christ according to merely human criteria, that is, by the results of his life, must explain why they have determined to exclude the transcendent category of the divine. What grounds can they give for such a move? The successors of Lessing and Troeltsch, in the various quests of the historical Jesus, will need to do better than simply parrot the post-Enlightenment mantra that 'we have no need of the God-hypothesis'.[60] Anti-Climacus contends that such a procedure cannot do justice to the reality of Jesus himself. Even from the point of view of a neutral observer (were such a position possible), it must be judged unscholarly to decide *a priori* that God is not involved in the reality with which we are concerned in Jesus Christ. For Kierkegaard's own part he is utterly unrelenting in his insistence that the truth of the god-man can be known only through faith. One 'knows' that Christ is Lord, for instance, only when, through a life of discipleship, one has discovered the authority and the trustworthiness of Christ.

Kierkegaard's rejection of historical, critical inquiry raises the question whether he is not himself guilty of Docetism, of supposing, that is, that the historical features of Christ's existence are incidental to his identity. For while it may be true that Christ is not *merely* human, he is still *truly* human. At least, that was the view upheld by the Council of Chalcedon in 451 and accepted by the church as the proper claim of faith. Why then should not the accepted methods of inquiry into historical figures be able to make *some* contribution to understanding who Jesus is, always noting that such methods may not be able to account for the fullness of the reality of Christ? Why should one insist that historical inquiry is to no avail at all? Or to put it in the terms of Anti-Climacus himself, why should any attempt 'to approach Jesus Christ by means of what is known about him from history' be counted as 'blasphemy'?[61] The charge has been levelled against Kierkegaard that he discounts historical inquiry altogether and thus dehistoricises Jesus Christ. Gordon Michalson, for instance, attributes to Kierkegaard the view that historical evidence concerning Jesus Christ is theologically irrelevant.[62] The consequence of this would be that 'the Moment', which has taken place in the midst of history, and by which Johannes Climacus places so much store, is not decisive after all. This conclusion Kierkegaard certainly does not want. But how can he be saved from it in the face of Anti-Climacus' polemic?

Two points may be offered in Kierkegaard's defence. First, Anti-Climacus is surely right when he says that the extraordinary thing about Jesus Christ is not that he was a man; the extraordinary thing (and the salvifically decisive thing) is that it is God who became this man.[63] If that is true, then any inquirer who is not open to this possibility has precluded him or herself from understanding what is truly extraordinary about Christ. Such an inquirer will at best become an admirer but certainly not a disciple. To make Christ's humanity the primary object of interest, therefore – as the assessment of Jesus' life according to its results seems to do – and without regard for the divine extraordinariness of that life 'in-itself',[64] is to forfeit one's claim on the truth. It is to suppose, falsely, that the extraordinariness of Christ's life is established by the accumulation of its results with the passing of time. Kierkegaard's point is that the extraordinariness of Christ – his divinity – has nothing whatever to do with results.

In addition, Anti-Climacus maintains that the fact of Christ's divinity is not for demonstration (or proof) but for faith. It cannot be an object of knowledge. 'One cannot *know* anything at all about *Christ*', he says.[65] Further: 'history can indeed richly communicate knowledge, but knowledge annihilates Jesus Christ'.[66] An objection might be raised at this point. If Anti-Climacus confines 'knowledge' to the realm of the provable and means, therefore, only that the divinity of Christ – thus, the extraordinary reality of Christ – cannot be proven, then this seems unproblematic. Or if, further, he considers 'knowledge' to place the object of our knowing at our disposal, or to give us intellectual command over it, then again, we may agree that knowledge of Christ is not like that. But with the help of theologians such as Karl Barth, and of philosophers such as Michael Polanyi, one might prefer to set forth a broader definition of what may count as knowledge than Anti-Climacus offers here – a definition that refers to the form of knowing that obtains between persons and which is characterised not by command but by love.[67] Kierkegaard does later concede – once his polemical purpose here has been served – that faith does yield a knowledge of truth.

Second, when Anti-Climacus rejects 'history' as a means of inquiry into the reality of Jesus Christ, he has in mind a particular form of historical inquiry, that which, in *Practice in Christianity*, he calls 'secular' or 'profane' history. '[T]hroughout the book', he says, ' "history" is to be understood as profane history, world history, history directly understood in contradistinction to sacred history'.[68] What Anti-Climacus refers to is that form of historical inquiry, abundantly evident in the critical biblical scholarship of Kierkegaard's day and ours, that counts it improper to refer to the being and action of God.[69] Such an approach could only be justified if it were known to be the case that God does not act in human history. That matter, however, cannot be decided in advance. It is both the scholarly and the theological illegitimacy of this move that renders 'profane history' an unsuitable means of inquiry into who Jesus is. A form of historical inquiry that did not set out with such a presupposition might well be a different matter. In that case, investigation of the reality of Christ would not primarily be a matter of assessing the *results* of his life, but rather of attending to the testimony of those who have claim to be reliable witnesses. It is Kierkegaard's own view that precisely in doing that, the reader will be brought to encounter Jesus as he truly is in his abasement. Such an encounter is explored by Kierkegaard through the category of 'contemporaneity'.

## e. Being Contemporary with Christ

In the background of Anti-Climacus's polemic against the historical approach to Jesus Christ lies the Hegelian concept of the world-historical which supposes that the passing of time effects an inevitable improvement in our understanding, and thus makes certain what was not – or not readily – apparent in Christ's own time. On such a view, those who live eighteen hundred years after Christ reap an epistemic benefit from the passing of time. '[H]istory makes it absolutely certain that he was the great one', and people conclude, 'Ergo this is the right thing. That is, it is the right, the noble, the sublime, the true, when it is he who does it'.[70] This is the delusion of Christendom. A person inherits understanding of Christ as a birthright and becomes a Christian just by being born in Denmark. Everything becomes 'as simple as pulling on one's socks'.[71]

> [What] we really do not care to find out in a deeper
> sense [is] what it is he does; even less do we try with the
> help of God and according to our humble capacities to
> imitate him in doing the right, the noble, the sublime,
> the true. [ . . . ] We are content to admire and extol
> and – as was said of a translator who timidly translated an
> author word-for-word, therefore meaninglessly – are "too
> scrupulous", perhaps also are too cowardly and flabby
> really to want to understand.[72]

'As a result', Anti-Climacus continues, 'one must attempt again to introduce Christianity into Christendom'.[73] What that means is evident not only in *Practice in Christianity* but also in Kierkegaard's other writings: the emphasis must again be placed on imitation.[74] The emphasis must be placed, not on having an *idea* of the right, the noble, the sublime and the true, but rather on following the one who is and does these things. This following is what Anti-Climacus means when he speaks of becoming contemporary. Put another way, to be contemporary is to *believe*, where believing means putting one foot in front of the other, setting out upon the road as a follower of Christ, venturing out over the 70,000 fathoms of water. It does not mean sitting in one's study and contemplating Christ. It does not mean being part of a generation and a nation that has inherited Christ's good name. It does not mean becoming an admirer of the influence Christ has had through history. Such veneration, the veneration afforded by and satisfied with historical distance, 'is not worth a pickled herring'.[75] Christ seeks imitators not admirers, 'not adherents of a teaching but imitators of a life'.[76]

Christ invites us then to come to him, but Anti-Climacus, as we have seen above, stresses that the invitation is made by Christ in his abasement. Hearers of the invitation are not invited by Christ in his glory, but rather in his lowliness. The invitation, therefore, is to become lowly oneself, to take up one's cross,[77] and thus to take on the servant form that Christ himself took on. Only those who have ventured on that road are entitled to call themselves Christians. It is important to note here, that the emphasis is placed on *venturing* rather than on completing the journey.[78] Kierkegaard is well aware that even the best of Christians journey hesitatingly; they stumble and fall behind and think often of turning back. But there is all the difference in the world – the difference between being a Christian and not – between the person who has started to follow Christ in lowliness and the one who has ventured nothing. 'If you cannot bear contemporaneity [ . . . ] then you are not *essentially* Christian'.[79]

To be contemporary with Christ is a high demand. It is not easy, for example, to sell all one's possessions and give the money to the poor (Mt. 19.21). The demand of contemporaneity goes well beyond – indeed is of a different order to – the ethical.[80] It involves a change of condition, as the following passage shows:

> 'Come here *to me*'. Amazing! Human sympathy does,
> after all, willingly do something for those who labor
> and are burdened; we feed the hungry, clothe the naked,
> make philanthropic donations, build philanthropic
> institutions, and if the sympathy is deeper we probably
> also visit those who labor and are burdened. But to
> invite them to come to one, that cannot be done; then
> one's entire household and way of life would have to be
> altered. It will not do, when one is living in abundance
> oneself or at least in joy and gladness, to reside together
> in a house and live together in a common life and in daily
> association with the poor and wretched, with those who
> labor and are burdened. In order to invite them to come
> to one in this way, one must oneself live in the very same

manner, poor as the poorest, poorly regarded as the lowly man among the people, experienced in life's sorrow and anguish, sharing the very same condition as those one invites to come to one.[81]

In his descriptions of what it is to be a Christian Anti-Climacus can occasionally sound harsh and uncompromising. But his articulation of the demands of faith follows closely the biblical account of what it is to be a disciple, and especially the words of Christ himself. Kierkegaard's wish is that we see ourselves in the mirror of the biblical word.[82] After the harsh word has been heard and acknowledged however, Kierkegaard can also be gentle. His advice, through Anti-Climacus, to those who 'cannot bear contemporaneity' is this:

> What you have to do, then, is to confess this unconditionally to yourself so that you above all maintain humility and fear and trembling in relation to what it truly means to be Christian. For it is along that way that you must go in order to learn and to practice resorting to grace in such a way that you do not take it in vain . . .[83]

The reference to grace is indispensable. For all that contemporaneity is a striving, 'a prodigious exertion',[84] Anti-Climacus does not suppose that contemporaneity is something that we *achieve*. Similarly, Kierkegaard writes in his *Journals*,

> On closer inspection all this talk about wishing to have been contemporary with Christ is presumptuous; for what is it but fancying oneself to be good enough to be an apostle. And even the apostles fell away, and they had to be equipped with extraordinary divine powers in order to be, that is, to be able to keep on being, contemporary with him – the best evidence that no one can keep on being contemporary with him all by himself.[85]

Imitation is thus a vital word, but it is neither the first word nor the last. It is not the first because in the matter of becoming a contemporary it is Christ who takes the initiative. He is the one who invites. '[H]e is himself the one who goes around and, calling, almost pleading, says: Come here. He, the only one who is able to help and help with the one thing needful'.[86] Moreover, as readers of Climacus's *Philosophical Fragments* will already have understood, becoming contemporary is contingent on receiving the condition from 'the god'.[87] Neither is imitation the *last* word, for when a person's striving leaves him or her still short of the glory of God (Rom. 3.23), then 'Christ's life has another meaning as well; it is atonement. If Christ were only the prototype, then it was cruel of Him to force the issue to such an extreme; but He had to die – in order to save the world'.[88] Christianly conceived, those who venture out even the merest distance in imitation of Christ suddenly find that the fullness of the life of Christ has been given to them. Atonement is theirs. Grace has abounded after all. Venturing the decisive act of imitation becomes the means by which the disciple 'flees to grace'.[89]

The emphasis on Christ as prototype makes clear that Christian faith is vitally concerned with the historical figure of Christ. Climacus explains, '[t]he follower [ . . . ] is in faith related to that teacher in such a way that he is eternally occupied with his historical existence'.[90] But, despite this 'eternal occupation' it is not the endeavour of historical inquiry that will make one a follower. '[K]nowing a historical fact – indeed, knowing all the historical facts with the trustworthiness of an eyewitness – by no means makes the eyewitness a follower'.[91] Only faith does that. For to be a follower is not to know all the historical facts about Christ, but to live with Christ, in contemporaneity. It is to venture the decisive act.

# Chapter 5

# The Human Predicament

In February 1843, Kierkegaard published the first work in what he would come to call his 'authorship'. It was *Either/Or* published by the pseudonymous editor Victor Eremita who has collected together a series of papers representing 'aesthetic' and ethical points of view. At the time of its writing, Kierkegaard spoke of it to his friend Emil Boesen and said, 'I hope you will keep this between us. Anonymity is of the utmost importance to me'.[1] Apparently the 'life-views' presented in *Either/Or* are not ones that Kierkegaard wants to put his own name to. They represent *possible* conceptions of what it is to be a human being, but they are not life-views that Kierkegaard himself wishes to commend. For his own part he says,

> An authorship that began with *Either/Or* and advanced
> step by step seeks here its consummating place of rest at
> the foot of the altar, where the author, personally most
> aware of his own imperfection and guilt, certainly does
> not call himself a witness to the truth but only a singular
> kind of poet and thinker who, 'without authority',
> has had nothing new to bring but 'has wanted to
> read through once again, if possible in a more inward
> way, the original text of individual human existence-
> relationships, the old, familiar text handed down from
> the fathers . . .'[2]

The exploration of 'individual human existence-relationships' was in fact the concern of the whole authorship, always however, with the express aim to make clear what it is to be a Christian. The clarification of what Christian existence consists in involved

Kierkegaard in setting out the alternative possibilities, namely the aesthetic, the ethical, and what Kierkegaard called 'Religiousness A', a form of religiousness he distinguishes from Christianity or 'Religiousness B'. Each of these categories represents a 'life-view' or an 'existence-sphere' as they are predominantly referred to in *Stages on Life's Way*. Initially there are three such spheres of existence, the aesthetic, the ethical and the religious although, when exploring the character of the 'religious' sphere Kierkegaard distinguishes between religiousness A and religiousness B.[3] Judge William,[4] one of the characters in *Either/Or*, refers to the aesthetic, the ethical and the religious as 'the three great allies', and comments,

> . . . if you do not know how to preserve the unity of the different manifestations everything gains in these different spheres, then life is without meaning and one must completely agree with your pet theory that of everything it can be said: Do it, or do not do it – you will regret it either way.[5]

A life-view consists, apparently, in a framework for the interpretation of one's existence and the meaningful determination of one's choices in life.[6] Without commitment to some life-view or other, be it aesthetic, ethical or religious, life simply becomes meaningless, and one has no reason to act in one way and not another – 'you will regret it either way'. Thus, '[e]very human being, no matter how slightly gifted he is, however subordinate his position in life may be, has a natural need to formulate a life-view, a conception of the meaning of life and of its purpose'.[7] It is important to note (again) here that commitment to a life-view does not mean holding to it as an idea; it means rather that the life-view is expressed in one's existence. Johannes Climacus describes *Either/Or* as 'an indirect polemic against speculative thought, which is indifferent to existence'.[8] The point is 'to exist in what one understands'.[9] We will survey here only briefly what the aesthetic and ethical forms of existence consist in, for our task in this chapter is to proceed to an analysis of what it means to exist 'before God'.

## a. The Aesthetic

Again in *Either/Or* Judge William asks,

> But what does it mean to live esthetically, and what does
> it mean to live ethically? What is the esthetic in a person,
> and what is the ethical? To that I would respond: the
> esthetic in a person is that by which he spontaneously and
> immediately is what he is; the ethical is that by which he
> becomes what he becomes.[10]

The person who lives within the sphere of the aesthetic is
concerned only with the immediate. Such a person is motivated
by what will bring pleasure, comfort, and immediate satisfaction. The popular expression for the aesthetic is, 'one must
enjoy life'.[11] Judge William explains further: 'The personality
is immediately qualified, not mentally–spiritually but physic-
ally. Here we have a life-view that teaches that health is the
most precious good, is that around which everything revolves.
A more poetic expression of the same view reads: Beauty is the
ultimate'.[12] Further expressions too are possible, as can easily
be imagined – the all-consuming desire for wealth, fame, success in one's career, for common example. 'But the person who
says that he wants to enjoy life [in these ways] always posits a
condition that either lies outside the individual or is within
the individual in such a way that it is not there by virtue of the
individual himself'.[13] That is, the condition for the enjoyment
of life lies outside the individual. An external good is 'made
life's task and its content'.[14]

Kierkegaard is not altogether disapproving of the aesthetic
life. The aesthete has at least the virtue of being committed to a
life-view, of showing some passion, of existing in what he or she
understands. The esthetic life-view is thus an 'ally' of the ethical
and the religious in providing a framework by which one's life
has some meaning. But, along with Judge William, Kierkegaard
urges consideration of a higher view, a view determined by the
ethical – at least, or, better still, by the awareness of one's existence before God.

## b. The Ethical

The ethical, we have seen already, is that by which a person 'becomes what he becomes'. But this needs some explanation. According to Judge William, the ethicist teaches us that 'there is a calling for every human being' and we are to choose it ethically.[15] To be ethical, in other words, is to accept the responsibilities of one's calling. In contrast with the aesthete in *Either/Or* who counsels against getting involved in friendship, or marriage, and against taking an official post,[16] for each of these will constrain one in some measure and hinder the realization of one's quest for pleasure, the ethicist commends conformity to the roles and practices of an established social order. Judge William refers again and again to marriage as an exemplification of the ethical life-view. Commitment, faithfulness and the fulfilment of a particular role as husband or wife are the virtues especially in view here.[17] This emphasis on the relation of the human personality to its social context is Hegelian in character. Hegel drew a distinction between 'morality' (*Moralitaet*) and the 'ethical life' (*Sittlichkeit*). Morality, though not entirely dismissed by Hegel, refers to the abstractions of Kantian ethics, whereas *Sittlichkeit* is concerned with 'the concrete relations of a living social order'.[18] Human beings find their true fulfilment, according to Hegel, 'not in the abstractions of Kantian morality, but in conformity to the laws and customs of society'.[19]

Hegel rejects Kant's view that it is possible and necessary for the individual to supply his or her own morality. We find criteria for ethical action, rather, in the established social practices of a well-ordered community. The values imposed upon us by virtue of our membership of that community are those necessary to its good ordering. Conformity to these values or ethical principles is a process of self-actualisation. For Hegel, then, true personhood is actualized only by being given concrete embodiment in the roles of a harmonious social system or ethical life. It makes no sense, to ask, what must I do to be good? We should ask instead, what must I do to be a good father or a good teacher, or a good shopkeeper? Goodness is not some abstract notion but a predicate attaching to roles within a particular social system. This is Judge William's view. To be ethical is to accept the responsibilities of one's calling. Judge William writes:

> When a person has a calling, he generally has a norm outside himself, which, without making him a slave, nevertheless gives him some indication of what he has to do, maps out his time for him, often provides him with an occasion to begin. If at some time he fails in his task, he hopes to do it better the next time . . .[20]

Judge William further contends that the identification of one's calling 'reconciles the person with life', for it places her securely within the category of the universal. For all the differences in the callings of particular individuals, there remains the universal, that it is a calling. The individual has a part to play within the social order. We see here again a conception of human life that Kierkegaard himself resists strongly. Within Judge William's conception of the world it is easy to conceive what it is to be a Christian in just these terms. To be a Christian is simply to fulfil one's calling, to take one's place in the social order, and when the social order is Christendom, being a Christian is as easy as pulling on one's socks. We will return to this critique of the ethical in chapter six below when we will consider Kierkegaard's estimation of Abraham.

Meanwhile let us note two further points about the ethical as it is presented by Judge William. Although Judge William himself doesn't realize it, absorption into the universal constitutes a loss of personal identity. To identify one's calling with the acceptance of some role within the established social order is precisely to lose one's identity. The contemporary Orthodox theologian John Zizioulas has recently made this point in his account of human personhood. The uniqueness of the person 'is relativized in social life', Zizioulas contends.[21] In any of the social roles one may adopt, as husband, teacher, shopkeeper and so on, one is replaceable. The role does not secure one's unique identity. The person is not 'saved' by his or her fulfilment of a social role. Kierkegaard does not develop an account of personhood in the same way that Zizioulas does, but his determination to safeguard the uniqueness of the individual against the tyranny of the universal that he saw at work in Hegelian philosophy, anticipates Zizioulas's similar critique of a view, ever more prevalent in the modern world, that reduces the person to a useful object within a social order.

This brings us to a second point. To recognize that a person is not saved by her fulfilment of a social role, is a reiteration of the Pauline contention that we are not saved by works. Frater Taciturnus, another of Kierkegaard's pseudonyms, hints at this when he writes in *Stages on Life's Way*, '. . . the ethical [is] the sphere of requirement (and this requirement is so infinite that the individual always goes bankrupt) . . .'[22] In the same place Taciturnus says, 'The ethical is only a transition sphere, and therefore its highest expression is repentance . . .' Again, we may note a correspondence to the Pauline claim that 'all have sinned and fall short of the glory of God'.[23] Although Judge William doesn't explicitly recognize that the ethical striving he commends always ends in 'bankruptcy', he does find reason to ponder just that possibility when at the very end of his counsel to the young aesthete in *Either/Or* he sends to his correspondent a sermon written by 'an older friend who is a pastor in Jylland'. The sermon is titled, 'The Upbuilding That Lies in the Thought That in Relation to God We Are Always in the Wrong'.[24] Frater Taciturnus, we have seen, noted that the requirement of the ethical is infinite; it can never be fulfilled and so the individual striving to accomplish the ethical 'always goes bankrupt'. There is an echo here of Martin Luther's struggle to make himself righteous before God.

I myself was a monk; for twenty years I tortured myself with prayers, fastings, vigils, and freezing; the frost alone might have killed me. It caused me pain such as I will never inflict on myself again even if I could. What else did I seek by doing this than God, who was supposed to note my strict observance of the monastic order and my austere life. I constantly walked in a dream and lived in real idolatry for I did not believe in Christ. I regarded him only as a severe and terrible judge, portrayed as seated on a rainbow. Therefore I cast about for other intercessors, Mary and various other saints, also my own works and the merits of my order. And I did all this for the sake of God not for money or for goods.[25]

The received wisdom of Luther's theological schooling told him that God was a stern and angry judge who could accept only those who were righteous. This 'wisdom' served only to torment Luther for he could never justify himself before the infinite requirement. Luther's struggle might have been in the mind of the pastor in Jylland when in his sermon he describes the torments of 'the doubter':

> Thus he ascertained that this wisdom was a treacherous
> friend who under the guise of helping him entangled
> him in doubt, worried him into an unremitting cycle
> of confusion. What had been obscure to him previously
> but had not troubled him did not become any clearer
> now, but his mind became anguished and careworn
> in doubt. Only in an infinite relationship with God
> could the doubt be calmed; only in an infinitely free
> relationship with God could the God who cares be
> turned to joy. He is in an infinite relationship with God
> when he acknowledges that God is always right; he is
> in an infinitely free relationship with God when he
> acknowledges that he is always wrong.[26]

What does this freedom consist in? It is freedom from the burden of having to justify oneself. It is the freedom that ensues when one recognizes that before God one has been justified already and has been loved unconditionally all the while. And so at the end of Judge William's lengthy commendation of the ethical life-view, the sermon of an older friend presents the possibility that the ethical as such cannot save us from despair. Something beyond the ethical is needed, something we have customarily called the religious.

We must not suppose that the ethicist, Judge William, had not previously been interested in religion. Being 'religious' was in Christendom, a social convention happily endorsed and taken seriously by the Judge. The practice of religion, particularly attendance at church on Sunday, was an important constituent of good citizenship and another measure of ethical achievement. For Judge William, God is the architect and ultimate guarantor of the moral order of the universe. The convention of marriage, for instance, is established by God[27] and conformity to the moral order is conceived as a responsibility we hold before God.[28] But, as David Gouwens has noted, Judge William's ethical formation before God 'assumes an essential *self*-reliance'.[29] He still believes that the person has the power to put himself in right-relation with God. It is the pastor in Jylland who introduces the thought that before God we are *always* in the wrong, and that we stand in need therefore, of God's forgiveness and God's help. The pastor's sermon throws into question Judge William's confidence that we have the capacity ourselves to form an ethical character before God.[30]

## c. The Consciousness of Sin

The recognition that before God we are always in the wrong, or, more precisely, the recognition of sin, is identified by Johannes Climacus as the point of departure and the crucial expression for religious existence.[31] But we must be more precise still. One enters the religious sphere not by coming to some abstract conception of the category of sin, but rather by understanding oneself as a sinner. 'It is important', Climacus insists, 'that sin not be conceived in abstract categories, in which it cannot be conceived at all, that is, decisively, because it stands in an essential relation to existing'.[32] Climacus here directs his reader to 'a book titled *The Concept of Anxiety*' penned also by Kierkegaard but this time under the pseudonym Vigilius Haufniensis. That work is subtitled, 'A Simple Psychologically Orienting Deliberation on the Dogmatic Issue of Hereditary Sin'. That it is the 'dogmatic issue' Kierkegaard is concerned with here is important. Sin is properly the subject of revelation. 'Only the god could teach it', Climacus tells us in *Philosophical Fragments*[33] which suggests already that sin is not an ethical category but has to do with one's relation to God. Climacus has also told us that sin is 'to exist in untruth',[34] to exist, that is, in alienation from the one who is himself the Truth.

The true nature of sin is revealed by God and yet manifests itself as anxiety. Vigilius Haufniensis tells us that subjective anxiety is the consequence of sin. Objective anxiety, on the other hand, is 'the reflection of the sinfulness of the generation in the whole world'. [35] The first formulation indicates that sin afflicts the individual, and the second indicates that it afflicts the human race, and indeed the whole creation. Haufniensis refers to Rom. 8.19 where creation is depicted as waiting with eager longing . . .[36] The same passage speaks of creation's groaning in travail. Creation as a whole has been 'subjected to futility' (Rom. 8.20); it 'sank into corruption' as Haufniensis puts it, and this on account of Adam's sin.[37] Kierkegaard clearly thinks of Adam as a particular historical individual and is concerned in *The Concept of Anxiety* to show that despite Adam's uniqueness as the originator of hereditary sin, there is no *essential* difference between Adam and all other sinful human beings. Although the race, since Adam, is afflicted by sin, and although each of us is caught up in that sinfulness, Kierkegaard rejects the idea that sin is part of our human substance.[38] The similarity to Adam is twofold: sin does not belong to the essence of our humanity, and we are therefore culpable for sin. There is for each of us a 'qualitative leap' into sin. Sin is not the expression of our essential nature, but a movement into another category, namely disobedience. Thus, 'the guilt that breaks forth in anxiety by the qualitative leap retains the same accountability as that of Adam . . .'[39] Kierkegaard hereby maintains the orthodox dogmatic conception: sin is our fault, not that of the Creator.

To explain further Kierkegaard's conception of sin we need to invoke his account of the self. In *The Sickness Unto Death*, Kierkegaard, through his pseudonym Anti-Climacus, offers his well-known but conceptually difficult definition of the self.

A human being is spirit. But what is spirit? Spirit is the self. But what is the self? The self is a relation that relates itself to itself or is the relation's relating itself to itself in the relation; the self is not the relation but is the relation's relating itself to itself. A human being is a synthesis of the infinite and the finite, of the temporal and the eternal, of freedom and necessity, in short, a synthesis. A synthesis is a relation between two. Considered in this way, a human being is still not a self.

> In the relation between two, the relation is the third as a negative unity, and the two relate to the relation and in the relation to the relation; thus under the qualification of the psychical the relation between the psychical and the physical is a relation. If, however, the relation relates itself to itself, this relation is the positive third, and this is the self.[40]

In explication of this conception of the self, let us consider first the claim that a human being is a synthesis of the infinite and the finite, of the temporal and the eternal, of freedom and necessity. Anti-Climacus here reflects an ancient wisdom represented, for instance, in the biblical tradition which says of human beings, 'dust you are and to dust you shall return' (Gen. 3.19), and yet also confesses that they 'have been made a little lower than God' and have been 'crowned with glory and honour' (Ps. 8.5). We are 'of the earth', finite, temporal and bound by the conditions of created existence, and yet the constitution of our humanity extends beyond the merely material. We exist in relation to God and are endowed with freedom to respond to God in love – or in defiance. Both things are true of each human subject; we are at once both finite, limited, material beings and yet endowed with freedom and called to life in communion with God.[41] These two aspects of human being are to be held in relation – 'the self is a relation . . .'. Anti-Climacus suggests, but adds, 'the self is a relation *that relates itself to itself*'. There is a third aspect to the constitution of the self, beyond the synthesis of the related pairs. This third aspect is consciousness. Human beings are capable of *self*-consciousness. That is, they may become aware of themselves as a synthesis of the finite, and the infinite, and so on . . . Precisely in virtue of that self-awareness, the synthesis becomes a task that we are to work at and maintain in proper balance. In a conception that would be taken up by the existentialist thinkers who came after him, Anti-Climacus, and clearly Kierkegaard himself,[42] rejects the idea that the self is a completed, static entity, a finished product, as it were, that has only to express itself. Rather, the self is a life-long project for which the individual is responsible. The later existentialists were divided however about whether to accept or reject the further claim that the self is a relation that 'has been established by another'.[43] For Kierkegaard, however, this affirmation is of paramount importance. We exist before God, and the goal of the self is 'to rest transparently in the power that established it'. We may note the echo here of Augustine's famous confession, 'Thou hast made us for Thyself, and restless is our heart until it comes to rest in Thee'.[44]

The restlessness to which Augustine refers, is analysed by Kierkegaard under the concepts of 'anxiety' and 'despair'. Both are manifestations of the self's alienation from the power that established it. 'Anxiety may be compared with dizziness' Haufniensis observes. It is a dizziness that occurs when the self becomes aware of the freedom in which it has been created and grasps hold of the finite in order to support itself.[45] Much like Fyodor Dostoyevsky's later tale of the Grand Inquisitor in which Christ is accused of imposing too great a burden upon human beings by granting them freedom,[46] Kierkegaard contends that we typically exercise our God-given freedom by plunging ourselves into bondage. The forms this may take are endless, but they commonly involve the attachment of ultimate importance to finite things. We stake our identity on our possessions, our reputation and our career. We forgo our freedom and become enslaved to finite goods that will one day pass away. These things are not evil but they become the cause of our enslavement if we attach ultimate importance to them. Just so, we fall into sin. Sin may be conceived, then, as a mis-relation between the finite and the infinite, the temporal and the eternal, freedom and necessity. To over-emphasize the infinite and the eternal is to suppose oneself to be a god; it is to be puffed up, to claim inordinate power and to imagine oneself superior to others. To over-emphasize the finite and the temporal, on the other hand, is to conceive of oneself and one's identity entirely in material terms. Those guilty of such mis-relation exist in despair. This does not mean that they will appear to be miserable; such people may indeed be, and often are, very comfortable and happy. Their despair consists, rather, in their misplaced and thus false hope. They have staked their existence on something that will not endure. Kierkegaard is in no doubt that we are all to be numbered in this group. We all fall short. We have all plunged ourselves into the bondage of sin, and stand in need, therefore, of forgiveness and re-creation. We are all afflicted with 'the sickness unto death'. This description comes, of course, from John's gospel, more particularly from the story of the raising of Lazarus (Jn. 11.4). When it is reported to Jesus that his friend Lazarus is ill, he responds, 'this sickness is not unto death'. Yet, as the story unfolds, we learn that Lazarus does die. The term 'death' clearly means in this context something other than the cessation of biological existence. Kierkegaard himself explains that '. . . in Christian terminology death is . . . the expression for the state of deepest spiritual wretchedness'.[47]

Spiritual wretchedness is the state of indifference toward God or of imagining oneself independent of God, of not needing God, of being defiant in face of God's forgiveness. It is to be unaware that one's highest perfection as a human being is to need God.[48] Why is this called 'death'? It is because without spirit we are mere matter, bunches of cells, walking around without meaning or purpose. As Shakespeare's Macbeth puts it, 'Life is but a poor tale, told by an idiot, signifying nothing'. The tragedy is, Kierkegaard thinks, that whatever we may confess to the contrary, we commonly live as though that were true. We live without spirit. Considering the applicability of Kierke-gaard's insight to our own consumerist age, we may note that in the Western world, our hearts commonly lie where our material treasure is.

However various may be the manifestations of misplaced trust, that is, of despair, there are two principal forms, Kierke-gaard suggests, of this sickness unto death. The first is despair in weakness: sin is 'in despair not to will to be oneself'.[49] This despair, 'in weakness' manifests itself as a failure to recognize or accept one's true identity before God. This can be 'despair over the earthly'[50] a classic instance of which is being anxious for tomorrow. One of the biblical texts to which Kierkegaard made frequent reference and about which he wrote numerous discourses[51] is Mt. 6.24–34. The text describes various ways in which we may be anxious over earthly things without realizing that God knows our every need. Despair in weakness may also be a despair 'of the eternal or over oneself'.[52] Here one recognizes one's weakness or one's sinfulness but despairs that God cannot help. The person who despairs in this way wallows in weakness, is filled with self-loathing and thereby loses both 'the eternal and himself'.[53] At its maximum such despair is 'inclosing reserve' [*Indesluttethed*].[54] Anti-Climacus here echoes Luther's account of sin as *homo incurvatus in se*, the human turned in upon itself.[55] St Augustine likewise contended that the root of all evil was self-enclosure.[56]

The second form of despair is defiant and is described thus: sin is 'in despair to will to be oneself'.[57] Anti-Climacus refers here to the sin of self-assertion, to the propensity of human beings to go their own way, without God, and to fashion for themselves an illusory and impossible identity and existence. It is, Anti-Climacus says, 'a misuse of the eternal'[58] and the determination to be one's own master.[59] The sinfulness here described is represented in the serpent's words in Gen. 3.5: 'When you eat of the tree, your eyes will be opened and you will be like God . . .' Raskolnikov in Dostoyevsky's novel, *Crime and Punishment* provides a good example of this form of defiant despair. Imagining himself to be a Napoleonic figure, Raskolnikov believed that his greatness as a human being placed him beyond the obligations and reach of the law. Christianly conceived, the despair of willing to be oneself is the sin of supposing that we can invest our own lives with meaning and purpose in defiance of the truly human life established and revealed in Jesus Christ.

## d. Everything Must Serve for Upbuilding

Anti-Climacus's intention in *The Sickness Unto Death* is to offer an exposition of the sickness that afflicts human beings. But his intent is pastoral. His exposition is 'for upbuilding and awakening'. In the Preface, he writes,

> From the Christian point of view, everything, indeed everything, ought to serve for upbuilding . . . Everything essentially Christian must have in its presentation a

resemblance to the way a physician speaks at the sickbed; even if only medical experts understand it, it must never be forgotten that the situation is the bedside of a sick person.[60]

As is pointed out by Howard and Edna Hong in their introduction to *The Sickness Unto Death*, a student sermon given by Kierkegaard in 1841 reveals Kierkegaard's deep insight into the human predicament and serves as an apt summary of the condition of sin and alienation from God. It is worth quoting at length.

Or was there not a time also in your consciousness, my listener, when cheerfully and without care you were glad with the glad, when you wept with those who wept, when the thought of God blended irrelevantly with your other conceptions, blended with your happiness but did not sanctify it, blended with your grief but did not comfort it? And later, was there not a time when this in some sense guiltless life, which never called itself to account, vanished? Did there not come a time when your mind was unfruitful and sterile, your will incapable of all good, your emotions cold and weak, when hope was dead in your breast and recollection painfully clutched at a few solitary memories of happiness and soon these also became loathsome, when everything was of no consequence to you, and the secular bases of comfort found their way to your soul only to wound even more your troubled mind which impatiently and bitterly turned away from them? Was there not a time when you found no one to whom you could turn, when the darkness of quiet despair brooded over your soul, and you did not have the courage to let it go but would rather hang onto it and you even brooded once more over your despair? When heaven was shut for you, and the prayer died on your lips, or it became a shriek of anxiety that demanded an accounting from heaven, and yet you sometimes found within you a longing, an intimation to which you might ascribe meaning, but this was soon crushed by the thought that you were a nothing and your soul lost in infinite space? Was there not a time when you felt that the world did not

understand your grief, could not heal it, could not give
you any peace, that this had to be in heaven, if heaven
was anywhere to be found; alas, it seemed to you that
the distance between heaven and earth was infinite, and
just as you yourself lost yourself in contemplating the
immeasurable world, just so God had forgotten you and
did not care about you? And in spite of all this, was there
not a defiance in you that forbade you to humble yourself
under God's mighty hand? Was this not so? And what
would you call this condition if you do not call it death,
and how would you describe it except as darkness?[61]

Beyond diagnosis, and because of his pastoral concern to
make clear what Christianity is, Kierkegaard is interested also
in the cure to this state of 'deepest spiritual wretchedness'.
The cure he says, in that same student sermon, and again in *The
Sickness Unto Death*, is 'simply to die, to die to the world'.[62] The
text for the student sermon was Phil. 1.19–25 and at its centre
stands the verse upon which Kierkegaard focuses: 'For to me,
to live is Christ and to die is gain'. The message of the apostles
is not given, Kierkegaard writes, 'in order that we should be
appalled by our own wretchedness but in order that we should
praise and thank God . . . You know – and this is sufficient for
you – that you too are called with a divine call, that the spirit is
the same even if the gifts of grace are different; you know that
you too are God's co-worker'.[63] This, ultimately, is the cure for
despair – divine grace, and dying to the world. For we cannot
receive God's grace unless we let go of works, unless we let go
of our reliance upon those things that enable us to get ahead
and provide a kind of security in the world. We cannot receive
God's grace unless we let go of, die to, the effort to justify ourselves. The Christian prescription for the spiritual wretchedness
is death, and then new life – in Christ.

## e. Consciousness of the Self

It follows, for Kierkegaard, that one cannot come to a true
knowledge of oneself except before Christ. '[T]he intensification

of the consciousness of the self is the knowledge of Christ, a self directly before Christ'.[64] And further:

> A self directly before Christ is a self intensified by the inordinate concession from God, intensified by the inordinate accent that falls upon it because God allowed himself to be born, become man, suffer and die also for the sake of this self. As stated previously, the greater the conception of God, the more self; so it holds true here: the greater the conception of Christ the more self. Qualitatively a self is what its criterion is. That Christ is the criterion is the expression, attested by God, for the staggering reality that a self has, for only in Christ is it true that God is man's goal and criterion, or the criterion and goal.[65]

Of particular note here is Kierkegaard's contention, again in agreement with Anti-Climacus, that the true criterion and goal of the self is found in Christ, in what God has done for humanity in Christ. In answer to the question, what is it to be human, Kierkegaard leads us to answer, to be human is to be one for whose sake, 'God allowed himself to be born, become man, suffer and die'. Kierkegaard's anthropology, his definition of the self, is in the end, as it was in the beginning but under different terminology, thoroughly christological. Christ is the criterion for what it is to be human. A century later Karl Barth, who learned much from Kierkegaard, made the same point: A genuine knowledge of humanity, says Barth, '. . . can be based only on the particular knowledge of the man Jesus Christ, and therefore on Christology'.[66]

## f. Forgiveness

But let us explore further what it means for the individual that 'God allowed himself to be born, become man, suffer and die'. Briefly put, as it is in *The Sickness Unto Death*, it means that 'God offers reconciliation in the forgiveness of sin'.[67] Anti-Climacus is not much interested in the 'mechanism' by which forgiveness of sin takes place. He does not enter into discussion, for instance, about the metaphors of atonement presented in the Bible. He *is* interested, however, in the declaration of forgiveness presented to the individual.[68] Here above all, there is no refuge in the crowd. In the teaching about sin, Christianity is concerned with the single individual.[69] Concerning the forgiveness of sin, Christianity addresses the individual and says, 'You shall believe – that is, either you shall be offended or you shall believe. Not one word more; there is nothing more to add. "Now I have spoken," declares God in heaven; "we shall discuss it again in eternity. In the meantime, you can do what you want to, but judgement is at hand"'.[70] Anti-Climacus here reflects the fact that whatever may be said about the logic of forgiveness, ultimately the forgiveness of sin is simply a declaration, as, for instance, in Jesus' encounter with the paralytic: 'Your sins are forgiven' (Mk. 2.5) or the woman caught in adultery: 'Neither do I condemn you. Go your way and from now on do not sin again' (Jn. 8.11). This is not a matter for negotiation. 'You shall believe – that is, either you shall be offended or you shall believe'. Belief in the declaration of forgiveness is bound up with belief in the person who makes the declaration. Here, for Anti-Climacus, the possibility of offence is at its most acute. That which can be declared only by God (Mk. 2.7) is declared by one who comes among us in the form of a lowly servant, who is poor, who is forsaken and who surrenders to humanity's violence.[71] This lowly, nondescript, servant of humanity declares, 'your sins are forgiven', and adds, 'blessed is the one who takes no offense at me'. The opposite of sin – its overcoming – is not virtue, Anti-Climacus insists. It is faith; more particularly, it is faith in Christ. This, says Anti-Climacus, is the theme throughout *The Sickness Unto Death*. '[T]he formula for the state in which there is no despair at all: in relating itself to itself and in willing to be itself, the self *rests transparently in the power that established it*. This formula in turn . . . is the definition of faith'.[72]

We noted above that the fact and nature of sin is not a matter of general knowledge. 'Neither paganism nor the natural man knows what sin is . . . '[73] Moral failure and petty misdemeanours may be a matter of public observation but sin is a different category. Sin has to do with one's existence before God. Christianity assumes, therefore, 'that there has to be a revelation from God to show what sin is'.[74] In his *Journals* he writes,

> Just as the first impression of a true and deep love is the feeling of one's own unworthiness, in the same way the need for forgiveness of sins betokens that one loves God. But all by himself no man can ever come to think that God loves him. This must be proclaimed to men. This is the gospel, this is revelation. But precisely because no human being can by himself come to the idea that God loves him, in like manner no human being can come to know how great a sinner he is. Consequently the Augsburg Confession teaches that it must be revealed to a man how great a sinner he is. For without the divine yard-stick, no human being is the great sinner (this he is – only before God).[75]

Kierkegaard's view contrasts with the traditional Western *ordo salutis* (order of salvation) in which it is supposed that the process of salvation commences when, in virtue of their own powers of discernment, individuals recognize and repent of their sin. Only then does God offer forgiveness and reconciliation. Grace and forgiveness are presumed to be conditional upon the sinner's contrition. The New Testament, however, has it the other way around. It is in the light of Christ and *following* the word of forgiveness that the sinner is able to learn what sin is and repent. In the story of Zacchaeus, for exemplary instance, it is only after Jesus' gesture of reconciliation that Zacchaeus understands his sinfulness and repents of his wrong-doing (Lk. 19.1–10). Likewise, from the cross Jesus prays for the forgiveness of his persecutors, even while they remain ignorant of what they do (Lk. 23.34). The Western *ordo salutis*, requiring sinners to understand and repent of sin before God comes to their aid, is a return to the Socratic account of how one learns the truth so carefully distinguished from Christianity in *Philosophical Fragments*.[76] The truth [of sin] cannot be known without the condition; the condition is faith, a gift given by God himself, and faith, along with repentance, is a *response* to the declaration of forgiveness. Despite the prevalence of the western *ordo salutis* – also in our own day

– Kierkegaard regards it is a mistaken view: 'Heterodoxly one may say that conversion precedes and conditions the forgiveness of sins; orthodoxly one may say: the forgiveness of sins precedes conversion and strengthens men truly to be converted'.[77]

That repentance follows rather than precedes divine grace is a point made clearly by John Calvin who writes, '. . . a man cannot truly devote himself to repentance, unless he knows himself to be of God. Now, no man is truly persuaded that he is of God, except he has previously received his grace'.[78] Luther too contends that repentance is possible only on account of grace, rather than in anticipation of grace. In explanation of *metanoia*, the New Testament term for repentance Luther says, 'metanoia signifies a changing of the mind and heart, because it seemed to indicate not only a change of heart, but also a manner of changing it, i.e., the grace of God'.[79]

The themes of divine grace and human incapacity recur frequently in Kierkegaard's discourses, especially in those composed with the sacrament of the Eucharist or communion in mind. 'At the Communion table you are capable of doing nothing at all. And yet it is there at the Communion table that declaration is made of satisfaction for guilt and sin, for your guilt and your sin'.[80] The tax collector who went up to the temple to pray (Lk. 18), and the 'woman who was a sinner' (Lk. 7) are exemplary figures for Kierkegaard, for they approach God knowing they can do nothing on their own. That they know that much, however, is already an indication that God has been at work with them, enabling them to learn the truth; if not, then we return to the 'Socratic'.

## g. Atonement

We have noted above that Kierkegaard is concerned above all with how one responds to the declaration of forgiveness and grace rather than with the mechanics of how atonement is accomplished. With respect to 'the mystery of the Atonement', Kierkegaard says, 'My soul rests entirely in faith, understands itself entirely in believing'.[81] The believer believes 'because he *shall* believe, rather than . . . *because he can comprehend*'.[82]

Nevertheless, together with the discourses on the penitent tax collector and the woman who was a sinner, in 'Three Discourses at the Communion on Fridays', we find a discourse on Christ as the high priest in which we gain some indication of how Kierkegaard conceives the atonement doctrinally. The text for the discourse is Heb. 4.15: 'We have not a high priest who is unable to have sympathy with our weaknesses, but one who has been tested in all things in the same way, yet without sin'. The principal idea through which Kierkegaard explores the atonement is found in the formula, 'Christ has put himself in our place'. There is a threefold aspect to this substitution, established by the biblical text. First, Christ, the high priest, puts himself in the place of the one who suffers. He has 'sympathy with our weaknesses'. Kierkegaard here anticipates the theme explored extensively in our own day by Jürgen Moltmann[83] and by liberation theology. The Saviour is one who suffers with the sufferer. 'This is . . . what true sympathy [*Medlidenhed*] wants; it wants so very much to put itself completely in the place of the sufferer [*Lidende*] in order to be able really to comfort'.[84] Second, Christ puts himself in the place of those who are tempted. He is 'tested in all things, in the same way'. Christ 'knows the magnitude of every temptation',[85] Kierkegaard writes. There is no place of temptation in which you may find yourself, therefore, in which Christ cannot stand with you. The Saviour defeats sin, not only through forgiveness, but by standing with you against temptation, should you allow it.

Third, Christ stands in the place of sinners. The text of Hebrews, of course, says that Christ was 'without sin'. Thus Kierkegaard observes: '. . . in this respect, then, he did not put himself in your place, he cannot put himself completely in your place, he, the Holy One . . .'[86] And yet,

> If he, if the Redeemer's suffering and death is the
> satisfaction for your sin and guilt – if it is the satisfaction,
> then he does indeed step into your place for you, or he,
> the one who makes satisfaction, steps into your place,
> suffering in your place the punishment of sin so that you
> might be saved, suffering in your place death so that you
> might live.[87]

Although this claim enjoins the concept of penal substitution, the emphasis here, and in Kierkegaard's further elucidation of the matter, is placed not at all upon the punitive aspect of the satisfaction but entirely upon the compassion of the Saviour who bears for us the cost of sin.

> Thus when the punitive justice here in the world or in judgement in the next seeks the place where I, a sinner, stand with all my guilt, with my many sins – it does not find me. I no longer stand in that place; I have left it and someone else stands in my place, someone who puts himself completely in my place. I stand beside this other one, beside him, my Redeemer, who put himself completely in my place – for this accept my gratitude, Lord Jesus Christ![88]

## h. Judgement

The emphasis upon the compassion of Christ, made known through his death, is evident also in Kierkegaard's account of the judgement of God proclaimed through the cross. In a prayer preceding the discourse, 'But one who is forgiven little loves little' (Lk. 7.47), we read, 'Lord Jesus Christ, you who certainly did not come into the world in order to judge, yet by being love that was not loved you were a judgement upon the world'.[89] The truth of our human situation is laid bare by the love of Christ. Again, Christ is not the judge in some punitive sense; rather, the infinite and unconditional nature of his love reveals the poverty of our own love. It is love then that provides the most severe judgement. In pronouncing that 'your sins are forgiven', love comprehends everything, leaves nothing secret, and declares the truth. The person who loves little, is the one who turns away from this love, who does not accept love's verdict, and thus also shuns the forgiveness. The consequence, that there is no forgiveness for such a person, is self-inflicted. 'Love says: It is self-inflicted – it is not thereby thinking of his many sins – ah, no, it is willing to forget them all, it has forgotten them all; and yet it is self-inflicted says love'.[90]

Kierkegaard here contrasts love with justice. Justice, he suggests, *is* punitive. 'When justice judges, it balances the account . . .'[91] Clearly, he is working here with a concept of justice derived from Roman law, and rendered in the Vulgate as *iustitia*. The judgement of love, however, is portrayed more faithfully through the Hebrew word, *tsedekah* and its usual Greek translation in the Septuagint, *dikaiosune*. These terms are essentially relational and indicate the re-establishment of right relationship. The 'justi-fication' (*dikaiosis*) of sinners, therefore, involves their being set once more in right relationship with God. Kierkegaard captures well this biblical meaning with his exposition of the judgement of love. The word of judgement is, accordingly, also a word of comfort.[92]

## i. Grace

Although Kierkegaard deserves his reputation as a fierce critic of human pretentiousness, especially of the self-satisfied pre-tentiousness of those who suppose that their getting along well in the world provides evidence of God's favour, the word of judgement is always two-edged. We are judged in the light of God's love. We might put it as Barth would do later: God's 'No' to human sinfulness is always enclosed within his 'Yes', within the promise of forgiveness and reconciliation. 'The No [of judge-ment] is not said for the sake of the No, but for the sake of the Yes [of reconciliation].'[93] The dialectical relationship between judgement and grace is a recurrent theme in Kierkegaard's work. It corresponds to the relationship between God's infinite, qualit-ative distance from humanity and the intimacy of the relationship God establishes with human beings. This correspondence is evid-ent, for example, in a Journal entry from 1849:

> The fact that Jesus died for my sins certainly expresses the
> magnitude of grace, but that he will involve himself with
> me only on this condition also expresses the magnitude
> of my sins, the infinite distance between myself and
> God . . . The remarkable thing about it is that just
> when God expresses his condescension he also expresses

indirectly his infinite elevation. I am willing to become reconciled with men, he says (what a condescension!) on the condition that my son be allowed to be sacrificed for you – what an infinite distance of elevation, if this is the sole condition![94]

The reader must go especially to the Discourses in order to discover the extent of Kierkegaard's attention to God's compassion, and to the comfort extended through divine grace. It is in the Discourses, typically intended for those who have come to receive communion, that Kierkegaard testifies to the sufficiency of grace. Only those who, in humility, present themselves to God with their need only[95] are in a position to hear the word of grace. More commonly, however, the word of grace is drowned out by protestations – even those silently uttered – of our own worthiness.

The person who recognizes that before God, he or she is always in the wrong has moved from the ethical to the religious sphere. No longer supposing that ethical performance, good works, are a sufficient means of securing God's favour, the religious person recognizes her need of God's help. In a Discourse, titled, 'To Need God is a Human Being's Highest Perfection', Kierkegaard writes,

> Just as knowing oneself in one's own nothingness is the condition for knowing God, so knowing God is the condition for the sanctification of a human being by God's assistance and according to his intention. Wherever God is in truth, there he is always creating. He does not want a person to be spiritually soft and to bathe in the contemplation of his glory, but in becoming known by a person he wants to create in him a new human being.[96]

The first qualification of the religious life then is the recognition both of one's need of transformation, and of one's need of God's help. That much is common to two forms of religiousness that Kierkegaard goes on to distinguish and which he calls, 'Religiousness A' and 'Religiousness B'. The former may be characterized as 'immanent religiousness' while the latter is

Christianity. What is the difference between these two? Essentially the difference consists in a differing conception of how one relates to the eternal. Here we return to the issue in *Philosophical Fragments*. Kierkegaard there distinguishes between a Socratic conception of how the Truth may be learned – of how the individual, that is, may enter into relation with the eternal – and an alternative conception that resembles in its key particulars the position presented in the New Testament. An essential difference between these two conceptions is the 'decisiveness of the Moment'. Whereas, in the first, Socratic view, the condition for learning the Truth lies within the individual – is immanent, in the second view, the condition must be given to the learner. A change must therefore be brought about, a change that takes place within the course of history. The Moment in which this change occurs becomes, therefore, the decisive condition of the individual's discovery of the Truth, or, to put it in the terms with which Kierkegaard is ultimately concerned: it becomes the decisive condition of the individual's reconciliation with God.

In contrast with the religiousness of immanence,

> In Religiousness B , the upbuilding is something
> outside the individual; the individual does not find the
> upbuilding by finding the relationship with God within
> himself but relates himself to something outside himself
> in order to find the upbuilding . . . The paradoxical
> upbuilding . . . corresponds to the category of God in
> time as an individual human being, because, if that is the
> case, the individual relates himself to something outside
> himself.[97]

Religiousness A, despite being aware of the individual's need of God, is characterized by a residual confidence that the condition for the God-relationship is some human capacity or other. In Hegel, as has been common in Western thought, the condition was thought to be our rationality. In Schleiermacher, the condition was the individual's consciousness of absolute dependence. In Lessing and in Kant the condition was thought to be our moral capacity. Kierkegaard contends, however, that the condition is faith, and faith is no immanent capacity but a gift made available through encounter with the paradoxical figure of the God who has become a lowly human being. The paradox of the God in time, furthermore, is not something that can be comprehended by or assimilated into some prior view of the world. The paradox of the God-man can be responded to only by taking offence, thus maintaining one's allegiance to that world-view, or by faith, where faith is not the acceptance of some proposition or some doctrine, but a form of life characterized above all by obedience to Christ. The further characteristics of such a life will be the subject of the next chapter.

# Chapter 6

# Practice in Christianity

Our concern in this chapter and the next is to consider Kierke-gaard's conception of what the living of Christian life entails. The title for the chapter is Kierkegaard's own, that of a book pub-lished, as we have seen, under the pseudonym Anti-Climacus. Anti-Climacus, we recall, is described by Kierkegaard as a Christian 'on an extraordinary level'. Describing himself as the 'editor', Kierkegaard writes in the Preface, 'In this book, origin-ating in the year 1848, the requirement for being a Christian is forced up by the pseudonymous author to a supreme ideality'.[1] One might expect a heavy burden to be subsequently imposed upon the reader, or at least upon the reader who actually wants to be a Christian. We might expect to encounter here, where 'the requirement for being a Christian is forced to a supreme ideality', the 'severity of Kierkegaard's demands'.[2] And we do – to some extent. But Kierkegaard signals in the Preface that the 'severity of Christianity's requirement' is not the main thing to be learned. The main thing is grace. 'The requirement should be heard – and I understand what is said as spoken to me alone – so that I might learn not only to resort to *grace* but to resort to it in relation to the use of *grace*'.[3] Karl Barth complained that in Kierkegaard we hear predominantly of God's 'No' to human-ity's sinfulness and hypocrisy, while other teachers are needed to hear of God's 'Yes', the 'Yes' of forgiveness and grace.[4] Bar-th's usually astute judgement is questionable here, however, perhaps because he did not read all of Kierkegaard's work and so overlooked the pastoral affirmation frequently offered by Kierkegaard to the genuine seeker after truth, the seeker, that is, who leaves pretension aside and comes only with 'personal admission and confession'.[5] To such an enquirer, Kierkegaard can testify with great compassion to the assurance of forgive-ness and grace.

## a. The Requirement

Evidence for that assertion can be found in the choice of text under which Anti-Climacus, in *Practice in Christianity*, sets out 'the requirement for being a Christian'. He chooses Mt. 11.28: 'Come here to me, all who labour and are burdened, and I will give you rest'. This is 'the requirement'. Uttered by Jesus himself, the requirement simply is, 'come here to me'. Kierkegaard's severity, to which Barth draws attention, is reserved for those who don't want salvation on Jesus' terms. It is directed against those who insist that some credit must be given for their intellectual prowess, their good standing in society, or their moral rectitude. It is directed against those whose 'Christianity' consists principally in the conventional observance of religious ritual. Kierkegaard's severity, like that found in the gospel, is directed against those who count it more important to bury their dead, complete a business transaction, get married, secure their future prosperity, and who imagine that they will then have time to come to Jesus. Or, it is directed against those who count all these things first in importance and yet imagine that they are following Jesus as well. Barth has understood *this* point well and commends Kierkegaard to the attention of those theologians who have yet to discover the disruptive demands of the Gospel.

> Their vocation as such constitutes no challenge to them. They know 'what is what', and thus are not aware of any embarrassments. They know Christianity and their positions as its representatives to be securely fitted into the structure of the other elements and functions of human society. They are glad to see Christianity, and with it their own activity, sanctioned and basically approved by all good men. Among these good men they are not in an alien place, but rather at home as part of them. Apart from occasional harmless disturbances, they are at peace with themselves, with the Church, with the world, and so also with God.[6]

The requirement, as Kierkegaard states it, is apparently very simple: 'come here to me'. But it is almost impossibly difficult to leave behind all those things upon which we commonly stake our identity – our profession, our learning, our good reputation, our prosperity – and even more difficult when we behold the inviter and see that he is a lowly servant, despised and rejected and bearing a cross. Here again we encounter the paradox: the one offering help appears to be in desperate need of help himself; the one offering salvation, 'cannot save himself' (Mt. 27.42). It becomes an almost impossibly difficult thing to stake one's life on this offer of help. But that is the requirement, Kierkegaard insists.

*Practice in Christianity* explores at length the obstacles to obedience briefly mentioned here. The greatest obstacle is that to be a follower of Christ, one must become lowly and humble oneself. Increasingly through the course of Kierkegaard's authorship, and especially towards the end of his life when its expression became somewhat bitter, Kierkegaard held to the belief that suffering and martyrdom were the marks of authentic discipleship. Because the invitation to follow Christ involves suffering, and because also there is no human reckoning by which it can be shown that following Christ will bring salvation in the end – we have only Christ's word for it – the commitment of one's life to his Lordship can be undertaken only with fear and trembling.

That conviction is explored at length in Kierkegaard's study of Abraham who, in the New Testament, is held up by the apostle Paul as the archetype of faith.[7] Paul refers especially to the story in Gen. 22 which recounts Abraham's readiness to sacrifice Isaac his beloved son in obedience to the command of God. Isaac, the child born to Abraham and Sarah after long years of barrenness, was to be the one through whom God's earlier promise would be fulfilled. 'You shall be the father of many nations', God had said to Abraham; 'I will give to you, and to your offspring after you, the land where you are now an alien, all the land of Canaan, for a perpetual holding; and I will be their God'.[8] That promise was placed in jeopardy by the command Abraham then receives to take Isaac and sacrifice him at Mt Moriah. Clearly, such a command confounds both convention and common sense, as also our refined ethical sensibilities. According to Kierkegaard, therefore, Abraham believes by virtue of the absurd. He sets out for Mt Moriah without all rational objections having been answered. He ventures the

decisive act with nothing to cling to but the inexplicable promise of God. The virtue of Abraham's faith does not consist in
his having out-thought the well-meaning, rational objectors.
He has not come up with an argument by which his action may
be defended. The virtue of his faith consists rather in his readiness to trust God even when his own reason cannot fathom
how God's purposes will be worked out. Or so Kierkegaard
presents it. The ventures of discipleship are risky: 'forgive your
enemies'; 'bless those who persecute you'; 'sell your possessions
and give the money to the poor'; 'take up your cross and follow me'. 'Christianity requires that the individual, existing,
venture everything . . .'9 But, because there is no guarantee
that in following such commands things will come out right,
and because, indeed, such imperatives of faith commonly conflict with worldly sagacity, one can venture, Kierkegaard says,
only 'by virtue of the absurd'. One ventures the act of discipleship trusting in the one who has nowhere to lay his head, who
is mocked, spat upon and crucified, and who yet proclaims,
'Come to me all who labour and are heavy laden, and I will give
you rest'. The warrant for enacting these imperatives of faith is
simply that they are commended by Christ. There is nothing
for it, therefore, but to trust the outcome to him. In face of this
'absurdity', Anti-Climacus observes, one ought to pray:

> 'God in heaven, I thank you for not requiring a person
> to comprehend Christianity, for if that were required, I
> would be the most miserable of all. The more I seek to
> comprehend it, the more incomprehensible it appears to
> me and the more I discover only the possibility of offense.
> Therefore I thank you for requiring only faith, and I pray
> that you will continue to increase it'.10

Commenting on this passage, David McCracken writes:

> [The prayer] contains central truths and the dilemma that
> faces each individual: (1) Christianity is incomprehensible,
> it is not a part of the category of understanding; (2) the
> more one tries to understand it, the more one encounters
> the possibility of offense; and (3) the only alternative to

offense, and the only requirement for Christianity, is faith. That, in a nutshell, is Kierkegaard's position, and it is the dialectical dilemma that Kierkegaard's 'single individual' faces.[11]

The dilemma is rendered more acute when one realizes that faith is not something achieved once – in a moment of conversion, perhaps – but is a mode of existence that must be undertaken continually. Faith involves the continual regeneration of the individual who at every moment remains a sinner. Thus, as Henry Allison observes,

. . . since that which must be continually begun anew can never be completed, the decisive expression for this form of religiousness is the consciousness of guilt. This consciousness of guilt, the awareness of being in the wrong over and against God, is the highest development of the religiousness of inwardness, and we are thus led to the paradoxical conclusion that the deepest expression of the individual's God-relationship is to be found in the consciousness of the disrelationship.[12]

Corresponding to the claim that Christ is both prototype and redeemer, Kierkegaard portrays Christian life as at once a prodigious striving and a continual reliance upon grace.

[I]t must be firmly maintained that Christ has not come into the world only to set an example [*Exempel*] for us. In that case we would have law and works-righteousness again. He comes to save us and to present the example. This very example should humble us, teach us how infinitely far away we are from resembling the ideal. When we humble ourselves, then Christ is pure compassion. And in our striving to approach the prototype [*Forbilledet*], the prototype itself is again our very help. It alternates; when we are striving, then he is the prototype; and when we stumble, lose courage, etc., then he is the love which helps us up, and then he is the prototype again.[13]

Two themes, corresponding approximately to the commended reliance upon grace and to the striving, will provide a framework in what follows for the further exploration of Kierkegaard's conception of the Christian life. We will consider first, the life of devotion about which Kierkegaard has a great deal to say, and second, returning once more to Abraham, Kierkegaard's account of the necessity of obedience.

## b. The Life of Devotion

In a discourse titled, 'What is Required', which eventually has something to say about the 'works' commended in James, Chapter 1, Kierkegaard begins by focussing on the requirements of attentiveness to God. Consistent with the claim adduced earlier that the requirement is simply to heed Jesus' invitation to come to him, Kierkegaard remarks, 'In order to become a doer of the Word one must first of all be a hearer or reader of it'.[14] Taking up the analogy in Jas. 1.23 of those who look at themselves in the mirror [of the Word] and then forget what they were like, Kierkegaard proceeds to offer an account of what it means to look at oneself in this mirror. *'The first requirement is that you must not look at the mirror, observe the mirror, but must see yourself in the mirror'.*[15] Kierkegaard makes clear (again!)[16] his impatience with the myriad ways in which scholarship typically becomes obsessed with the former and consistently overlooks the latter. 'One could almost be tempted to assume that the full force of human craftiness has a hand in it'.[17] Scholarly devices, may serve a purpose – that of translating the biblical Hebrew and Greek, for example – but their employment is only a preliminary to the real point of reading God's Word as one reads a letter from one's beloved. This analogy reveals the essence of Kierkegaard's view of Christian Scripture. Scripture, he believes, is an instrument of God's self-communication. 'The words of Scripture . . . are at their maximum Jesus' own words'.[18] There is an implicit acknowledgement here that the words of Scripture are a human cultural production, but this does not preclude them from being also, *at their maximum*, words through which we are addressed by Christ. Indeed it is consistent with Kierkegaard's Christology generally that Christ should make himself known through the lowly form of human words.[19] In order to hear the divine address, a first requirement is that we are 'silent' before it. That is to say, we must set aside our preconceptions and our sophisticated scholarly apparatus and let it speak for itself. Kierkegaard here turns Paul's admonition that women should keep silent in church (I Cor. 14.34) to positive effect. The silence of attentiveness to God's Word, that Kierkegaard imagines is exemplified in a woman,[20] is much to be preferred to the blathering of preachers who have not listened before mounting the pulpit steps.

Continuing with the analogy of a letter from the beloved, Kierkegaard observes that the 'letter' of God's Word contains not only an expression of affection, but also a wish, 'something the beloved wished her lover to do'.[21] 'God's Word is given in order that you shall act according to it . . .'[22] But that requires first, attentiveness – not the attentiveness of scholarship, which always keeps Scripture at arm's length, but the attentiveness of devotion, the attentiveness of one who is personally addressed by the Word. Thus,

> *The second requirement is that in order to see yourself in the mirror when you read God's Word you must (so that you actually do come to see yourself in the mirror) remember to say to yourself incessantly: It is I to whom it is speaking; it is I about whom it is speaking.*[23]

As an instrument of God's self-communication, the reading of Scripture contributes also, for Kierkegaard, to the formation of the self, and to the upbuilding of the individual in faith. The person of faith is a creature of the Word of God; she is called into being and is both nourished and sustained by the Word.

> . . . provided you keep on reading God's Word this way for a time (and this is the first requirement) – you will read a fear and trembling into your soul so that, with God's help, you will succeed in becoming a human being, a personality, rescued from being this dreadful nonentity into which we humans, created in the image of God, have been bewitched, an impersonal, an objective something.[24]

The importance of reading Scripture 'as if it is I to whom it is speaking' is a feature of Kierkegaard's account of the formation of the self that is seldom noted by commentators upon his work. Not much has yet been done to redress the neglect of Kierkegaard's biblical interpretation noted by Paul Minear in 1953,[25] although progress has been made with the appearance of Timothy Polk's *The Biblical Kierkegaard*.[26] Polk locates Kierkegaard within the tradition of reading Scripture by the rule of faith, and cites the following account of what this tradition entails:

> Augustine urges just such a strategy, for example, in *On Christian Doctrine* where he delivers the 'rule of faith' which is of course a rule of interpretation. It is dazzlingly simple: everything in the Scriptures, and indeed in the world when it is properly read, points to (bears the meaning of) God's love for us and our answering responsibility to love our fellow creatures for His sake.[27]

The key point here is that Scripture is given by God for our instruction, principally our instruction in love – God's love for us, and, our 'answering responsibility' to love our fellow creatures for God's sake. We will come to the matter of our *answering responsibility* below, but, first, there is more to be learned from Kierkegaard about the modes of attentiveness to divine instruction.

Alongside the reading of Scripture, Christian life is nourished also by prayer. Kierkegaard quotes Luther approvingly in this regard: 'In the sermon on the Epistle for the Sixth Sunday after Easter, Luther expresses very beautifully that the Christian must maintain the practice every day either of God's speaking with him (by reading God's Word) or of speaking with God (by praying)'.[28] Elsewhere, Kierkegaard modifies Luther's account of prayer in order to emphasize that in prayer our own speaking turns again to hearing and then to obedience.

> The spontaneous, immediate person believes and imagines that when he prays the main thing, the thing he has to work at especially, is that *God hears* [*hører*] what it is **he** *is praying about*. And yet in truth's eternal sense

it is just the opposite: the true prayer-relationship does not exist when God hears what is being prayed about but when the *pray-er* continues to pray until he is the *one who hears*, who hears what God wills. The immediate, spontaneous person uses a lot of words and therefore is actually demanding when he prays. The true pray-er is simply *obedient* [*hørig*].[29]

Two prominent features of Kierkegaard's conception of Christian life are again evident here; it is a life shaped by God's address to the individual, and it issues in obedience. It is also evident, both in Kierkegaard's comments on prayer, and in the examples of the prayers accompanying his discourses, that Kierkegaard conceives of prayer, not as a burden, nor even as a task, but as the fruit of divine grace. Prayer, we might say, is the speech of love – not a burden, but a glad response to God's love. The point is apparent, for instance, in the prayer preceding the first of two discourses based upon Lk. 7.36–50 and titled, 'The Woman Who Was a Sinner'. Notably, given Kierkegaard's reputation as a harsh judge,[30] he chooses the text precisely in order to emphasize God's merciful compassion. He begins with the prayer: 'Lord Jesus Christ, in order to be able to pray aright to you about everything, we pray to you first about one thing: help us so that we might love you much . . .', and further, '. . . you are love of such a kind that you yourself love forth the love that loves you, encourages it to love you much'.[31] Consistent with the discovery by Johannes Climacus that the individual can do nothing for him or herself, but must rely utterly on God's gift both of the condition of faith, and of Godself, Kierkegaard here recognizes that God takes responsibility even for our 'answering response'. 'Lord Jesus Christ . . . you yourself love forth the love that loves you . . .'

In *Philosophical Fragments* Climacus spoke of the teacher (Christ), not only as the one who gives the condition, but also as the saviour, deliverer and reconciler, thereby hinting at the comprehensive scope of Christ's work. While, without doubt, something is asked of us, Christ takes charge, in Kierkegaard's view, of the whole drama of redemption in which human beings are restored to right relationship with God. Also in prayer, Christ puts himself in our place and bears the responsibility of putting our cause before God. Thus,

> What it means to pray in Jesus' name is perhaps illustrated most simply in this way. A public official orders this and that *in the name of the King* – what does it mean? In the first place it means: I myself am nothing, I have no power, nothing to say on my own – but it is in the name of the King. It is the same with praying in the name of Jesus: I do not dare approach God except through an intermediary . . . Finally, when a public official commands in the name of the King, it means that the King takes the responsibility upon himself. So it is also with praying in Jesus' name: Jesus takes upon himself the responsibility and all the consequences; he steps forward for us, steps forward in place of the one who is praying.[32]

Although Kierkegaard, does not set the matter out in systematic doctrinal terms, there is an unmistakeable echo here of the Reformation emphasis upon the sole priesthood of Christ.[33] Kierkegaard's bitter reaction to the excesses and distortions of the ordained priesthood of his own day is counter-balanced by the strong theological conviction that the priesthood of Christ is sufficient for the individual who, in humility, avails herself of that priesthood. It often is 'her' rather than 'his' piety that Kierkegaard commends: 'From a woman you learn concern for the one thing needful, from Mary, sister of Lazarus, who sat silent at Christ's feet with her heart's choice: the one thing needful'.[34] We see too, in the citation above, a recurrence of Kierkegaard's preferred language for the redemptive action of Christ. Christ puts himself in our place. The representative action of Christ 'for us' extends also to the place of prayer. Christ's priesthood is efficacious even in the place set aside for *our* 'answering response'. Precisely on account of that priesthood, a place at the communion table is set aside for us.

> My listener, this is the kind of high priest of sympathy we have. Whoever you are and however you are suffering, he can put himself completely in your place. Whoever

you are and however you are being tempted, he can put himself completely in your place. Whoever you are, O sinner, as we all are, he puts himself completely in your place! Now you go to the Communion table; the bread is handed to you and then the wine, his holy body and blood, once again as an eternal pledge that by his suffering and death he did put himself also in your place, so that you, behind him saved, the judgement past, may enter into life, where once again he has prepared a place for you.[35]

Along with reading Scripture and prayer, the sacrament of communion was understood by Kierkegaard as a particular and special means through which God meets with us and undertakes his transforming work. At the communion table one is enabled by grace to hear Christ's voice[36] and to confess before God both one's sin, and – what amounts to the same thing – one's need of God. For all Kierkegaard's bitter assessment of the failures of the church in Christendom, he could conceive a legitimate and important role for the church if only its clergy understood clearly the requirement of Christianity and were honest in portraying the degree to which we commonly fail to meet the requirement. Despite the failings of the clergy, however, Kierkegaard continued to attend church for most of his life with the expectation, perhaps, that even the most incompetent and hypocritical of pastors could not finally defeat God's intent to speak through Word and Sacrament.

> . . . here in God's house, whether the pastor preaches or the sexton, the most renowned pastor or the least-known student, there is always One who preaches, always one and the same – God in heaven. That God is present, this is the sermon; and that you are before God, this is the content of the sermon.[37]

## c. Obedience

The first requirement of Christian faith is to attend to God's voice, the voice that addresses us in Scripture, through the

Sacraments and in prayer. Beyond attentiveness, however, God requires obedience. We come now to consider what obedience entails. It is tempting to suppose that obedience means nothing more demanding than good citizenship. If we don't kill, don't steal, don't lie, and so on, as the Decalogue commands, then we may easily suppose that we have fulfilled the requirement of obedience. We then get on with our lives having satisfied ourselves that we are not like other men and women who fail in this or that particular of the law. Against that smug falsification of the Christian requirement Kierkegaard sets the example of Abraham, mentioned briefly above as the archetype or hero of faith. Kierkegaard's reflections upon Abraham in *Fear and Trembling* guard against our propensity to 'set the bar too low', against our propensity to scale back the requirement of discipleship so that we can meet it without any serious threat to the comfortable forms of life in which we have become ensconced. Kierkegaard contends throughout his authorship that a reduction in the requirements of faith could be achieved only by offering a counterfeit in its place. This 'historically specific form of human deviousness', as Merold Westphal nicely puts it,[38] stoops so low as to suggest that in order to be a Christian one has merely to be born in a Christian country and then go along with the crowd.

It is typical of such deviousness that it finds a more sophisticated expression in, and may perhaps be inspired by, the ruling philosophy of the day. We have seen already that Kierkegaard attributed much of the malaise of Danish Christendom to the popularity of the philosophy of G. W. F. Hegel. *Fear and Trembling* has thus to be seen as part of Kierkegaard's broad polemic against Hegel, especially in this instance, against Hegel's claim that faith has been clearly understood and incorporated into the system. Equally important for the understanding of *Fear and Trembling*, however, is the preceding effort of Immanuel Kant to subsume Christian faith within a philosophical scheme or, as he himself put it, to construct 'religion within the limits of reason alone'. That too, in Kierkegaard's view, is a curtailment and distortion of Christian faith; it is a procrustean trimming of the Gospel in order to make it look just like the ideas of the 'good' life that we have come up with ourselves. In Kant's case, of course, the good life to which all religion is directed is simply the consistent application of the categorical imperative, that product of practical reason through which right and wrong may be precisely defined. While, according to Kant, God is supposed to approve this scheme and act as the remote guarantor of its coherence, this does not allow to God the prerogative of disclosing his own view on what might constitute the life well lived. Such an intervention in the affairs of human beings – traditionally called revelation – would constitute, in Kant's view, an intolerable violation of human autonomy. Faith on this account, 'pure religious faith' as Kant calls it, in contrast with the historical or empirical faith of the church, must be purely rational and does not differ from the principle of a good course of life.

Kierkegaard's strategy in *Fear and Trembling* is to confront such an account of faith with the Biblical story of Abraham and Isaac in order to see whether it is really true that the faith of the person who follows a religion within the limits of reason alone looks just like the faith of Abraham, the one whom the Bible itself calls the archetype of faith. It is important to remember here that the church in Christendom was still prepared to admit that the Bible is in some manner authoritative. After all, Kierkegaard points out, we still hear sermons on Abraham; he is still promoted as the paragon of faith, even if the whole story is recited in clichés.[39] In a world that assumed either cautiously with Kant or enthusiastically with Hegel, that in relation to the Bible, the deliverances of philosophy are simply a way of saying the same thing in other words, albeit more simply and clearly, then Kierkegaard's proposal of a conflict between philosophy and the Bible was an attempt to unmask an improper illusion.

## d. The Limits of the Ethical

In *Fear and Trembling*, Kierkegaard himself sets forth three problems thrown up by the story of Abraham and Isaac. First there is the question, 'Is there a teleological suspension of the ethical?'; second, 'Is there an absolute duty to God?' and third, 'Was it ethically defensible for Abraham to conceal his understanding from Sarah, from Eliezer, and from Isaac?'

What does it mean, first of all, to ask about a teleological suspension of the ethical? Kierkegaard explains, '[t]he ethical as such is the universal, and as the universal it applies to everyone, which from another angle means that it applies at all times'.[40] The convictions of both Kant and Hegel are readily apparent in this description of the ethical. For Kant, practical reason identifies the 'categorical imperative' which is defined precisely as that maxim which 'could always hold . . . as a principle establishing universal law'.[41] All people in all places and times are obligated to act according to such a maxim whatever the particulars of their own experience or circumstances. The ethical is universally binding. For all that there are differences between the ethical systems of Kant and Hegel,[42] they have in common both that Hegel too envisages no exceptions to the universal obligations of ethics, and that those obligations themselves are reliably identified by human reason.[43]

It is implied by the ethical systems of both Kant and Hegel that the ethical task of the individual is to 'annul his [or her] singularity in order to become the universal'.[44] Kierkegaard explains:

> As soon as the single individual asserts himself in his singularity before the universal, he sins, and only by acknowledging this can he be reconciled again with the universal. Every time the single individual, after having entered the universal, feels an impulse to assert himself as the single individual, he is in a spiritual trial from which he can work himself only by repentantly surrendering as the single individual in the universal.[45]

Here we have a polemic against anybody who considers his or her case to be an exception from ethical norms. Furthermore, Kierkegaard remarks – and here we come to the nub of the issue – 'If this is the highest that can be said of man and his existence, then the ethical is of the same nature as a person's eternal salvation . . . [46] This is pure Kant. What Christianity offers under the name of salvation is attained quite simply through the determination of the individual to act according to the dictates of practical reason. Or as Kant himself puts it, 'there exists absolutely no salvation for man apart from the sincerest adoption of genuinely moral principles into his disposition'.[47] Over against this however, is Abraham, willing to draw the knife against his own son and yet precisely because of this ethically indefensible action he is celebrated as the archetype of faith. Kierkegaard confronts his age with the dilemma: what is to be done with Abraham? What is to be done with this knight of faith who cannot be accommodated within the prevailing account of what constitutes a life well-pleasing to God. Hence the question: is there a teleological suspicion of the ethical? Can there ever be a demand upon us that properly requires a suspension of the categorical imperative?

For Kant himself there is no dilemma. The universal demand of ethics is the highest claim upon us. There is no case in which the categorical imperative could be overturned. His verdict upon Abraham, therefore, is straightforward: Abraham made a mistake in believing that the instruction to sacrifice Isaac had come from God.[48] 'God's holy will', Kant remarks, is incapable of any maxim conflicting with the moral law'.[49] Kant contends therefore, that Abraham ought to have replied to the supposedly divine voice by saying, 'It is quite certain that I ought not to kill my innocent son, but I am not certain and I cannot ever become certain that you, the "you" who is appearing to me, are God'.[50] The implication of Kant's confidence is that the deliverances of practical reason enable us to know good from evil with incontrovertible assurance, and further, that this is just the same thing as seeing with the eye of God. One might imagine it possible to claim the support of Gen. 3:5 for Kant's position, 'when you eat of the tree of the knowledge of good and evil your eyes will be opened, and you will be like God'. But that, of course, is the serpent's argument. It is not clear that the knowledge we have attained of good and evil has in fact made us like God. And it is not clear, therefore, that Kant is justified in claiming that the impossibility of defending Abraham on ethical grounds means assuredly that Abraham had mistaken the command of God.

Kierkegaard, for one, is not so sure. Kant's interpretation leaves him with a fundamental problem. In the Biblical story of Abraham and Isaac, the divine origin of the demand to sacrifice Isaac is never called into question. Abraham did what he did because God commanded it. The Bible clearly does not offer the story as an example of how archetypes of faith can sometimes be mistaken. Kant looks like being wrong on exegetical grounds. But if Kant's interpretation is mistaken on this point then he is left with the alternative that religion within the limits of reason alone is not after all compatible with Biblical faith. Kant himself is not likely to have been troubled too much by this conclusion – his own efforts to show the compatibility between Christianity and a purely rational faith do not really bear the stamp of conviction – but Kierkegaard's contemporaries in Danish Christendom would likely find the problem a great deal more disturbing. They, by Kierkegaard's own account, were sailing happily along under the assumption that Biblical Christianity demanded no more of them than conformity to the dictates of popular morality. That was a view undergirded, if that were really necessary, by the good names of Hegel and Kant. Abraham, however, is another matter altogether. And this of course is Kierkegaard's point: Christianity itself is another matter altogether.

## e. Can Abraham be Justified?

Having made this point, however, Kierkegaard's deliberations are not yet at an end. All that has been done so far is to ensure that faith is no longer offered at bargain price. Kierkegaard himself offers the analogy of the spice merchants in Holland, who responded to a slump in prices, by arranging for a few cargoes of spice to be sunk at sea, thus shortening supply and jacking up the price. If, by comparison with the Biblical portrayal of faith, the religious ships of Kant and Hegel have been sunk, that at least means that Christianity will no longer be sold off cheaply, but we have still to confront the enigma of Abraham who, though acting in obedience to a divine command, does not give us warrant to say that he was ethically in the right. There is still the problem whether faith might sometimes require us to act against the best insights of ethical reflection, whether it might require us, in other words, to do what cannot be justified ethically.

Kierkegaard does not allow us to resolve the problem by suggesting that Abraham acted according to a higher ethical duty, higher than the duty not to kill, and higher too than the duty of a father to seek only the good for his children. It is possible to conceive of cases where a child has been sacrificed to a higher cause. Kierkegaard offers the examples of Jephthah, Agamemnon and Brutus. In each of these three examples a father sacrifices a child or children so that many more lives might be saved, or in Jephthah's case, sacrifices the child in fulfilment of a vow made in anticipation of many lives being saved. (It must be admitted that the moral ambiguities of Jephthah's story do not render him the best example of a tragic hero in support of Kierkegaard's case, but the point remains that we have sometimes to choose between competing ethical duties and must renounce one in favour of another.) In the cases cited, Kierkegaard means to show forth the terrible dilemma of a father who has to choose between the life of his own child and the lives of the people he leads. If he chooses against his own child then he has at least the ethical defence of choosing the lesser evil, and that among his options can be reckoned as the highest good. In this way he can be understood as a tragic hero putting the needs of his people before his own love. The tragedy of the father's action notwithstanding, that action is both comprehensible and ethically justifiable. It does not involve, therefore, a teleological suspension of the ethical. The requirements of ethics as such are not suspended. Rather, one ethical claim is counted as having precedence over another.

Abraham, in contrast, can offer no such defence. He is not acting according to some higher ethical demand. He can offer no account of his action except that he believes it to have been commanded by God. Because Abraham is a God fearing man, he regards the requirement to obey God as absolute. In contrast to the sympathy offered to the tragic hero, however, Abraham's action gives rise to the judgement that he is either bad or mad.

Kierkegaard is well known for preferring the judgement of madness to be made upon faith rather than allowing faith to be cheapened for the sake of popular approval. Indeed, there are many commentators who attribute to Kierkegaard a Tertullianesque glorification of the absurd. But Kierkegaard's frank admission of the *apparent* absurdity of faith is not a concession that faith is inherently irrational. A proper defence of this claim requires more space than I have available here, but two remarks may indicate the general direction a defence might take.[51] First, the renowned remarks about Christianity appearing paradoxical or absurd appear almost without exception under the names of Kierkegaard's various pseudonyms, most of whom are not Christians but view faith from the outside. That it appears absurd to them does not settle the matter of whether faith is absurd in itself. Indeed, Kierkegaard himself says that 'When the believer has faith, the absurd is not the absurd – faith transforms it . . .'[52] Second, Kierkegaard himself does not concur with the popular conception that reason gives a God's eye view of the world. The way in which human beings exercise their capacity for rational thought is shaped to an important degree by the world-view within which they are operating. If that were not so, if instead we all operated on neutral ground, then we should expect a much greater conformity of opinion among philosophers at least, and then among all who are determined to be rational. That widespread disagreement remains gives cause to doubt that reason can easily and conclusively distinguish between absurdity and truth. Kierkegaard, for his part, is adamant that reason has no such capacity.

Back to Abraham then; can his action be reckoned as irrational or absurd? It may well appear to be so, and we have established that no ethical defence is available to him, yet Kierkegaard seems to answer, 'not necessarily'. It is important to note that Kierkegaard does not go beyond this. He does hold Abraham up as the knight of faith but he does not at any stage provide a warrant for his action. He confesses, or rather his pseudonym Johannes de Silentio confesses, not to be able to provide any warrant. 'I cannot understand Abraham', de Silentio says. I accept that he is the archetype of faith but his decision to sacrifice his son is not intelligible to me. 'Whereof one cannot speak, thereof one must be silent', Wittgenstein once remarked.[53] It seems that Johannes the Silent One comes to the same conclusion with respect to Abraham. If Abraham is the archetype of faith, then his faith bursts the bounds of human reason. Outside of those limits, Abraham's faith is no longer to be found among the things that we can give an intelligible account of.

It is not just de Silentio who comes to this conclusion. It is the position confirmed by Abraham himself whose silence is a striking feature of the journey to Mt Moriah. That silence is broken only once when Abraham answers Isaac's query about the lamb for the sacrifice by saying 'God will provide a lamb for the sacrifice, my son'. This, however, is by no means an explanation of his action; it is simply a reiteration of his faith. And so Kierkegaard's question: Was it ethically defensible for Abraham to conceal his understanding from Sarah, from Eliezer and from Isaac?[54]

The conclusion arrived at is, again, while no ethical defence is possible, this is not sufficient reason for Abraham to be condemned. Kierkegaard is prepared to assume that Abraham has reasons that reason cannot tell. Abraham himself seems to know that he has passed beyond the limits of an intelligible defence of his actions. What this may suggest is that even Abraham himself cannot be sure that he is acting aright. His conviction that he is acting in obedience to the command of God cannot be supported rationally and nor can it be easily supported by precedent, for this word of God seems to be in conflict with every other word that he has so far heard, most especially of course, the word that Isaac is the child of promise, the one through whom all nations will be blessed. Will God now take away that promise or has Abraham himself misunderstood? When Kierkegaard says that Abraham believes by virtue of the absurd, he has this in mind; that Abraham trusts God in two apparently contradictory directions, first that Isaac is the first of many generations who will be blessed because of Abraham, and second that Isaac is to be sacrificed on an altar before the Lord. Trusting God in both these things, 'Abraham *cannot* speak, because he cannot say that which would explain everything (that is, so it is understandable)'.[55]

Without a reasonable defence available to him, without any intelligible explanation to be secured for himself and offered to others, Abraham has nothing other than faith. But he goes on, obediently he believes, but with fear and trembling for everything is at risk. One of Kierkegaard's complaints against the clichéd recital of the Abraham story in the pulpits of his time was that they did not pay any attention to Abraham's anxiety. They did not appreciate the risk of obedience. The intelligible pattern of Abraham's life to date, his relationship with God, with Sarah, and of course with Isaac; all of this may be lost. And yet the voice of God beckons him onward and Abraham with fear and trembling obeys. Why? We don't know. Johannes de Silentio doesn't know. And if Abraham himself knows, he is unable to make it intelligible to anyone else, perhaps not even to himself. We have here, perhaps, an instance of what Peter van Inwagen has referred to as 'inarticulable reasons'.[56] Van Inwagen's defence of inarticulable reasons suggests that while Abraham may not have been able to explain his action, while he may not have been able to give an intelligible account of why he believes what he does, he is not for that reason irrational. Nor can his beliefs therefore be said to be false. Abraham acts because he believes God has so commanded him to act, and the truth of this belief is not necessarily undermined just because he cannot give a reasoned defence of it.

Kierkegaard's story can end there. It is not his intention to resolve the enigma, but rather to set it before us in all its force. Kant and Hegel have long been left behind. Both have opted out of this model of faith. But those who persevere with Abraham's story are faced with the question whether faith might require of them too an act whose justification lies beyond their capacity to understand. What might Kierkegaard have in mind? Perhaps those harsh sayings of Jesus, about leaving the dead to bury the dead, or giving away all one's possessions and following him, or taking up one's cross; all these are particular forms of the injunction that whoever loses his own life for my sake and for the gospel will save it.[57] From the standpoint of unbelief, that outcome doesn't look likely. Reason cannot confirm it. Indeed reason seems to be able to muster some very good arguments against it. Yet the Biblical story of Abraham searches the depths of our own commitment to God alongside our care for those whom we love. Can these ever be in conflict? Will God ever ask of us anything that might violate our values or our morality? Will faith ever require a sacrifice?

These are the questions that Kierkegaard leaves us with. Has Abraham been justified? The answer for Kierkegaard himself, must be No! For to provide a justification of Abraham's action would be to bring him back within the limits of reason alone, to measure him against an articulable and universal standard. Those standards, as proffered by Kant and Hegel at least, cannot condone but can only condemn Abraham. For them he cannot be the archetype of faith. But the Bible says he is. That leaves us with two options. Either we must decide against the Bible and in favour of our very best ethical insights. Or we may venture the suggestion that there will be times in the life of faith when the individual must proceed without all reasonable objections having been resolved. Faith proceeds even though doubt has not been absolutely refuted. That is risky. To journey out beyond ethics and beyond common sense is to find oneself alone – perhaps even without God, perhaps just alone.[58] People of faith are capable of, and often do get it wrong. But faith means trusting in God with the hope that one's action is justified, not in the end by our own reason, but by God.

Paul Holmer has remarked that Kierkegaard believed that what happened to Abraham on Mt Moriah could also happen elsewhere. 'The logic that makes it even conceivable', Holmer adds, 'is the rational accompaniment to the emotions that were Abraham's – the peculiar fear and trembling that were a sign that his life was being judged and formed',[59] judged and formed, I would add, by a standard that is not our own.[60]

## f. Further Questions

What can we say about Kierkegaard's position? Four questions in particular warrant further attention. (1) How legitimate is an appeal to inarticulable reasons? (2) Might the inarticulable reasons defence be strengthened by a clearer articulation of the need to consider particular instances of divine command not in isolation but in relation to the life of faith in general? (3) What value might there be in matters of faith, in an appeal, not to the public as such, but to the ecclesia? (4) If the command of God is not always fathomable, what safeguards are there against lunacy and evil? What, for instance, might Kierkegaard have to say about Jonestown and Waco where crowds of devoted followers were led to their deaths by people whom we are inclined to regard as crazed and tragically mistaken religious leaders?

Considering first the legitimacy of appeal to inarticulable reasons, it seems possible here to appeal to common practice.

Despite the concern most people probably share that their actions should for the most part be considered to be rational, it also seems to be the case that many human actions do not have available to them a rational defence. This is especially the case, I think, in the sphere of interpersonal relations. One could offer many examples, I will suggest just one. Keri Hulme's novel *The Bone People*,[61] winner of the Booker prize in 1985, tells the story of a young boy, Simon, who was subjected to frequent physical abuse by his adoptive and alcoholic, solo father. The child remains devoted to his father, however, and can even be said to love him deeply. His love persists in the face of many reasonable objections that even Simon himself can think of. It is a love that seems to be irrational and Simon himself cannot offer an intelligible account of it, but he loves and trusts nevertheless. Are there not many comparable examples in the sphere of human relationships? Here especially, human beings often act in accordance with reasons that cannot be easily explained.

The inarticulable reasons defence of Abraham might, however, be strengthened by appeal to a wider context. Had Abraham heard the command of God to sacrifice Isaac 'out of the blue' as it were, apart, that is, from a history of relationality between God and Abraham characterized as it was by love and trust, then it is much less likely that Abraham could have regarded the word he heard as a command from God. The context of Abraham's covenantal relationship lends a degree of intelligibility to the command. It is not complete intelligibility of course, certainly not enough to render his action comprehensible to those who have not shared in the covenant, perhaps not even enough to render it comprehensible to himself, but it is enough for Abraham to be going on with. It is enough for him to obey. How might this be the case?

Abraham's life has taken on a particular shape and has followed a particular direction under the conditions of divine guidance and human trust. His decision to leave the land of his birth, to set out in obedience to the call of God without knowing whither he was going; the divine gift of the child Isaac and the promise of blessing through him, had all combined to give Abraham's life an overall coherence and intelligibility. At one level, of course, the command to sacrifice Isaac represents a terrible breach in the framework of intelligibility, it commands an action that will certainly undermine all that has been hoped and promised. At another level, however, Abraham has always proceeded in obedience to God's call upon him. So while he has some very good reasons to doubt the command now given, he has always been able to trust God before. Why should he not trust God now, even though he cannot comprehend how God's command coheres with the pattern already established? When Abraham tells Isaac that God will provide a lamb for the sacrifice, this is neither an avoidance of the terrible reality, nor a sign that Abraham foresees the outcome of his journey, but rather a confession of the utter trustworthiness of God, even beyond his capacity to comprehend God's plans. Abraham's whole life provides a context that gives such trust just enough intelligibility for Abraham to go on but falls short of the level of intelligibility that would enable him to explain the matter to others.

I am suggesting here that extraordinary levels of love for and trust of another – beyond reason sometimes – have at least a partial intelligibility within the context of a relationship that has stood the test of time, while nevertheless being wholly unintelligible to anyone outside of the relationship itself.

This leads to my further question about whether such extreme situations as Abraham found himself in might be tested by appeal to the ecclesia, by appeal, that is to those who also share in that particular covenantal relationship which, I have argued, may lend some intelligibility to Abraham's faith. Such a defence is certainly not offered by Kierkegaard himself, but Kierkegaard clearly does belong to that community of faith that finds trust in God admirable even when it exceeds the bounds of rationality. 'Although I cannot understand Abraham', Johannes de Silentio says, 'I do admire him'. Silentio goes further, saying, 'My soul feels its kinship with [Abraham] and in all humility is certain that the cause for which the hero strives is also my cause, and when I consider it, I cry out to myself: *jam tua res agitur* [now your cause is at stake]'.[62] These are Johannes de Silentio's words but they represent an attitude that Kierkegaard himself appears to share.

'Abraham's cause is my cause'. There is a community of faith extended through succeeding generations of both Judaism and

Christianity that is willing to say that. However much members of that community also approach the matter with fear and trembling, and although they too may admit to not understanding Abraham, in recognizing his cause as their own, they constitute themselves as a community that upholds and admires Abraham even though he acts in a way that is not fully comprehensible. Wherever there are prophetic figures whose stand of faith isolates them so dramatically from the opinions of the general public, then a partial, though by no means infallible, criterion of the authenticity of their faith is whether or not they are upheld by the community that attends regularly to the Word of God. Appeal must be made here not simply to the church community found in the immediate vicinity – which may have gone astray, and that may be, in fact, the foil against which so dramatic a stand is made – but rather to the communion of saints, stretched out over time and space. It is to the broader community and tradition of Christian faith that one must appeal in order to see whether in that extensive communion there might be shared the conviction that a particular follower's cause is also its cause. One might see Martin Luther as a case in point, as also, Kierkegaard himself. Both men stood against the stream, were vilified and condemned by a particular local church, but have been judged over time and by the wider community of faith to be authentic and salutary voices in the tradition of Christian faith.

That criterion of authentic faith brings us some way towards an answer to the fourth question posed above, that of whether there are in Kierkegaard's position any safeguards against the mistaken faith of the communities at Jonestown or Waco and their like. The judgement of the ecclesia is a partial answer to this problem, but outside of *Fear and Trembling* Kierkegaard himself offers some further suggestions.

We have had cause already to consider the case of Adolph Adler who claimed to have received a personal revelation from Jesus. In *The Book on Adler*, Kierkegaard offers four criteria by which to assess the legitimacy of such claims to private revelation. While the first three criteria are less relevant to the case of Abraham – having more obvious application to sectarian movements – the fourth does offer an important consideration, and seems to be the one that Kierkegaard himself regards as paramount. Simply stated, Kierkegaard recommends consideration of whether the claimant to such a revelation otherwise exhibits a mature and godly life. The test of that is Christological, by which standard it is rather easy to weed out the money-making tele-evangelists, potential tyrants and the like.[63] Kierkegaard seems very confident about the power of this adjudicatory tool and comments as follows:

> If Christ had not been victorious by being crucified, but in modern style had been victorious through officiousness and a frightful gift of the gab so that none of the voters could refrain from voting for him, through a cunning that could make people believe whatever it might be, if Christianity had victoriously entered the world *in that way*, and Christ had been regarded as the Son of God – in that case it would not have entered into the world at all and Christ would precisely not have been the Son of God. What would have been victorious would not have been Christianity but a parody of Christianity.[64]

Godliness, then, that kind of Godliness so easily distinguishable from a life dominated by worldly interests and worldly notions of success, is considered by Kierkegaard to be the primary criterion for distinguishing the person who has received authentic revelation of God from the fraudster or the deluded. Like the confirmation of the ecclesia, it is not an infallible criterion but both signs of authenticity serve well in most cases.

Despite these provisos, the call to obedience will always encounter incredulity. To cite Kierkegaard once more, to be obedient in faith is to 'venture out over seventy thousand fathoms', out beyond the security of convention and of common sense. Such obedience has only the Word of God to cling to, and might be mistaken. Kierkegaard suggests, however, that authentic faith in God consists precisely in this.

# Chapter 7

# Works of Love and the Assistance of Grace

The model of Abraham as the archetype of faith distinguishes the requirements of faith from the universal obligations of ethics. Obedience to God might require a course of action in conflict with our best ethical insights. If not, then Abraham is no hero and ought to be condemned. Although Kierkegaard will allow no compromise of this sharp distinction between Godly obedience and ethics this does not entail that the person of faith will be distinguished by their flouting of all ethical rules. Life in the sphere of the religious does not require that the ethical be abandoned but that the demands of ethics no longer be absolute. God alone is absolute, and so it is only the command of God that can claim our absolute allegiance.

For the most part, Kierkegaard does not expect that we shall hear from God the fearful command to take our child to Mt Moriah, but there is one command, above all, that is issued to us all: 'You shall love'. In September 1847 Kierkegaard published *Works of Love*, a series of '*Christian deliberations . . .* not about *love* but about *works of love*'.[1] Kierkegaard conceives this book as a counter to the anticipated criticism of his uncompromising emphasis upon the individual. Kierkegaard is still in our own day commonly accused of individualism.[2] It is alleged that he has no conception of the relational constitution of human being such as has been developed in recent theology,[3] that he has no ecclesiology, and that he conceives the life of faith as heroically individualistic. There is no doubt that proof texts can be adduced in support of such claims, but proof texting is not the way to do justice to the matter. Kierkegaard himself complains that,

> . . . people ought to have learned about my maieutic
> carefulness, by proceeding slowly and continually letting
> it seem as if I knew nothing more, not the next thing –
> now on the occasion of my new upbuilding discourses
> [published in March 1847] they will probably bawl out
> that I do not know what comes next, that I know nothing
> about sociality. The fools! Yet on the other hand I owe
> it to myself to confess before God that in a certain sense
> there is some truth in it, only not as people understand
> it – namely, that continually when I have first presented
> one aspect clearly and sharply, then the other affirms itself
> even more strongly.[4]

Merold Westphal and Martin Matuštík have correctly observed that Kierkegaard's 'individualism' 'is a protest against a particular mode of human togetherness that he calls by such names as Christendom, the public, the present age, and even, anticipating Nietzsche, the herd. This individualism turns out to be the flip side of a thoroughly relational conception of the self . . .'[5]

## a. Becoming a Self Through Love

*Fear and Trembling* represents the clear and sharp presentation of the individual's singular responsibility before God to the point where Abraham is presented solely in terms of the infinite passion of inwardness. He can say nothing of his obedience to Isaac, to Sarah or to Eliezer, much less to anyone else.[6] The self in *Fear and Trembling* thus appears as a self-enclosed individual answerable only to God. But Kierkegaard contends that the presentation of the demands of faith in this way is a corrective to an excessive emphasis upon objectivity, upon the objectivity of creedal claims, for instance, or upon the objectivity of customary expressions of religious life that one can assent to and participate in without any change of heart. A change of heart, by contrast, the transformation of one's existence represented in the New Testament concept of *metanoia*, is a matter that concerns us personally.

> The Gospel [says Kierkegaard] does not need to add what the prophet Nathan added to his parable, 'You are the man', since it is already contained in the form of the statement and in its being a word of the Gospel. The divine authority of the Gospel does not speak to one person about another, does not speak to you, my listener, about me, or to me about you – no, when the Gospel speaks, it speaks to the single individual.[7]

Kierkegaard confronts the crowd with the requirement of individual responsibility before God. But he does not thereby deny that the self is formed through love of one's neighbour. The most comprehensive commentary upon *Works of Love* so far to appear is M. Jamie Ferreira's work *Love's Grateful Striving*.[8] Ferreira argues, rightly in my view, that becoming a self not only allows concern for others, but that it requires it. The self is conceived by Kierkegaard, not as an isolated individual, but as one established in relation to God. Ferreira demonstrates that 'before God' the individual is bound also to the neighbour. Love of neighbour, with God as the 'middle term' is thus seen as the means by which the individual is constituted as a self. Such love is not an option that the self may choose to exercise or not; it is a requirement of becoming a self. The Kierke-gaardian emphasis on individuality and inwardness, therefore, and the claim that 'you have to do only with yourself before God',[9] often quoted by those who are critical of Kierkegaard's ethic, entails neither self-centredness nor antisocial individual-ism. When read in context, as Ferreira shows us how to do, it is clear that Kierkegaard is concerned merely to emphasize that one should occupy oneself only with the fulfilment of one's own responsibilities; 'you are not responsible for ensuring that others do what they should'.[10]

We have learned already that Kierkegaard writes about the *works of love*, that is, about what love does. He has no interest in treatises on love itself conceived merely abstractly. In order to learn what love is one must observe what love does. For Kierkegaard, of course, this is a theological matter and is expressed quite specifically in Trinitarian terms. The deliberations begin with prayer:

> How could one speak properly of love if you were forgotten, you God of love, source of all love in heaven and on earth; you who spared nothing but in love gave everything; you who are love, so that one who loves is what he is only by being in you! How could one speak properly about love if you were forgotten, you who revealed what love is, you our Saviour and Redeemer, who gave yourself in order to save all. How could one speak properly of love if you were forgotten, you Spirit of love, who take nothing of your own but remind us of that love-sacrifice, remind the believer to love as he is loved and his neighbour as himself! . . .[11]

Ferreira observes that 'Kierkegaard's opening prayer makes it impossible to ignore his wholehearted embrace of the Lutheran principle of the priority of grace . . .'[12] The 'one who loves is what he is only by being in you'. God's love enables us to love, so it cannot ever be the case that our works of love stir God from inaction and prompt God to love us. Rather, God loves us first. That becomes a recurring theme in *Works of Love* and is a principle that ought to be remembered through the reading of Kierkegaard's whole corpus. All that he has to say about imitating Christ, about obedience, and about the striving of faith, is misunderstood if construed as a burden imposed by a stern and uncompassionate God. Ferreira again puts it well: 'The prayer, with its emphasis on the gift of God's love to us and the commandment to love the neighbor, places the whole set of deliberations within a great parenthesis of GIFT and STRIVING, gifted love and grateful works'.[13] The point is reiterated time and again throughout the series of Discourses. The way of obedience may be arduous and full of suffering but those who walk in that way with purity of heart will be sustained by the grace and the love of God.

## b. Love Your Neighbour

The relational aspect of Kierkegaard's conception of the self, counter-balancing the presentation in *Fear and Trembling*, becomes apparent very early in *Works of Love*. 'Christianity presupposes that a person loves himself and then adds to this only the phrase about the neighbour *as yourself*. And yet there is the change of eternity between the former and the latter'.[14] The phrase about the neighbour changes everything and puts the conception of the self on a whole new footing. The self is realized through love, not merely of oneself, which, on its own, would be the 'inclosing reserve' condemned as sinful, but rather through love of neighbour. The command to love one's neighbour is preceded in the Bible, of course, by the command to love God with all your heart and all your soul and all your mind. The order of the commandments is important, for the love of God is the deep well from which all love springs. 'Just as the quiet lake originates deep down in hidden springs no eye has seen, so also does a person's love originate even more deeply in God's love'.[15] Thus does God give what he also commands.

Faced with the command to love your neighbour as yourself, the individual will ask, who is my neighbour. It was, indeed, an expert in the law who put that question to Jesus, and he did so 'wanting to justify himself' (Lk. 10.29). Jesus responds by telling the parable of the good Samaritan which Kierkegaard interprets as undermining the inclination to show preference to some neighbours over others. 'Christianity has thrust erotic love and friendship from the throne, the love based on drives and inclination, preferential love, in order to place the spirit's love in its stead'.[16] Kierkegaard's apparent dismissal of preferential love has attracted criticism.[17] In Chapter 4 of *Love's Grateful Striving* Jamie Ferreira considers the criticism and asks whether Kierkegaard's emphasis upon the blindness of neighbour love, that is, its refusal to show partiality or preference for one over against another, obscures the distinctiveness of the particular individual. Kierkegaard writes, '. . . one sees the neighbour only with closed eyes or by looking *away from* the dissimilarities'.[18] While applauding the emphasis on human equality Ferreira worries about this inattention to the distinctive character of the individual because, she says, it is in danger of leading to abstraction. Ferreira here echoes the criticism of Theodor Adorno who claims that 'Kierkegaard's doctrine of love remains totally abstract'.[19] In response Ferreira suggests that '[w]hat we need is something to guarantee that these equal individuals or particulars are also recognized in their distinctiveness, that their concrete differences are seen to be morally relevant'.[20] As it turns out, I think Ferreira gets Kierkegaard exactly right when she explains that 'we are urged to close our eyes to dissimilarity and distinction so as not to contract the scope of the commandment; such blindness guarantees that no one can be excluded'.[21] Ferreira asks further, however, whether this recognition implies that concrete differences are not morally relevant? To be sure, we need to attend to concrete difference when deciding how *best* to love our neighbour, but such differences are of no account in deciding whether we *should* love our neighbour. There is no distinctive circumstance of any individual that could ever occasion a diminution of our duty to love, no concrete difference, that is, that would ever require us to love less. Kierkegaard's insistence on the blindness of love is thus indicative of the highest moral imperative, the same imperative presented in the Gospel under the command that we should love our enemies (Mt. 5.44). Kierkegaard comments, 'The Christian doctrine . . . is to love the neighbour, to love the whole human race, all people, even the enemy, and not to make exceptions, neither of preference nor of aversion'.[22] Although Kierkegaard certainly does insist that love must be blind to the differences between people, so that those differences do not become an excuse to love some more than or instead of others, he nevertheless deliberates at some length on the apostolic injunction to 'love the people we see'.[23] The point of emphasis here is that we are commanded to love people just as we see them with all their imperfections and weaknesses. Here Kierkegaard counters the accusation that his commendation of love deals only with an abstract ideal of human being.

The non-preferential and unconditional nature of the command to love one's neighbour reflects the non-preferential and unconditional character of God's love. Lest we suppose that God's election of Israel constitutes preferential treatment, we must remember that Israel is not chosen by God simply for its own sake but is elected to an obedience and faithfulness that will stand as a sign of God's promise to all the peoples of the earth (Gen. 18.18). Israel's election consists in God's call upon her to be responsible before God but also to neighbour.

Despite objections among some critics to Kierkegaard's emphasis upon the non-preferential nature of God's love and to the consequent obligation upon us to love without discrimination, Kierkegaard's insight here anticipates the post-modern condemnation of discrimination against the 'other'. Emmanuel Levinas, for instance, a reader of Kierkegaard, has influenced numerous post-modern theorists in insisting that we must show no partiality in extending hospitality to the stranger.[24] The basis for the non-partiality of neighbour-love is, for Kierkegaard, the equality of all before God. 'The neighbor . . . is your neighbor on the basis of equality with you before God, but unconditionally every person has this equality and has it unconditionally'.[25] 'In being king, beggar, rich man, poor man, male, female, etc., we are not like each other – therein we are indeed different. But in being the neighbor we are all unconditionally like each other . . . The neighbor is eternity's mark – on every human being'.[26] This is a human being's highest dignity, and her highest perfection, that she exists before God. That is true of the lowliest (humanly speaking), and of the most distinguished. Before God there is no difference between them. Therefore, says Kierkegaard, the neighbour to you is every person.[27]

Love of neighbour is illustrated in Luke's Gospel with these words of Christ: 'When you give a dinner or supper, do not invite your friends or your companions or your relatives or rich neighbours, lest they invite you in return and you be repaid. But when you give a banquet, invite the poor, the crippled, the lame, the blind' (Lk. 14.12–13). Commenting on these verses, Kierkegaard makes much of Jesus' use of the term 'banquet'.

[I]n the beginning an even less festive term, 'dinner' or 'supper' is used, and not until mention is made of inviting the poor and crippled is the word 'banquet' used. Do you not think it is as if Christ wanted to suggest that inviting the poor and the crippled is not only what we should do but is also something far more festive than eating dinner or supper with friends and relatives and rich neighbors, something one would not call a banquet, because inviting the poor – that is giving a banquet.[28]

Love for neighbour is distinguished here from charitable giving in which the paternalistic relations between benefactor and recipient are maintained.

The one who feeds the poor – but still has not been victorious over his mind in such a way that he calls this meal a banquet – sees the poor and lowly only as the poor and lowly. The one who gives a banquet sees the neighbor in the poor and lowly – however ludicrous this may seem in the eyes of the world.[29]

True love for one's neighbour, and true joy, is expressed in hosting a *banquet* for the poor, a banquet in which the poor and the crippled are honoured as equals. Kierkegaard here discerns the radical edge of Jesus' teaching. True love of neighbour expresses the fact that there is no essential dissimilarity between the lowly and the distinguished, for they are equal before God. A 'charitable giver', on the other hand, a giver of the kind who would not countenance actually eating with the poor, maintains the relations of inferiority and superiority and thus transgresses against God's conception of the matter. To love the neighbour is, by contrast, 'while remaining in the earthly dissimilarity allotted to one, essentially to will to exist equally for unconditionally every human being'.[30] The christological pattern is unmistakeable here. Kierkegaard has already established the principle that one learns what love is by attending to God's love. The gestures of love that Kierkegaard here develops are drawn from the life of the divine Son of God who became incarnate among us. Phil. 2.1–8 lies in the background of Kierkegaard's thought:

If then there is any encouragement in Christ, any consolation from love, any sharing in the Spirit, any compassion and sympathy, make my joy complete: be of the same mind, having the same love, being in full accord and of one mind. Do nothing from selfish ambition or conceit, but in humility regard others as better than yourselves. Let each of you look not to your own interests, but to the interests of others. Let the same mind be in you that was in Christ Jesus, who, though he was in the form of God, did not regard equality with God as something to be exploited, but emptied himself, taking the form of a slave, being born in human likeness. And being found in human form, he humbled himself and became obedient to the point of death – even death on a cross.

Having the same mind that was in Christ Jesus means, as Kierkegaard puts it, being victorious over one's mind in such a way that one calls a meal with the poor a banquet. It is worth making the point again here that Kierkegaard's theological concerns lie not in the precise formulation of Christian doctrine – he readily accepts the standard formulations – but rather in the clarification of how the doctrine is to be expressed through one's existence. 'The essentially Christian . . . is not related to knowing but to acting'.[31] Doctrinally we may identify Jesus as the one who, though being in the form of God, emptied himself, taking the form of a slave. Existentially, the emphasis lies on having the same mind that was in Christ Jesus, and in actually loving your neighbour as yourself.

## c. God is the Middle Term

In Chapter III A of *Works of Love* Kierkegaard introduces a theme that is central to his understanding of the relationship of love. '*Worldly wisdom*', he says, '*is of the opinion that love is a relationship between persons; Christianity teaches that love is a relationship between: a person – God – a person, that is, that God is the middle term*'.[32] This claim has attracted the criticism that Kierkegaard makes it impossible to love others directly, that is, for their own sake. If God is always the middle term, does this make the other merely an occasion for our love of God?[33] Three points may be made in defence of Kierkegaard's position. First, it is true for Kierkegaard that love of neighbour is an expression of one's love for God, but this does not mean that the neighbour becomes incidental. Rather, the neighbour can be loved – directly, and genuinely for his or her own sake – only when the neighbour is recognized as a beloved child of God, only when she is seen as equal with you before God. Apart from such recognition of divinely bestowed equality, worldly differences intervene and we are inclined to love out of self-interest, to curry favour with one who is superior to us (humanly speaking), because we want something the other has, because we enjoy the sense of self-worth and magnanimity that derives from helping those inferior to us, and so on. Only as our equals before God can we truly love others for their own sake.

A second reason why love of neighbour *with God as the middle term* facilitates rather than undermines true love, is that, as noted above, God is the source and criterion of true love. 'A human being's love originates mysteriously in God's love',[34] and, only in the light of God's love, can it be discerned what true love is.[35] For these reasons, 'no love and no expression of love may merely humanly and in a worldly way be withdrawn from the relationship to God'.[36] This leads to a third point: one does not genuinely love one's neighbour unless by that love the neighbour is enabled to understand herself as loved by God, that is, unless by that love, she learns that the mark of eternity is upon her, that she is made in God's image and, just so, is of infinite value to God. Through that realization she too will be enabled to love God. That was the outcome of Jesus' banqueting with the poor, with the outcasts and with sinners, and it is the outcome towards which all love of neighbour ought to be directed. 'The essentially Christian is this: truly to love oneself is to love God; truly to love another person is with every sacrifice . . . to help the other person to love God or in loving God'.[37]

## d. Works Righteousness?

*Works of Love* goes some way, I suggest, to correcting the impression some have gained from Kierkegaard that his heavy emphasis upon obedience, upon striving, and upon the imitation of Christ, leads to a doctrine of 'works righteousness'. *Works of Love* repeatedly emphasizes, however, that the works of love required of the Christian, indeed *commanded* by God are made possible in virtue of God's love. God's action precedes and enables our own action. Nevertheless, the impression continues among critics that Kierkegaard's conception of Christian faith, formulated as a corrective to what he perceived as a widespread abuse of the Reformation teaching on grace, errs in the opposite direction and turns the requirement of works into a heavy burden with little recourse to grace. Might it be that Kierkegaard himself falls foul of the parable he cites from Luther about the drunken peasant who is helped back onto his horse from the one side only to fall off the other?[38] Although Vernard Eller proceeds to defend Kierkegaard against the charge, he acknowledges that 'anyone who promotes as emphatic a doctrine of works (which is precisely what "obedience" amounts to) as did S. K. . . . inevitably opens himself to the risk and the accusation of works-righteousness'.[39] Such may be the impression gained when reading *For Self-Examination* and *Judge for Yourself!* which stress 'the requirement of Christianity', the necessity of works, and the need for imitation of Christ the prototype? Karl Barth voices the concern that Kierkegaard's gospel consists in a burdensome law rather than the freedom of grace:

Was it permissible to formulate more strictly still the conditions for thinking and living in faith, in love, and in hope? Was it permissible to make and thus again and again effect the truly necessary *negations* about the subject of theology and thereby to cause the poor wretches who became Christians, or might want to think of themselves as such, to taste again and again the bitterness of the training required? Was that permissible, if the aim was to proclaim and interpret the Gospel of God and thus the Gospel of his free grace? It is odd how easily one is caught in the wheels of a law that can only deaden and make one sour, gloomy, and sad.[40]

The persistence of these questions among theologians commenting on Kierkegaard requires that we give some attention to the relationship between gospel and law in Kierkegaard's thought.

How does he conceive the relation between grace and works and between Christ as prototype and Christ as redeemer?

Although it was Vernard Eller who raised the question of whether Kierkegaard advances a doctrine of works-righteousness, Eller himself does not believe this to be the case. There is in Kierkegaard's treatment of the matter, Eller points out, a dialectical relation between faith and works such that works both 'feed into grace' and 'proceed from grace'. We are summoned to follow Christ and so first comes an honest striving. But precisely in our failure to meet the requirement of imitating Christ we recognize our need of grace. Then after grace comes striving again – a striving born of gratitude that despite our failing Christ has become our redeemer.

There is no suggestion here that one is saved through works. We are saved by grace alone and yet it seems that in Kierkegaard's view the striving to imitate Christ is an indispensable part of what it means to be saved, both as preparation for grace and in consequence of grace. While he is clear that we are not saved by works, can it be the case that without works we are not saved? Can such a position be maintained? The question here is one of systematic balance. If gospel and law, grace and works both have their place in the definition of what constitutes a Christian, how should we conceive the relationship between them?

## e. A Corrective

That depends, possibly, upon the context in which Christianity is proclaimed. 'Times are different', Kierkegaard says in *For Self-Examination*, 'and different times have different requirements'[41] Kierkegaard is in no doubt that Luther was right in his own time to place all the emphasis on grace, for that 'was a time when the Gospel, *grace*, was changed into a new Law, more rigorous with people than the old Law . . . Everything had become works'.[42] Thus, says Kierkegaard,

> . . . the error from which Luther turned was an exaggeration with regard to works. And he was entirely right; he did not make a mistake – a person is justified

solely and only by faith. That is the way he talked and taught – and believed. And that this was not taking grace in vain – to that his life witnessed. Splendid![43]

The trouble Kierkegaard saw in his own age however, was that works, or more precisely, imitation or following Christ (*Efterfølgelse*) is done away with altogether.[44] And thus Kierkegaard wonders whether faith 'is to be found on earth'.[45] How do works function in this conception of things? Surely not as the means to salvation – that is by faith alone – but rather as the sign of faith. Faith gives rise to striving, not to secure salvation, but rather as the outworking of faith.

Karl Barth can surely not have overlooked the fact that Kierkegaard insisted again and again that salvation is by faith alone and depends entirely upon the grace of God. Barth's objection, therefore, must refer not to a doctrinal error in Kierkegaard but rather to what Barth perceives as an imbalance in Kierkegaard's presentation of the gospel. His objection seems to be that Christianity is presented by Kierkegaard as an altogether too gloomy affair, that it leaves the reader overwhelmed by the burden of following Christ rather than set free by grace from the concern to justify oneself. However much Barth might agree with Kierkegaard's diagnosis of Christendom's laxity, the end result of the proclamation of the gospel must always be, in Barth's view, that the hearer is uplifted by the announcement of the forgiveness and reconciliation that has been given through Christ. Is this the gospel that Kierkegaard too proclaims? Or does he leave us, in the end, without good news and despairing at our unworthiness? There is no doubt that Kierkegaard strives to impress upon his reader the stringency of the Christian requirement but does this emphasis obscure the centrality of grace? In consideration of this concern let us turn to the final discourse in *Judge for Yourself!*, 'Christ as the Prototype'.

## f. No One Can Serve Two Masters

Like most of Kierkegaard's discourses, this one is preceded by a prayer, the content of which gives a clue to the interpretation of the discourse itself. The opening line of the prayer is salutary for those mindful of Barth's criticism: 'Lord Jesus Christ, it was not to torment us human beings but to save us that you said the words "No one can serve two masters"'. Then follows:

> O Redeemer, by your holy suffering and death you have made satisfaction for everyone and everything; no eternal salvation either can or shall be earned – it has been earned. Yet you left your footprints, you, the holy prototype for the human race and for every individual, so that by your Atonement the saved might at every moment find the confidence and boldness to want to strive to follow you.[46] (JFY, 147)

The discourse that follows is about striving to follow Christ the prototype, but here in Kierkegaard's prayer we are given notice that Kierkegaard does not suppose that salvation is gained through the imitation of Christ. Salvation is by grace alone and the Atonement won for all by Christ gives both confidence and boldness to want to strive to follow him.

The text upon which the discourse is based is Mt. 6.24–34. Kierkegaard focuses first upon verse 24, 'No one can serve two masters', and turns his attention later to the example of the birds of the air and the lilies of the field. This progress is important, because, as we shall see, it moves the reader *from* a recognition of the stringency of the requirement *to* the uplifting that comes with the realization of divine grace.

'No one can serve two masters'. In this statement from Christ himself the requirement is made clear: Christian discipleship involves an absolute and unconditional allegiance. Anything less is not simply an imperfect discipleship but is impossible. No one *can* serve two masters. To propose in one moment to serve God and in another to serve mammon is, apparently, not to serve God at all. The requirement is absolute allegiance. The understanding of Christian faith presented in Kierkegaard's discussion of this text centres on what is to be done, rather than upon what is to be believed. This is a characteristic Kierkegaardian emphasis for which he here claims biblical support. It is expressed later in the discourse as the requirement to 'venture a decisive act'.

[This] means that one does not become a Christian
by hearing something about Christianity, by reading
something about it, by thinking about it . . . No, a *setting*
[*Bestedelse*] (*situation*) is required – venture a decisive act;
the proof does not precede but follows, is in and with the
imitation that follows Christ.[47]

This is the minimum, Kierkegaard explains, to venture out
in faith 'over the 70,000 fathoms of water'. The maximum, the
absolute, is expressed however, in the injunction that no one
can serve two masters. Here the requirement is that one's every
act be undertaken in unconditional obedience to God. But this,
Kierkegaard insists, is never achieved: watch carefully and you
will see that even for the most devout among us, their lives
express, 'But this is too lofty for us human beings; it is impossible
to serve only one master. No one can do it'.[48] Kierkegaard does
no more here than echo the words of the apostle Paul, 'There
is no one who is righteous, not even one . . .' (Rom. 3:10), but
it leads him to ask, 'Is, then, the requirement so cruel, or is the
Gospel not really good news?'[49] This question anticipates Barth's
complaint. Kierkegaard himself asks whether his proclamation
of 'the requirement' is simply too harsh, whether it lands upon
us crushingly rather than sets us free. And yet, so far, Kierkegaard has done nothing other than draw our attention to the
word of the New Testament itself. There may be more to the
gospel than the proclamation of this absolute requirement, but
there certainly is not less. That is Kierkegaard's primary point!

But it is not the end of the matter! Knowing well what it
really is to be a human being, knowing how infinitely far every
human being is from truly serving only one master, the gospel
goes on to say, 'that is precisely why I proclaim an Atonement:
is this not good news?'[50] If the requirement were anything less,
if it were not absolute and unconditional there would be no
need of atonement; we could meet the requirement ourselves.
And thus, according to Kierkegaard, the abominable thing in
Christendom is that the requirement has been scaled down,
that it is made no higher than what everyone achieves by being
born in a Christian country, by being baptized and by attending
church as convention requires. That is hardly our situation at the

onset of the twenty-first century, however. To be Christian is no longer the matter of course that it was thought to be in nineteenth century Denmark. We could argue now, perhaps, that the standard has become more rigorous again. To confess to being a Christian in today's world is, once more, to stand apart from the crowd. I doubt, however that Kierkegaard would be impressed. He would very likely remark that there is no substantive difference between a standard set at two feet high and one at four if the height to be cleared is one hundred feet or more. The falling short is what matters. Whether we fall short by ninety-six feet or ninety-eight makes no difference if, to continue the metaphor, the requirement was to clear the bar at one hundred feet. 'The confusion lies', Kierkegaard says, 'in the fact that you compare yourself with others – alone before God the matter is utterly simple'.[51] And further: 'Before God, at the moment when humanly speaking I have come the furthest, I have not come one inch, not one millionth of an inch, closer to God than the person who never strove, indeed, than the one who strove with all his might for the opposite'.[52] In a discourse that stresses an honest striving as the *conditio sine qua non* of authentic Christian faith, these are crucial words. Striving avails us nothing so far as salvation is concerned. The value and importance of striving must therefore be accounted for in some other way. We shall return below to offer such an accounting.

In the meantime, let us note that in relation to anyone who might be discouraged by the truth that no amount of striving will bring us any closer to God, Kierkegaard asks, 'is it not because he has placed himself in a wrong relation to it so that by putting himself in a wrong place he receives the pressure in a wrong place and the requirement crushes him instead of humblingly exerting a pressure that lifts up in joy over and in bold confidence through *grace*?'[53] There is an echo here of the previously mentioned sermon inserted as the conclusion to *Either/Or*, 'The Upbuilding that Lies in the Thought that in Relation to God We are Always in the Wrong'.[54] Far from being a thought that 'can only deaden and make one sour, gloomy, and sad' as Barth suspected, Kierkegaard's emphasis upon the utter failure of human beings to fulfil the requirement of imitation is directed towards uplifting. The intention of the Gospel, Kierkegaard writes, 'is that by means of the requirement and my humiliation I shall be lifted, believing and worshiping – and then I am light as a bird. What lifts up more, the thought of my own good deeds or the thought of God's grace'.[55]

Another reaction is possible however. Rather than being lifted up by the thought of how far short we fall of the requirement, and thus by the thought of the magnitude of grace, Christendom takes umbrage at the thought of our failure and consequently attempts to lessen the requirement – to such an extent, Kierkegaard alleges, that Christianity is no longer distinguishable from the secular mentality. There is nothing to distinguish a Christian from an ordinary citizen, and thus according to Kierkegaard, Christianity no longer exists.[56] '[I]t is abolished!'[57] It is to this situation that Kierkegaard directs his own literary efforts. He has endeavoured, he says, to present Christianity 'unaltered in all its unconditionality so that each and every one can ponder privately whether or not he wants to be involved with it'.[58] But,

> what stands between Christianity and people in these
> sensible times is that they have lost the conception of the
> unconditioned requirement, that they cannot get it into
> their heads why the requirement is the unconditioned
> (of what use is it, since no one, after all, fulfils it), that
> the unconditioned has become for them the impractical,
> a foolishness, a ridiculousness, so that they, mutinously
> or conceitedly, reverse the relation, seek the fault in the
> requirement and themselves become the claimants who
> demand that the requirement be changed.[59]

The fault in Christendom is not that the requirement is not met; 'Christianity can deal with that'.[60] The fault is that the requirement is changed to suit our own laxity. The truth, however, is that we can be involved with God only on His terms. '[I]f I am to be involved with God, then I must also countenance that the requirement is the unconditioned'.[61] The theological truth to which Kierkegaard here draws our attention is not in the first place a truth about the stringency of God's law. Rather it is a truth about who God is. God is absolute sovereign so that to offer anything other than absolute allegiance is a denial of that sovereignty. It is to confess another authority greater than or in conflict with God. But, and this is Kierkegaard's text for the discourse, 'no one *can* serve two masters'. The effort to do so therefore makes clear that we are not involved with God after all. God is not our Lord at all. Thus Kierkegaard pleads,

> No, no, O God in heaven, above all never rescind the unconditioned requirement! In wanting to abolish the unconditioned requirement, it is really you that people want to abolish, and this is why I cling so firmly to it and denounce sensibleness, which by abolishing the unconditioned requirement wants to abolish you.[62]

This is the grave reality of sin tragically enacted at Calvary, not that we fail to keep the law, but that we deny the Lordship of God and want to do away with him. And this is why Kierkegaard thinks that 'to make and thus again and again effect the truly necessary *negations* about the subject of theology' (Barth) is not an improper imposition upon the sensibility of 'those poor wretches who became Christians' but a necessary indication of the 'infinite qualitative difference' between God and humanity and of the Lordship of God. These are themes that Barth himself insists upon – explicitly following Kierkegaard! It might be argued of Barth, therefore, that he has overlooked Kierkegaard's insistence that the sovereignty of God is at stake through all his berating of Christendom?

## g. Cheap Grace/Costly Grace

While Barth himself increasingly moved away from Kierkegaard's influence, there is another of that same tumultuous era in twentieth century history and theology in whom the influence of Kierkegaard persisted. Dietrich Bonhoeffer in *Discipleship*[63] (*Nachfolge* in the original German) is similarly concerned with the safeguarding of the requirement of Christian discipleship. Grace is free, Bonhoeffer argues, but it must not be cheapened. Bonhoeffer's words from his Preface to *Discipleship* indicate the relevance of his thought to the Barthian critique of Kierkegaard. Bonhoeffer writes:

> We desire to speak of the call to follow Jesus. In doing so, are we burdening people with a new heavier yoke? Should even harder more inexorable rules be added to all the human rules under which their souls and bodies groan? Should our admonition to follow Jesus only prick their uneasy and wounded consciences with an even sharper sting?[64]

Answering his own question Bonhoeffer writes further:

> In following Jesus, people are released from the hard yoke of their own laws to be under the gentle yoke of Jesus Christ. Does this disparage the seriousness of Jesus' commandments? No. Instead, only where Jesus' entire commandment and the call to unlimited discipleship remain intact are persons fully free to enter into Jesus' community.[65]

The requirement must be made clear! Like Kierkegaard, Bonhoeffer acknowledges that times are different and that this is the emphasis appropriate to his age. 'Cheap grace', he says in 1937, 'is the mortal enemy of our church. Our struggle today is for costly grace'.[66] 'Cheap grace means', he continues, 'grace as bargain-basement goods, cut-rate forgiveness, cut-rate comfort, cut-rate sacrament; grace as the church's inexhaustible pantry, from which it is doled out by careless hands without hesitation or limit'.[67] And further: 'Cheap grace means grace as doctrine, as principle, as system. It means forgiveness of sins as a general truth; it means God's love as merely a Christian idea of God. Those who affirm it have already had their sins forgiven.[68]

All these claims can be found in Kierkegaard. Indeed one suspects that they are simply paraphrases of what Bonhoeffer has learned from him.[69] Likewise the claim Bonhoeffer makes that,

> Luther's deed cannot be misunderstood more grievously than by thinking that through discovering the gospel

of pure grace, Luther proclaimed a dispensation from obeying Jesus' commandments in the world . . . Luther said that grace alone did it, and his followers repeated it literally, with the one difference that very soon they left out and did not consider and did not mention what Luther always included as a matter of course: discipleship. Yes, he no longer even needed to say it, because he always spoke as one whom grace had led into a most difficult following of Jesus.[70]

Bonhoeffer too regards it as essential to lay stress on the absolute requirement to follow Christ. That we are saved by faith through grace alone does not mean that the requirement of obedience is done away with. 'Whenever Christ calls us, his call leads us to death',[71] Bonhoeffer says. New life is not the adoption of an idea. It is a form of existence. There is an ethical imperative – renunciation of the world. This does not mean that the Christian flees the world – Bonhoeffer repeats Kierkegaard's respect for but final rejection of the monastic ideal[72] – but the life of the Christian in the world is ordered by a call and a command that are not of this world. The Christian is called to service of a new master.

## h. Does Christianity Exist?

This is the call, but as Kierkegaard makes clear there is no one in this world who has succeeded in serving only one master. Can it be then, that Christianity does not exist? Kierkegaard says so on occasion, but it seems to me that this is a rhetorical strategy. Certainly he is serious about his claim that no human being fulfils the requirement to follow Christ unconditionally, but his oft repeated assertion that Christianity does not exist seems designed to make clear just this, that nobody meets the requirement of unconditional obedience. As we have already observed, Kierkegaard is saying nothing different here than what Paul says, in Rom. 3.10 for instance, 'There is no one who is righteous, not even one', or in Rom. 3.23, 'For all have sinned and fall short of the glory of God'. The question is whether Kierkegaard will also say with Paul and give due stress to the declaration, 'but they are now justified by his grace as a gift, through the redemption that is in Christ Jesus' (Rom. 3.24). This is the high point of the gospel message – not the condemnation of human sinfulness, though that is essential, but the declaration of justification and grace. Has Barth correctly observed that Kierkegaard reverses this relationship and stresses condemnation at the expense of grace? Is it for this reason that Kierkegaard purports not to be able to find Christianity anywhere in the world? Does he condemn without ever lifting up? We may let Kierkegaard answer for himself:

> . . . just as suspicious characters must register with the police, I must report to Governance with regard to this dubiousness of my being a Christian. Governance, being sheer love and grace and compassion, will surely not refuse to have anything to do with me but requires that I be honest in the relationship.
>
> Christ is the prototype, to which corresponds *imitation*. There is really only one true way to be a Christian – to be a disciple. The disciple has among other marks also this: to suffer for the doctrine. Anyone who has not suffered for the doctrine[73] has in one way or another incurred the guilt of using his sagacity to spare himself in a secular way. That he therefore should not dare to call himself a Christian or that he will not be eternally saved is far from my idea – God forbid that I should dare to say something that would end up recoiling upon myself most of all.[74]

So what is Kierkegaard urging upon us? He is not arguing that our failures in discipleship preclude us from calling ourselves Christians, nor that our lack of good works mean that we will not be saved. What he urges upon us, however, is an admission – an admission that the requirement of Christianity is not bourgeois religion; it is unconditional obedience to Christ, and then also the admission that we fall far short of that vocation.

'Christ as prototype must be advanced, but not in order to alarm'. Kierkegaard says:

> No, the *prototype* must be advanced in order at least to procure some respect for Christianity, to make somewhat distinguishable what it means to be a Christian, to get Christianity moved out of the realm of scientific scholarship and doubt and nonsense (objective) and into the realm of the subjective,[75] where it belongs just as surely as the Savior of the world, our Lord Jesus Christ, did not bring any doctrine into the world and never delivered lectures, but as the *prototype* required *imitation*, yet by his *reconciliation* expels, if possible, all anxiety from a person's soul.[76]

It is the knowledge of reconciliation that expels anxiety. It is the proclamation of grace, in other words, that assuages for those who read Kierkegaard aright, the sourness, the gloominess and the sorrow that Barth alleged would be the outcome for those who dwell too long in Kierkegaard's school. The proclamation of reconciliation is thus Kierkegaard's last word in his discourse about Christ as prototype, but let us recall that it is also his first. Atonement and grace enter into Kierkegaard's discussion of the text of Mt. 6.24 from the beginning of the discourse.[77] And let us note too Kierkegaard's insistence that 'we continually call to mind . . . that Jesus Christ is not only the prototype but is also the Redeemer . . .'[78] To that we may add a note from Kierkegaard's Journals: 'Yes, I certainly do realize very well that to want to build one's salvation on any works, to dare come before God with anything like this, is the most abominable sin, for this means a scorning of Christ's Atonement'.[79]

Nevertheless, 'times are different', Kierkegaard remarks, and different times require different emphases. When the monastery is the deviation, faith must be affirmed but when the professor is the deviation, when Christianity is reduced to expositions about doctrine – to lip service – without the following of Christ, then works must be emphasized,[80] not because works have merit,[81] but because they are an indication that one's life really has been transformed by grace.[82] Even when the emphasis shifts, however,

Kierkegaard knows that faith and obedience, grace and works, reconciliation and discipleship, are always to be spoken of in the same breath.

The relation between grace and works then is precisely this in Kierkegaard's view: we are saved by grace alone, but salvation means new life, and new life is characterized by discipleship, faithfulness, obedience, works! Works are to be understood here not primarily as good deeds but as *acts* of trust. Without those, one must question whether faith is to be found on earth. Kierkegaard here, is simply expounding the principle: 'by their fruits you shall know them'. The position is again repeated in Bonhoeffer: '. . . *only the believers obey*, and *only the obedient believe*. It is really unfaithfulness to the Bible to have the first statement without the second'.[83]

## i. Obedience as Witness

While works function as a critical indicator of whether or not faith is present in a person, Kierkegaard is conscious too that works, particularly 'works of love', can be a sign for others, a witness to the truth. Speaking of those who call themselves Christian but who nevertheless have not suffered for the doctrine, Kierkegaard remarks that each must make an admission – must confess his or her sin before God.

> And if [the one who so confesses] happens to be one of those who have undertaken to proclaim Christianity, he must bear in mind that by sparing himself in this way he has weakened the impression of Christianity, which has become less recognisable to others . . .[84]

Kierkegaard shows a quite remarkable concern for this aspect of the matter. The category of witness becomes increasingly important to him in his battle against the perceived hypocrisy of Christendom, and comes to a head, of course, in his disgust with Prof. Martenson's eulogy for Bishop Mynster. We have noted repeatedly above that one of the chief concerns of Kierkegaard's life was to make it clear what Christianity is. Wherever people profess themselves to be Christian but behave just like all secular-minded people, the waters are muddied. A confused idea of what Christianity is gains currency and faith is sold off cheaply. The Christian and thus the true witness to truth, however, is one whose life expresses works as strenuously as possible but who then humbly confesses: 'But my being saved is nevertheless grace'.[85]

Kierkegaard draws upon Luther for this conception of the value of works: 'Luther wished to take "meritoriousness" away from works and apply them somewhat differently – namely, in the direction of witnessing for the truth . . .'[86] It is not by talking that Christianity is proclaimed, but by acting.[87] For the preacher who does not realize this, Kierkegaard can hardly contain his scorn: '. . . it is actual existence that preaches', he says, '– all that with the mouth and the arms is no good'.[88] This is hyperbole of course, as Kierkegaard himself certainly realizes. But the point is well made; one cannot expect the proclamation of Christianity on Sunday to be taken seriously if on Monday it makes no difference to the state of affairs, even in the life of the preacher! Better, then, an honest admission of one's failings set against the proclamation of the ideal, rather than the betrayal of the ideal through hypocrisy.

This is the first aspect of Kierkegaard's concern for a truthful witness. The second aspect is also important, however, and accords with Kierkegaard's contempt for the Enlightenment project of making everything objective. The effort to secure the truth of Christianity through reason is itself a falling away from the life of obedience, and simply renders the truth of Christianity less and less convincing. Commenting on the doctrine of the ascension for example, Kierkegaard writes,

> The demonstration of Christianity really lies in *imitation*. This was taken away. Then the need for 'reasons' was felt, but these reasons, or that there are reasons, are already a kind of doubt – and thus doubt arose and lived on reasons . . .

> But those whose lives are marked by imitation have not doubted the Ascension. And why not? In the first

place, because their lives were too strenuous, too much expended in daily sufferings to be able to sit in idleness keeping company with reasons and doubt, playing evens and odds. For them the Ascension stood firm . . .[89]

Doubt arises, Kierkegaard contends, when we coddle ourselves with respect to imitation. So, 'doubt is actually a self-indictment'.[90] Kierkegaard's prescription for the doubter, therefore, is: 'First of all go out and become an imitator of Christ in the stricter sense – only someone like that has the right to speak up – and none of these has doubted'.[91]

## j. God's Enabling

The story is not yet complete. Indeed its most important element has barely been mentioned. In a criticism of Kierkegaard made elsewhere than the one already quoted, Barth charges Kierkegaard as improperly conceiving works as a duty owed to God. Barth does not doubt that Christian faith involves imitation of Christ; '. . . in the action for which man is freed by the action of God'; Barth writes, 'we really have to do with imitation'.[92] But Barth also insists that the Bible envisages this action 'as a liberation which comes to man from God and not therefore as a demand which God addressed to him'.[93] And further,

If God's love as His free self-giving to and for man is the basis of man's love, it can have the character only of a liberation which man is given for an action which in correspondence to that of God can only be free and not one which is required or imposed from without, which he is constrained to fulfil. It would be a strange love which demanded love. And it would be a strange love which was merely a response to this demand. It is the nerve of the whole relationship between the love of God and that of man that by the love of God man is put in a position to love, that he may do so, that he is not bullied or prodded to do so by any compelling authority from without, that he is really free – made free – to do so of himself in imitation of the self-giving of God.[94]

It is from this perspective that Barth alleges against Kierkegaard and especially against the volume *Works of Love* that 'for all the individual beauties of the work' the appeal to the commandment 'Thou shalt love' gives to it 'the unlovely, inquisitorial and terribly judicial character which is so distinctive of Kierkegaard in general'.[95] While the question of the character of Kierkegaard's work is probably best left to personal judgement, Barth's dogmatic point about the proper construal of the imperative to love requires attention. What would need to be shown in order to support Barth's point is that Kierkegaard lays stress upon the duty of the individual *to find it within herself* to love as God has loved us while ignoring Barth's own and properly biblical emphasis upon the liberation that God's love of us effects within our hearts. Is that really the case with respect to Kierkegaard's treatment of the matter? My consideration of *Works of Love* above attempted to show that, on Kierkegaard's account of the matter, the command to love can be met only through God's enabling.

*For Self-Examination* and *Judge for Yourself!* provide further evidence that Kierkegaard does recognize that the works of love to which the Christian is called are not to be construed as a human achievement, but rather as the outworking of God's transforming and liberating activity. The same conclusion about the defensibility of Kierkegaard's position against Barth's criticism is drawn by Paul Martens in his study of *Works of Love*. Martens writes: 'It appears that Barth wrongly suggests that those schooled in Kierkegaard can not find comfort in what the majesty of God's free grace has done, is still doing, and shall do conclusively'.[96] The acknowledgement of grace does not entail, however, that human striving is of no account. Within the sphere of God's grace human striving is just what is required. It is within the indicative of grace that the imperative of the command is to be found.

Kierkegaard explains the matter by use of a series of analogies. The first comes from Mt. 6.28, a text that Kierkegaard commends again and again: 'Look at the lilies of the field, how they grow; they do not work, they do not spin. But I say to you that not even Solomon in all his glory was clothed as one of them'. Observing that the best trained seamstress cannot make clothes for Solomon as fine as those of the lilies, Kierkegaard asks whether there is someone who sews and spins for the lilies? 'That there is', he then proclaims:

> God in heaven. But human beings spin and sew, 'Yes, necessity teaches them that all right . . .' 'Fie! How can you look down on your task that way – as if being human, as if God, as if existence – as if it all were a penitentiary! No, consider the lilies of the field . . . learn from the lilies and the birds to understand that when human beings spin and sew it is nevertheless really God who spins and sews. Do you believe that the seamstress, if she understands this, will therefore become less diligent in her work, that she will lay her hands in her lap and think: Well, if it is God who really spins and sews, then it is best that I be excused? . . . But, she, our own dear seamstress with the childlike piety, our lovable seamstress, she understands that only when she herself is sewing will God sew for her, and therefore she becomes all the more diligent in her work, so that by continually sewing she may continually understand that – what a gracious jest! – it is God who sews, every stitch . . .'[97]

The first point to be noted here is that the works that Kierkegaard urges upon his readers, are properly construed not as feats of human prowess but as the work of God enacted through human obedience. They do not take place without human striving and yet they are recognized as works enabled by the grace of God. This point requires pneumatological elucidation and Kierkegaard does provide it, but let us first note a further point to be taken from the quoted passage: Though not stated explicitly, the tone of Kierkegaard's storytelling suggests that far from being an onerous duty, as Barth alleged in relation to Kierkegaard's account of Christian works, the seamstress will regard her work as a joy. That is implicit in the use of the biblical text about the birds of the air and the lilies of the field. What absurdity it would be to suggest that they find it burdensome to be arrayed as they are.

> 'Look at the birds of the air!' What, you are worried and dejected, your eyes are downcast! What is this? God did not create man this way . . . look at the bird in the sky. Oh, confess to yourself that God can no more be said to be the one who presses down than the arching sky can be said to press. No, the pressing down comes from the earth or from what in you is of the earth, but just as the arching sky lifts up, so God is the one who wants to lift up.[98]

In order to make the point more clearly that the works of discipleship should be regarded as sheer delight, Kierkegaard tells another story, this time about a child and his mother:

> Everyday little Ludvig is taken for a ride in his stroller, a delight that usually lasts an hour, and little Ludvig understands very well that it is delight. Yet the mother has hit upon something new that will definitely delight the little Ludvig even more: would he like to try to push the stroller himself? And he can! What! He can? Yes, look, Auntie, little Ludvig can push the stroller himself! Now, let us be down to earth but not upset the child, since we know very well that little Ludvig cannot do it, that it is his mother who is actually pushing the stroller, and that it is really only to delight him that she plays the game . . . It is the same with being able to work. Properly understood, understood in a godly way, it is pure delight, something God has thought of to delight human beings . . . ah, do not grieve his love; he thought that it would really make you happy! This is a godly understanding of what it means to work.[99]

Such passages must make one reluctant, firstly, to assent too readily to Barth's judgement that the character of Kierkegaard's work is 'unlovely, inquisitorial and terribly judicial'. But secondly, the theological import of these passages must not go unnoticed. Kierkegaard does urge upon his readers that the person of faith must strive to imitate Christ, but the striving is conceived, first, as itself enabled by the grace of God, and second, as a matter of sheer delight. Elsewhere we learn that the striving is motivated by gratitude for what God in Christ has done for us. Kierkegaard remarks in his Journals, 'The atonement is the decisive thing. Then, on the other side, precisely out of joy over the reconciliation, comes an honest striving . . .'[100]

## k. The Spirit Gives Life

We noted above the need for a pneumatological elucidation of God's enabling. We do not have far to seek for such elucidation; the second discourse of *For Self-Examination* is based on Acts 2.1–12 and is titled, 'It is the Spirit who gives life'. The discourse is a relatively short one; Kierkegaard's argument develops as follows. First he distinguishes between the spirit of the age and the Holy Spirit. The two are not to be confused as Kierkegaard thought had happened in his own age. The difference becomes apparent, Kierkegaard goes on to argue, when it is realized that the Spirit is given when we die to the world. 'A life-giving Spirit – that is the invitation; who would not willingly take hold of it! But die first – that is the halt!'[101] The point here is the same as that made in discussion of the text, 'No one can serve two masters'. The new life of discipleship involves forsaking allegiance to the life of old. Kierkegaard then proceeds to explain that the Spirit is the giver of faith, of hope and of love. These three gifts are representative, for Kierkegaard, of all the resources one needs to be a Christian, including, therefore, those very gifts which enable good works. Speaking of the apostles, Kierkegaard says, '. . . the life-giving Spirit brought them love. Thus the apostles, in conformity with their prototype, resolved to love, to suffer, to endure all things, to be sacrificed in order to save this unloving world. And this is love'.[102] It is the Spirit who thus provides precisely what the apostles are commanded to do.

The discourse then finishes with Kierkegaard's parable of the coachman:

> Once upon a time there was a rich man. At an exorbitant price he had purchased abroad a team of entirely flawless, splendid horses, which he had wanted for his own

pleasure and the pleasure of driving them himself. About a year or two passed by. If anyone who had known these horses earlier now saw him driving them, he would not be able to recognize them: their eyes had become dull and drowsy; their gait lacked style and precision; they had no staying power, no endurance; he could drive them scarcely four miles without having to stop on the way, and sometimes they came to a standstill just when he was driving his best; moreover they had acquired all sorts of quirks and bad habits, and although they of course had plenty of feed they grew thinner day by day.

Then he called in the royal coachman. He drove them for a month. In the whole countryside there was not a team of horses that carried their heads so proudly, whose eyes were so fiery, whose gait was so beautiful; there was no team of horses that could hold out running as they did, even thirty miles in a stretch without stopping. How did this happen? It is easy to see: the owner, who without being a coachman meddled with being a coachman, drove the horses according to the horses' understanding of what it is to drive; the royal coachman drove them according to the coachman's understanding of what it is to drive.[103]

In explanation of the parable Kierkegaard comments, 'So also with us human beings. When I think of myself and the count-less people I have come to know, I have often said to myself sadly: Here are capacities and talents and qualifications enough but the coachman is lacking'.[104] The parable is about the Holy Spirit, giving new life, giving gifts for discipleship, and draw-ing human beings into the works of love. Kierkegaard certainly does speak of those works in terms of human duty[105] – Barth is right – but should this be regarded as a fault? Kierkegaard is plain enough that it is the Spirit who enables us to take up that duty,[106] and that the duty itself is to be conceived, not as a burden, but as a joy. He is also right, that is to say, biblical, to insist that such works do not take place without the utmost human striving.

## 1. Christ Fulfils the Law

There is one further matter to which Kierkegaard draws our attention, and which completes, I think, the necessary counter to Barth's misgivings. In the midst of the discourse, 'Christ as the Prototype', we find Kierkegaard insisting that there is only one who has fulfilled the requirement, and that one is Jesus Christ. 'By looking at his life, we shall see the unconditioned requirement and see it fulfilled. We continually call to mind, however, that Jesus Christ is not only the prototype but is also the Redeemer, lest the prototype disquiet us to the point of despair . . .'[107] That Christ has fulfilled the law is recognized here as the basis of that liberation which Barth thought Kierkegaard had obscured. It is precisely because Christ himself both fulfils the law and commands obedience that Kierkegaard finds the command to love so uplifting. 'When eternity says, "You shall love,"' Kierkegaard explains, 'it is responsible for making sure that this can be done'.[108] Despair at the command is thus defeated precisely because the one who gives the command is also the one who fulfils it for us, thus making sure it can be done. That sounds paradoxical, but not when it is recognized that by virtue of his own redemptive action, fulfilling the law on our behalf, Christ's command becomes a promise. The gospel news is that because Christ has loved we shall love also. Kierkegaard's recognition of this is astonishingly liberating, as Timothy Polk explains:

> The story of Christ speaks of one more transformation – that of the imperative itself. What we first heard as a command has become a pledge and promise, historically enacted, eternally grounded, eschatologically secured, given on the highest authority: 'You shall love' – *agapeseis*, future declarative[109] Kierkegaard has made a subtle and enormously important observation, and what an enormous difference it makes: now, because of Christ, Christians read an imperative also as a promise; law has become Gospel in one and the same sentence, not in abrogation but in fulfilment. Therefore the Christian life of love, always presently striving, should also be one of hope and futurity, hope in the promise of the Gospel.[110]

'[W]herever the purely human loses courage', Kierkegaard says himself, 'the commandment strengthens . . .'.[111] We see confirmed here what is everywhere apparent, namely, that the whole of Kierkegaard's proclamation of the need for works is premised upon the grace of God in Christ and upon the promise of the Gospel that because Christ has loved, we shall love also. 'It is God who, so to speak, lovingly assumes love's requirement'.[112] David Gouwens thus writes: 'Kierkegaard's understanding of love is not, as Barth charges, sheer abstract demand or imperative, but is based upon the concrete realization of love in the life of Christ'.[113] 'Christ's life of love has been pledged to be fully ours at the last'.[114]

In all his berating of those who call themselves Christian, therefore, Kierkegaard does not doubt for a minute that they will in the end be saved.[115] The basis of that confidence is the grace of God. But like Paul[116] and Luther, as also Calvin[117] before him, Kierkegaard insists that grace is abused if it leads Christians to have no regard for the law.

## m. In Conclusion

Kierkegaard is not systematic in the presentation of his message; he is a writer of upbuilding discourses, not of volumes of systematic theology. But if by the term 'systematic' we understand, not of course the systematizing of the gospel within the limited span of human reason, but a concern for the coherence of the whole gospel and for how the parts are interrelated, then the elements of a systematic theology are certainly to be found in Kierkegaard. He is a rigorous thinker, relentless in his pursuit of a Christian conception of things, a conception of things, that is, which originates in and is responsible to the gospel of Jesus Christ. The question we have been concerned with in this chapter, however, is whether Kierkegaard is guilty of a systematic imbalance in his presentation of the gospel and most especially in his presentation of the relation between faith and works, between grace and law? Does he explicate the requirement of imitation in such a way that it distorts or obscures the fact that we are saved by grace alone? I have tried to show that he does not, but now it is time to acknowledge that this is the merely academic question. The more important question, the one for which Kierkegaard himself is especially concerned, is not about whether in offering his corrective to the errors of his age he has gone too far, but about whether the error he has identified currently abounds, whether it still stands in need of correction. The important question is whether through his corrective Kierkegaard still confronts us with the challenge of the gospel and by virtue of that challenge prompts action towards a giving of our whole lives, without merit as they are, into the hands of God. That in the end is not a matter of doctrinal debate but of prayer. Kierkegaard retreats and his reader is left alone before God.

# Chapter 8

# Reckoning with Kierkegaard

We come in this final chapter to consider Kierkegaard's place in the tradition of Christian theology. What were the influences upon him? What were the sources that he drew upon? What impact has he had upon the subsequent thought of the Christian community? What is to be learned from him still by those who engage in the task of Christian theology? Assessments of his place in the tradition are likely to be contentious. Kierkegaard has been aligned posthumously with all manner of causes and theological movements. Every commentator upon his work draws upon those themes and emphases that appeal most to their own theological or philosophical convictions and sensibilities. There is no point in pretending that I have not done the same in the preceding chapters. I regard him as one who is fundamentally orthodox in his theological convictions, as one who is committed to Christian faith as it has been handed down from the apostles, as one who upholds the authority of Scripture and as one who believes in the objective truth of a gospel that can be understood in truth only subjectively, only by the those who live it, by those for whom it has become an existence communication.

It is important to acknowledge nevertheless that Kierkegaard remains a profound critic of orthodoxy, especially where it has removed the offence of the gospel, hardened into dogma and become comfortably conventional. We must recognize Kierkegaard as a polemicist against every effort to domesticate God and to substitute religious observances for the costly obedience of Christian discipleship. We must also recognize, as he did himself, that he offers to the Christian tradition, not a systematic account of the gospel and all its entailments but a corrective, a corrective to the recurring propensity of those who call ourselves Christians to sell off the gospel at bargain price both in order to attract more members and, more commonly, to reduce the demands it makes upon us. Christianity he claims, 'has been harmed incalculably by being given a deep bow and meaningless respect. Meanwhile it has been deprived of all its characteristic marks . . .'[1] Although, or rather because, he confesses the need of correction himself, Kierkegaard remains an astute diagnostician of the human condition and an uncomfortable ally for those who count themselves as Christian. That is because his theological orthodoxy consists, above all, in a penetrating analysis of the myriad ways in which, though justified by and beloved of God, Christians remain sinners who are endlessly inventive both in their efforts at self-justification and in avoiding the plain sense of Jesus' radical ethic.

The corrective offered by Kierkegaard was a corrective, not of doctrine as such, but of the way Christian doctrine has been appropriated. Howard and Edna Hong explain that Kierkegaard's corrective was needed 'not because of doctrinal aberration but because of a lack of inward deepening, of a subjectivizing of the objectivity of doctrine, and because of an avoidance of the second danger, witnessing to the implications of the doctrine.'[2] Kierkegaard himself describes his task as the provision of an 'existential-corrective' to the established order[3] and remarks,

> The person who is to provide the 'corrective' must study the weak sides of the established order scrupulously and penetratingly and then one-sidedly present the opposite – with expert one-sidedness . . . If this is done properly, then a presumably sharp head can come along and object that 'the corrective' is one-sided and get the public to believe there is something in it. Ye gods! Nothing is easier for the one providing the corrective than to add the other side; but then it ceases to be precisely the corrective and itself becomes an established order.[4]

In a nice turn of phrase from Richard John Neuhaus, Kierkegaard 'shouted to the hard of hearing and drew startling pictures for the almost blind'.[5] The corrective character of Kierkegaard's writings means that we cannot make a systematic theologian out of him, but theologians should attend again and again to his prophetic voice calling for a more faithful and, especially, a more honest discipleship. They will do well also to keep in mind Kierkegaard's corrective as they attempt to articulate the claims and trace the existential requirements arising from faith in the lowly and suffering servant who is in person the strange, eternal Word of God, at once the Prototype and the Redeemer.

The essential character of any Christian theology is revealed, above all, by the approach it takes to christology. In Kierkegaard's own time Christian theology was dominated by the rival approaches of two professors at the University of Berlin, G. W. F. Hegel and F. D. E. Schleiermacher. For all their differences – Hegel was a rationalist, and Schleiermacher was a Romantic – they share one negative characteristic, negative, at least, in Kierkegaard's view. In developing their theologies Hegel and Schleiermacher both come to Christology *after* the foundations of their thought had been laid. The foundations of Hegel's rational system and of Scheleiermacher's Romantic piety are determined *before* consideration of Jesus himself, so that the Christology developed by each thinker necessarily involves an accommodation of Jesus to a prior theological conceptuality. Jesus plays no role in determining the essential structure of their theological thought. For Hegel, the determination of Geist as the all-encompassing reality and the unfolding of the world-historical dialectic provides the conceptual framework into which Jesus is then accommodated. For Schleiermacher, the anthropological affirmations involved in the conception of God as the ultimate ground of religious experience, likewise, determine in advance the shape of his Christology.

Schleiermacher develops his theology from the foundational contention that God's immediate presence underlies the religious experience of every human being. Fundamental to human consciousness is the sense that we are not independent beings, but that in some way we have come to be and are sustained through the agency of a being beyond ourselves. He further suggests that the question of the origin of our being results in the universal feeling of absolute dependence. This modification of the mind and heart consists in the feeling that we are not ourselves responsible for our own being but somehow exist in relation to an 'Other'. This feeling of absolute dependence, according to Schleiermacher, constitutes the fundamental human religious experience and is the ground upon which all theology must be built.

Having determined that God is the Other upon whom we are conscious of being absolutely dependent, Schleiermacher comes to the consideration of Christ after the theological foundations have been laid. Until that point the theology has been developed without reference to Christ, and so its essential structure and character have been determined apart from Christology. The method is succinctly revealed in Schleiermacher's summary definition of the identity of Jesus. 'The Redeemer is like all men [and women] in virtue of the identity of human nature, but distinguished from them all by the constant potency of his God consciousness, which was a veritable existence of God in him'.[6] Schleiermacher has already determined that all human beings are related to God by virtue of their God-consciousness. The human Jesus is then distinguished from all other humans simply by the 'constant potency' of his God consciousness. Jesus' divinity is thus understood as the qualification of an anthropological category.

Contemporary with Schleiermacher, Hegel was constructing a system which would find a place for God within one universal all-embracing understanding that would dissolve any dualism between the eternal and temporal worlds. This all-embracing system was to be thoroughly metaphysical and consistently rational. The consistent rationality of Hegel's system puts the emphasis on reason and the mind rather than on experience and the senses and the universal or 'absolute' nature of his system issues in the assertion that all reality is gathered up in the all-encompassing, impersonal reality of *Geist* (Absolute Mind or Spirit). The world-historical process is presented as the self-projection of Absolute Mind although nature, which is without mind stands initially over against this Absolute Mind. It is only with the emergence of the human mind in history that the world takes on a new self-awareness – an awareness of its own participation in and essential unity with the Absolute Mind.[7] This self-awareness of the world is imperfectly represented in all religion, more adequately sketched in Christianity and at last attains its fullness in Hegel's own system of 'Absolute Idealism'.

As with Schleiermacher, Hegel has constructed a theology into which Jesus Christ must now be incorporated. Within this system Jesus becomes the embodiment or expression of an 'idea' such that the embodiment is clearly less important than the idea itself. The idea is the idea of reconciliation, the eternal truth of the essential unity of God and humanity, of finite and infinite mind, of the rational and material worlds. This eternal idea was brought to light and exemplified concretely in the person of Jesus Christ. Through him the idea was made known to us. This is the essential point for Hegel. The life, death and resurrection of Jesus does not *bring about* reconciliation but presents us with the *idea* of reconciliation and alerts us to its possibility. The decisive transformation is a transformation of the human mind in so far as it recognizes and takes hold of its essential unity with Absolute Mind. Christ enables us to recognize the truth about the world and about ourselves, namely, that we share in and are products of the one great universal Mind that thinks itself. As Kierkegaard points out in *Philosophical Fragments*, both systems rest on the presupposition that the essential condition for learning the truth lies within humanity itself. For Hegel the condition is humanity's capacity for rational thought, and for Schleiermacher it is our religious sensibility, our innate awareness of God.

Opposing both systems, Kierkegaard places them alongside the New Testament account of the matter. Reading the New Testament, Kierkegaard discovers that Jesus cannot be accommodated within prior categories of thought and that the condition for recognizing the truth of Christ is a gift given by God rather than some innate human capacity. Flesh and blood cannot reveal this to you Jesus says. That truth is revealed 'by my Father in heaven' (Mt. 16.17). Following the logic of this New Testament account, Kierkegaard contends that 'the point of departure in theology is divine revelation, not a reading, be it ever so accurate, of the human heart [Schleiermacher] or human history [Hegel]'.[8] Robert Perkins offers the further observation that in Kierkegaard's view,

Theology must be done on its own terms, with its own categories and with its own sustained methodology.
Theology must neither be formed nor receive its content

from philosophical positions alien to its own nature. It is not the business of theology to become intellectually respectable to any time; because when properly understood, theology will be a scandal and a stumbling-block to the philosophy, the rationalism and the idolatry of any age. No longer must theology cut itself to the size and shape allowed by an Aristotle, a Hegel, or a Kant . . .[9]

Although Kierkegaard found few supporters in his own day, the lack of support does not indicate that the content of his theology was either unorthodox or unprecedented. Quite the contrary, in fact. Kierkegaard's concern was to call Christian theology and Christian practice back to its authentic roots in the apostolic tradition, not to strike out towards something new. The distinctive mark of an apostle, in Kierkegaard's view, is the apostle's absolute reliance on the authority of the divine Word. No attempt should be made to authenticate that Word through appeal to human authorities. The Word of God must be allowed to speak for itself; its authority must reveal itself. If it does not comply with human estimations of what is true; if it appears paradoxical or absurd in light of human conceptions of what God can and cannot say and do, then there is a choice to be made. One may believe or one may take offence, but the Word itself must be allowed to stand. The Word made flesh in Jesus and addressed to us through the witness of the New Testament cannot be adapted into something that can be believed without subverting its authority as the divine Word. The moment it is subordinated to human authority, it is done away with. Put in the dramatic terms of Kierkegaard himself, when that happens Christianity no longer exists.

Kierkegaard was a prophetic voice in his own time, and remains so for us. But his prophetic power consists precisely in his reading and re-presentation of 'the old familiar text handed down from the fathers'.[10] Kierkegaard's reading of that text, however, was not unmediated by Christian tradition. The church most prominent in Denmark and the tradition in which Kierkegaard was raised and educated was Lutheran. Despite extensive contact with the Moravians as a child, it was the Lutheran, state church of Denmark that Kierkegaard attended regularly as an adult and it was upon the Lutheran theological tradition that Kierkegaard drew in mounting his critique of what Christianity had become. The Lutheran dramatist, G. E. Lessing, was one source of inspiration for Kierkegaard's protest but, as we have seen, Kierkegaard himself took a quite different path in responding to the theological problems that Lessing raised, especially the problem of the relationship between Christianity and philosophy. But Kierkegaard praised Lessing who 'knew considerably more what the issue is about than the common herd of modern philosophers',[11] and he admired Lessing's honesty as a thinker. Honesty was also a quality that Kierkegaard admired in Socrates. Socrates did not claim to know more than could be known and yet saw clearly the problems of human existence.

Along with Lessing and Socrates, and with Hegel too, of course, Luther is the thinker mentioned most often in Kierkegaard's writings,[12] often with approval, but critically too. Yet according to Kierkegaard's own account he did not start reading Luther in earnest until 1847.[13] The Lutheran *tradition*, therefore, rather than a direct reading of Luther himself, is likely to have been the formative influence. While his theological education at University would certainly have provided a grounding in Lutheran theology, it has been argued by a number of scholars that Kierkegaard absorbed Luther's thought predominantly through the writings of J. G. Hamann. Walter Lowrie, for instance, claimed that 'Hamann was the only author by whom Søren Kierkegaard was profoundly influenced'.[14] More recent studies by Craig Hinkson and John Betz have traced that influence in some detail.[15] The category of the paradox, and the conflict between the gospel and the deliverances of human reason appear to have been developed by Kierkegaard through engagement with Hamann's work. Hamann was also a great admirer of Socrates and employed the methods of indirect communication, maieutic teaching, and irony, all of which were taken up by Kierkegaard. It seems plausible too that Hamann was for Kierkegaard the key tradent of Luther's thought prior to 1847.

Kierkegaard's agreement with Luther, or with the tradition stemming from Luther, applies to two themes in particular, namely, the lowliness of Christ and the priority of grace. On these matters especially, we are right, I think, to follow Jamie

Ferreira's advice 'that we should assume Kierkegaard's theological agreement with Luther except for those places where he specifically notes otherwise'.[16] Despite his many quibbles with Luther, the centrality and fecundity of these themes in Kierkegaard's work reveals just how important Luther's influence was, albeit indirectly. From the first theme, the lowliness of Christ, stems Kierkegaard's pervasive emphasis upon the paradoxical character of Christ's appearance in time. The incarnation of Christ in the form of a lowly servant who suffers a brutal and ignominious death by crucifixion confounds all human estimations of how God should behave and where God is to be found. From that revelatory drama stems in turn Kierkegaard's account of the rigorous demands of Christian discipleship. To follow this Christ is, necessarily, to become lowly oneself, to love and to serve others even to the point of suffering and death. Because Christ is the prototype,

> [y]ou are supposed to be like Christ. All right, then try this – at the very moment you yourself are suffering most of all, simply think about consoling others, for this is what he did. The task is not to seek consolation – but to be consolation. To seek the company of the cripples, the despised, the sinners and the publicans.[17]

But, of course, Kierkegaard realizes how difficult it is to be like Christ. He knows well that we fall short again and again – all the time in fact, and so enters the second major theme of his work, the priority of grace. It is on account of God's grace that the incarnation takes place at all. Humanity does nothing to deserve God's merciful and loving attention, and when, again and again, human beings fall short of the requirements of love, God in Christ, stoops low to redeem us, to gather us again like sheep that have gone astray, into the joyful embrace of his love. That is the story of the gospel. It is a further all-pervasive characteristic of our human condition, however, that we prefer to tell other stories about ourselves, stories in which the requirement is diminished and thus made easier to attain, stories in which our sin is diminished so that we can congratulate ourselves on being 'not like other men' (Lk. 18.11), stories in which obedience is diminished so that it means nothing more than observing the conventions of civil religion. Kierkegaard's rage against Christendom is directed especially at those – theologians and clergy in particular – who make out that these alternative stories are a faithful telling of the gospel. In the face of our failures, grace abounds, but honesty is required, honesty concerning the extent of our sin, and then, also, honesty concerning our need of atonement and grace. 'No person is saved except by grace . . . But there is one sin that makes grace impossible, that is dishonesty; and there is one thing that God unconditionally must require, that is honesty'.[18]

Kierkegaard finds this confirmed in Luther. He finds there too an insight that is salutary for those who read Kierkegaard today:

> What Luther says is excellent, the one thing needful
> and the sole explanation – that this whole doctrine
> (of the Atonement and in the main all Christianity)
> must be traced back to the struggle of the anguished
> conscience . . . The anguished conscience understands
> Christianity . . . But you say, 'I still cannot grasp the
> Atonement'. Here I must ask in which understanding – in
> the understanding of the anguished conscience or in the
> understanding of indifferent and objective speculation.
> How could anyone sitting placidly and objectively in
> his study and speculating ever be able to understand the
> necessity of an atonement, since an atonement is necessary
> only in the understanding of anguished conscience. If a
> man had the power to live without needing to eat, how
> could he understand the necessity of eating – something
> the hungry man easily understands.[19]

The same goes for reading Kierkegaard. Kierkegaard addresses the one who 'with joy and gratitude I call my reader'. Such a 'reader' is one who has an anguished conscience, who, in the midst of striving, knows her need of God and seeks the consolation of grace. Kierkegaard had no interest in academic readers. He despised the misunderstanding admirers who, he foresaw, would gather about his work and marvel at his genius, oblivious all the while to the fact that the work is for upbuilding. Kierke-gaard seeks readers who are prepared to submit themselves to the transforming discipline of divine grace. His authorship, under the direction of Governance, has no other purpose than that.

Kierkegaard found few readers in his own time who could keep up with his prodigious output or fathom the depths of his thought. His contemporaries in Copenhagen were bemused, intrigued, outraged, dismissive and offended.[20] We know less of whether there were some who waited upon his successive productions with the purity of heart and personal concern for upbuilding that he sought in his readers. Only such as these would be true companions in the endeavour of his authorship. It is impossible to trace the extent of Kierkegaard's influence among readers who have engaged with Kierkegaard according to his wishes, in solitude, and with Kierkegaard's writings as an aid to a more profound encounter with God. But his impact upon the public discourse of theology can more easily be seen.

Not until the early twentieth century did Kierkegaard's writ-ings gain attention outside of Denmark and engender the mixed reactions of a wider audience. His reception by philosophers, his influence particularly upon the existentialists of the early twen-tieth century[21] and upon subsequent continental philosophers is a story that has been told elsewhere.[22] Our interest here is in Kierkegaard's impact upon theology. The nineteenth century had been a century of extraordinary confidence in the prowess and perfectibility of humankind. The progress represented in the industrial revolution, the advance of modern science, the political revolutions in Europe had created a mood of optimism, pervasive confidence in inevitable progress, and a widespread belief that human beings were possessed not only of the tech-nological prowess but also of the moral capacity to solve the world's most pressing problems. Herbert Spencer, the English sociologist, captured well the mood in the mid-nineteenth cen-tury: 'Progress is not an accident but a necessity . . . surely must the things we call evil and immorality disappear . . . surely must man become perfect'.[23] Theologians, in the main, went along with Spencer. Variously drawing upon Hegel and Kant, and con-vinced by proponents of the Quest of the Historical Jesus that Jesus' proclamation was concerned above all with humanity's progress toward the kingdom of God, the establishment of that kingdom through human moral effort became a key theme among theologians of the nineteenth century.

The mood was not to last. With the First World War, European optimism, grand visions of the progress of history, and confidence in the perfectibility of humankind came to a catastrophic and bloody end. Much has been written of the young Karl Barth's disillusion in that period with the readiness of his liberal theological professors to sign up to the Kaiser's war policy, a capitulation that occasioned for Barth and for his German-speaking contemporaries a theological crisis.[24] The nineteenth century theological vision in which they had been schooled was found wanting, so completely had it and its god been identified with the cultural and nationalistic aspirations of the German people. The young theologians were in need of theological resources not provided to them by their professors, resources that could speak again of the sinfulness of humankind, of the otherness of a God who could not be domesticated, and of a divine judgement that revealed the depths of humanity's need of forgiveness and grace. They found those resources, first of all, by returning to the Bible, but they found them too in the writings of Søren Kierkegaard. Kierkegaard provided for them a means to speak of the infinite, qualitative difference between the ways of God and the ways of humankind, of the distance of God from all *human* conceptions of salvation, and of a lowly, suffering Saviour who unmasked the pretentiousness of human aspirations and offered instead a cross-shaped way to the kingdom of God.

A 'theology of crisis' thus evolved, a dialectical theology that stressed the otherness of God and the finitude of human beings. Formulated in the pages of Barth's commentary on the epistle to the Romans and developed also by Barth's contemporaries Emil Brunner, Friedrich Gogarten and Rudolf Bultmann, dialectical theology constituted a protest against 'cultural protestantism', against too close an identification of God with the culture of the day. This was also Kierkegaard's protest. God comes among us in human form not to confirm our innate proximity to the divine but precisely to overcome the great chasm that separates humanity from God. The incarnation is an act of divine love and mercy, but we must recognize in it as well God's wrath and word of judgement at what humanity has become. The God who comes among us thus, calls his followers not to a triumphal existence in the world, but rather to a costly obedience that creates scandal, engenders offence, and will likely lead to suffering in a world such as this.

While the dialectical theologians were profoundly inspired by Kierkegaard's theological critique of his age, each went on, in very different ways, to forge a path apart from and beyond Kierkegaard. We have already seen some of Barth's later criticisms, principal among which were the allegations, largely mistaken I believe, that Kierkegaard offered a joyless vision of Christian faith, that his account of Christian discipleship was too individualistic, and that it produced a fixation upon subjectivity.[25] Brunner, in dispute with Barth, and departing from Kierkegaard, eventually sought to give some credence to the truth human beings could discover for themselves (albeit through attention to general revelation) and which would establish a 'point of contact' for the advent of the special revelation given in Christ. Bultmann, for his part, retained a powerful interest in the existential challenge of the gospel, and saw that challenge addressed specifically to the individual's anxiety. This he learned from Kierkegaard, and he developed it through appropriation of a good dose of Heidegger. For Bultmann, however, everything was concentrated on the individual's moment of existential transformation, on the 'how' of appropriation. There is no refuge to be had in objective certainties. This is a Kierkegaardian emphasis, to be sure, but it is bereft of Kierkegaard's equal emphasis on the subjectively appropriated 'what' of the gospel, on the concrete historical reality of the incarnation. Bultmann and Kierkegaard were both exercised by the question of how faith is related to historically uncertain facts,[26] but, departing from Kierkegaard's conception of the matter, Bultmann's gospel came to depend less and less on the historical actuality of God's presence in time. The God-man's presence in time became a 'vanishing point' as Bultmann developed his conviction that the *preaching* of the gospel, the *kerygma*, was enough. The existentialist concern of Bultmann was evident also in Gogarten's theology, as was the influence of both Heidegger and Kierkegaard. Gogarten drew especially upon Kierkegaard's critique of Christendom and

argued that authentic Christian faith had to free itself of the false
gods of social institutions and civil religion, and live respons-
ibly before God in a secularized world. Kierkegaard's critique
of objectivity was also taken up by Gogarten who insisted that
the gospel could be appropriated only through faith. The assertion of the freedom and responsibility of the Christian in the
secular world, is again consistent with Kierkegaard's thought,
but Gogarten places more confidence in human capacity than
does Kierkegaard. Christ is the exemplar we are called to follow but there is less sense in Gogarten than in Kierkegaard, that
before God we are always in the wrong and stand, therefore, in
constant need of divine mercy and grace.

Paul Tillich was another from the same generation of
German-speaking theologians who found resources in Kierkegaard to critique the liberal theology of the nineteenth century
and to recover an account of the otherness of God. Tillich takes
up Kierkegaard's emphasis upon the existential challenge of
the Gospel. He accepted, as well, Kierkegaard's critique of cultural Protestantism, and his polemic against the domestication
of God. Tillich also upheld the infinite, qualitative difference
between God and the creature and the need for revelation, but
placed a great deal more faith in the deliverances of human reason and the insights of philosophy, than Kierkegaard could ever
have sanctioned. Tillich's gospel, furthermore, was increasingly
expressed in abstract terms, far removed from the kinds of communication Kierkegaard sought through his Discourses with
the common man or woman. Nevertheless, Tillich and the dialectical theologians in general, exercised a powerful and lasting
influence upon twentieth century theology and, despite their
respective divergences from Kierkegaard, their role in alerting
theologians to Kierkegaard's work remains important.

After the dialectical theology of the early twentieth century,
came a second wave of theologians inspired by Kierkegaard
to find ways of articulating the Christian gospel in the midst
of profound suffering and in an era deeply scarred by human
sinfulness. Dietrich Bonhoeffer, as has been noted earlier, and
Reinhold Niebuhr were prominent among them. Bonhoeffer's
emphasis upon the costliness of grace was worked out on the road
of suffering and imprisonment during the second world-war.

Bonhoeffer himself became a martyr, a witness to the truth of the kind, we might suppose, that Kierkegaard would have approved. Bonhoeffer shared as well Kierkegaard's view that as sinful human beings, 'always in the wrong before God', we are utterly reliant upon divine grace. That applied to Bonhoeffer's involvement in a plot to assassinate Hitler, an instance, perhaps, of the 'teleological suspension of the ethical'. Certainly, as Julia Watkin has suggested, 'Bonhoeffer himself provided a living illustration of what it can mean to take the gospel seriously in Kierkegaardian terms'.[27] Reinhold Niebuhr was also deeply influenced by Kierkegaard's account of human sinfulness and took up a great deal of Kierkegaard's theological anthropology. Niebuhr's major work, *The Nature and Destiny of Man* reveals his dependence on Kierkegaard's conceptions of the self, and of human freedom. Elsewhere, Niebuhr applies a Kierkegaardian critique to secular and Christian liberalism in America.[28]

Those so far mentioned have been Protestant theologians. It is fair to say that Kierkegaard's theological influence has been more pronounced among Protestants, but some Catholic writers, notably Louis Dupré and Erich Przywara, have produced significant studies of Kierkegaard's work.[29] While Dupre takes a quite different view, arguing that Kierkegaard is sometimes sympathetic but often antipathetic toward the idea of the Catholic Church, Przywara appealed to Kierkegaard's high view of ordination in arguing that Kierkegaard leans toward a Roman Catholic ecclesiology. Przywara also finds in Kierkegaard's account of the deep, inward struggle of faith, an affinity with St John of the Cross and his depiction of the 'dark night of the soul'.[30] A comprehensive survey of Kierkegaard's relation to Catholicism recently provided by Jack Mulder, Jr., takes further Dupré's assessment that between Kierkegaard's thought and Catholicism there are areas of agreement but also of tension.[31]

The influence of Kierkegaard upon present day theology is still taking shape, but there is certainly no diminution of interest in Kierkegaard's works. Only a portion of that interest is theological, but there is every likelihood that Kierkegaard's powerful critique of the negative impact upon theology of post-Enlightenment rationalism will continue to serve as a rich resource for a post-modern engagement with the God who is infinitely and qualitatively different both from human beings themselves, and from the gods we continually fabricate in service of our own interests. The God who *truly knows* what is in our interests is to be approached with fear and trembling, for the blessedness promised by Christianity, and God's upbringing in love, involve struggle and spiritual trial – so far do they take us from conventional religion, and from the universal. Kierkegaard reminds us, further, of a Truth that is available only through faith, a quite specific faith in the concrete, historical figure of Jesus. He reminds us of the wonder that God should be mindful of us, and he speaks to us of the costliness of that mindfulness, the cost borne by God, first of all, for God loves us first, treads the path of suffering and servanthood, and puts himself completely in our place. Kierkegaard speaks too of the cost to be borne by those who follow Christ – the cost involved in venturing out beyond the security of objective certainties, worldly possessions, finite aspirations and society's approval. These must be let go in order to become contemporary with Christ. The biggest obstacle to such discipleship, the greatest hindrance to communion with Christ and with one's neighbour, is simply sin. That concept does not enjoy the popularity that Kierkegaard himself does. But Kierkegaard would not be surprised. The concept of sin means nothing except to the one who comes before God with an anguished conscience. But whoever does come, confessing their need, will encounter the infinite mercy of God, and will learn that the overcoming of sin is wholly a matter of grace. They will learn too that grace calls forth obedience, prodigious striving, and endless works of love.

# Notes

## Chapter 1

1. Alastair Hannay, who in other respects has much valuable insight to offer on Kierkegaard's work, is one scholar who has advanced the incredible claim that Kierkegaard 'nurture[d] a lifelong ambivalence towards Christianity which allowed him to hold it at a distance . . .' This assessment unfortunately distorts Hannay's weighty and widely read biography of Kierkegaard. See Hannay, *Kierkegaard: A Biography* (Cambridge: Cambridge University Press, 2001), 39.
2. From the subtitle of *The Point of View of My Work as an Author*, 21.
3. *Point of View*, 23.
4. *Point of View*, 92.
5. *Point of View*, 93n.
6. *Point of View*, 92–3.
7. For a summary of the range of interpretations and interpretive methods applied to 'The Seducer's Diary' see Bradley R. Dewey, 'Seven Seducers: A Typology of Interpretations of the Aesthetic Stage in Kierkegaard's "The Seducer's Diary"', *International Kierkegaard Commentary* (ed. Robert L. Perkins; vol. 3 Either/Or I; Macon, GA: Mercer University Press, 1995), 159–99.
8. Kierkegaard, 'Preface' to *For Self-Examination*, 3. The desire for a reader of this kind is stressed repeatedly in Kierkegaard's signed works.
9. *Journals*, VI/6727, X⁴ A 33, n.d., 1851.
10. *Journals*, 3/3684, X³ A 431, n.d., 1850.

## Chapter 2

1. It is difficult to be precise about the number of books Kierkegaard wrote because his papers include unpublished drafts of books and what he did publish has been variously edited and combined in subsequent volumes.
2. *Journals and Papers*, VI/6205, IX A 171, n.d., 1848.
3. The point appears several times in Kierkegaard's writings. See, for instance, *Journals and Papers*, I/1030, IV A 164, n.d., 1843.
4. Kierkegaard was very particular about this. In each of the 'Prefaces' to the several series of Discourses in *Eighteen Upbuilding Discourses*

# Notes

Kierkegaard explains that 'this little book . . . is called "discourses", not sermons, because its author does not have authority to *preach*, "upbuilding discourses", not discourses for upbuilding, because the speaker by no means claims to be a *teacher* . . .'. Kierkegaard is here placing himself in the position of the learner who, along with his reader, stands in need of upbuilding in Christian faith. See *Eighteen Upbuilding Discourses*.

5. *Point of View*, 93n.
6. Kierkegaard seems clearly to be referring here to the providential guidance of God, one purpose of which is 'to bring [a person] up'. See JP, 1/188, $X^2$ A396, n.d., 1850.
7. *Point of View*, 79.
8. *Point of View*, 79.
9. Kierkegaard lived alone save for the assistance of a manservant who tended to household chores.
10. *Journals and Papers*, 5/5141, I A 161, n.d., 1836.
11. *Point of View*, 79.
12. *Journals and Papers*, 5/5874, $VII^1$ A 5, n.d., 1846.
13. *Journals and Papers*, 5/5430, II A 805, n.d., 1838.
14. See Julia Watkin, *Kierkegaard* (London: Geoffrey Chapman, 1997), 8.
15. I take this point from Watkin, *Kierkegaard*, 17 n.9, whose account of Kierkegaard's mother and his affection for her corrects the negative portrayals frequently offered elsewhere.
16. The mother of Hans Lassen Martensen reports that she 'had never in her life seen a person in such great distress as S. Kierkegaard was over his mother's death'. Hans Lassen Martenson, *Af mit Levnet* I–III (Copenhagen: Gyldendalske Boghandel Nordisk Forlag, 1882–83), I, 78–9. Cited in Watkin, *Kierkegaard*, 19, n.16.
17. See, for instance, *Journals*, VI/6355, $X^1$ A 137, n.d., 1849.
18. See, for instance, *Journals*, VI/6379, $X^1$ A 228, n.d., 1849.
19. *Point of View*, 82.
20. *Journals*, 6/6167, IX A 71, n.d., 1848.
21. *Journals*, 5/5335, II A 243, 11 August 1838.
22. *Journals*, 6/6164, IX A 68, n.d., 1848.
23. 'Johannes Climacus or De Omnibum Dubitandum est', *Philosophical Fragments, Johannes Climacus*, 120.
24. The autobiographical element has frequently been taken for granted by Kierkegaard's biographers. Joakim Garff reminds us, however, that the customary reading of the story as a description of Kierkegaard's own childhood, though entirely plausible, is nevertheless conjectural. See Joakim Garff, *Søren Kierkegaard: A Biography* (trans. Bruce H. Kirmmse; Princeton: Princeton University Press, 2005), 15. Alastair Hannay, on the other hand, contends that 'the autobiographical origins of this story are confirmed by several sources'. Hannay does not, however, give details of those sources. See Hannay, *Kierkegaard: A Biography*, 36.
25. See *Journals and Papers*, VI/6389 $X^1$ A 272, n.d., 1849. The childhood memories are again referred to in *Practice in Christianity*, 174–78. The

Notes

detection of autobiographical reference in these accounts again involves a degree of conjecture but numerous entries in Kierkegaard's corpus attest to the great impression made upon him by his father's instruction in Christianity.

26. The point here, along with the following citation from Saxtorp's sermon comes from Garff, *Søren Kierkegaard*, 12.
27. *Journals and Papers*, VI/6389, X$^1$ A 272, n.d., 1849.
28. Jørgen Bukdahl, *Søren Kierkegaard and the Common Man* (trans. Bruce H. Kirmmse; Grand Rapids, MI: Eerdmans, 2001), xiii.
29. Garff, *Søren Kierkegaard*, 320. Cf. Bukdahl, *Søren Kierkegaard and the Common Man*, 21–5.
30. *The Moment and Late Writings*, 49.
31. *Journals*, I/593, X$^1$ A 552, n.d., 1849.
32. *Journals*, I/600, X$^4$ A 246, n.d., 1851.
33. *Journals and Notebooks*, vol. 1, 17. AA: 12, 22 (1 June 1835).
34. Journal entry, 1 May 1935. Cited in Garff, *Søren Kierkegaard*, 30.
35. *Journals and Notebooks*, vol. 1, 19–20. AA: 12, 24 (1 June 1835).
36. The Moment and Late Writings, 28.
37. Cited by Garff, *Søren Kierkegaard*, 62.
38. Garff, Søren Kierkegaard, 63.
39. *Journals and Papers*, I/508, X$^1$ A 558, n.d., 1849.
40. I take the point from Garff, *Søren Kierkegaard*, 87.
41. *Journals and Papers*, V/5302, II A 209, April 1838.
42. Cited in Garff, *Søren Kierkegaard*, 126.
43. *Journals and Papers*, V/5313, II A 730, n.d., 1838. Garff reports that the entry was written on Sunday, April 22. See Garff, *Søren Kierkegaard*, 127.
44. *Journals and Papers*, V/5324, II A 228, 19 May 1838.
45. *Journals and Papers*, V/5329, II A 232, July 9, 1838.
46. Biographers commonly comment on the profligacy of Kierkegaard's early years at university but although his father was called upon to pay a debt accrued in 1836 exceeding the annual salary of a university professor, the largest balance was for books from Reitzel's bookshop. See Garff, *Søren Kierkegaard*, 103 and 123.
47. *Journals and Papers*, V/5330, II A 233, 10 July 1838.
48. *Journals and Papers*, V/5328, II A 231, 9 July 1838.
49. A few weeks before his death, Michael Kierkegaard complained in a letter to his sister of being 'weak in body and soul' and expressed the hope that 'my homeward journey is near at hand.' Cited in Garff, *Søren Kierkegaard*, 128.
50. *Journals and Papers*, V/5335, II A 243, 11 August 1838. The one person to whom Kierkegaard felt he could really talk was Emil Boesen (1812–81), a close friend of Kierkegaard from childhood and throughout his life.
51. For an explanation of the title, see Garff, *Søren Kierkegaard*, 144.
52. *Early Polemical Writings*, 76–7.
53. See Garff, *Søren Kierkegaard*, 144.

54. See *Journals and Papers*, V/5219, II A 67, 8 May 1837 and V/5220, II A 68, n.d., 1837.

55. *Journals and Papers*, VI/6472, X$^5$ A 149, n.d., 1849.

56. *Journals and Papers*, V/5368, II A 347, n.d., 1849.

57. Ibid.

58. Ibid.

59. *Journals and Papers*, VI/6163, IX A 67, n.d., 1848.

60. *Journals and Papers*, VI/6426, X$^1$ A 494, 25 June 1849.

61. Regine herself believed this to be the central reason for the ending of the engagement. In 1896, long after Kierkegaard had died, and after the death of her husband, Regine gave her own account of events to Hanne Mourier who then made a record of that account, addressed to Regine herself. 'You felt no bitterness, anger or reproach against him, but sorrow and pain. Kierkegaard's motivation for the break was his conception of his religious task; he dared not bind himself to anyone on earth in order not to be obstructed from his calling. He had to sacrifice the very best thing he owned in order to work as God demanded of him: therefore he sacrificed his love for you for the sake of his writing'. Hanne Mourier, *Encounters with Kierkegaard: A Life as Seen by His Contemporaries* (ed. Bruce H. Kirmmse; Princeton: Princeton University Press, 1996), 36–7.

62. *Journals and Papers*, VI/6472, X$^5$ A 149, n.d., 1849.

63. Regine confesses her 'unshakeable faith in him' in a letter to Henrik Lund (Kierkegaard's nephew) dated 10 September [1856]. See Bruce H. Kirmmse (ed.), *Encounters with Kierkegaard*, 50.

64. *Journals and Papers*, VI/6472, X$^5$ A 149, n.d., 1849, at paragraph 17.

65. *Søren Kierkegaard's Papirer*, XI$^3$ B 87, 133. Cited in Garff, *Søren Kierkegaard*, 191.

66. *Journals and Papers*, V/5552, *Letters*, no. 69, 27 February 1842.

67. See the Preface to *Either/Or*.

68. See *Journals and Papers*, VI/6472, X$^5$ A 149, n.d., 1849 (18 and 19).

69. Kierkegaard eventually published six volumes of Discourses all of which are meditations on biblical texts. He deliberately calls them discourses rather than sermons because, not having been ordained, he 'does not have authority to preach'. See the Preface to each series of Discourses.

70. See, *Point of View*, especially 29–37.

71. *Journals and Papers*, VI/6346, X$^1$ A 116, February 19, 1849. In the same entry Kierkegaard writes, 'I am deeply convinced . . . that there is an integral comprehensiveness in the whole production (by the special assistance of Governance), and that there is certainly something else to be said about it than this meager comment that the author has changed'.

72. *Journals and Papers*, VI/6533, X$^2$ A 196, n.d., 1849.

73. *Point of View*, 30.

74. *Without Authority*, 3.

75. *Journals and Papers*, VI/6533, X$^2$ A 196, n.d., 1849.

76. *Point of View*, 54.

77. *Point of View*, 9.
78. *Point of View*, 8.
79. Ibid.
80. Hans Rørdam writing to Peter Rørdam, 4 May 1855. Reproduced in Kirmmse (ed.), *Encounters with Kierkegaard*, 105.
81. The phrase, an unreferenced citation, appears in Kristian Arentzen's memoirs. See Kirmmse (ed.), *Encounters with Kierkegaard*, 115.
82. Emil Boesen as reproduced in Kirmmse (ed.), *Encounters with Kierkegaard*, 125–6.
83. See Kirmmse (ed.), *Encounters with Kierkegaard*, 125.
84. *Journals and Papers*, VI/6161, IX A 65, n.d., 1848.

## Chapter 3

1. *Point of View*, 23.
2. *Concluding Unscientific Postscript*, 17.
3. *Concluding Unscientific Postscript*, 17.
4. The Danish word *smuler*, translated as 'fragments', indicates a very meagre offering, merely a few scraps.
5. See G. E. Lessing, 'On the Proof of the Spirit and of Power', *Lessing's Theological Writings* (ed. Henry Chadwick; London: Adam and Charles Black, 1956), 51–61.
6. We will say more of this in Chapter 4 below.
7. *Philosophical Fragments*, 11.
8. As does Socrates himself throughout the dialogues. See, for exemplary instance, the demonstration of the maieutic method in *The Meno*, 82–85.
9. *Philosophical Fragments*, 12.
10. See *Philosophical Fragments*, 13–20.
11. *Philosophical Fragments*, 14–15.
12. *Philosophical Fragments*, 15.
13. *Philosophical Fragments*, 17
14. *Philosophical Fragments*, 59.
15. The several series of Discourses from 1843 to 1844 are published in English translation as *Eighteen Upbuilding Discourses*, ed. and trans, Howard V. Hong and Edna H. Hong (Princeton, NJ: Princeton University Press, 1990).
16. Kierkegaard, 'To Need God Is a Human Being's Highest Perfection', *Eighteen Upbuilding Discourses*, 325.
17. See *Concluding Unscientific Postscript*, 21.
18. *Concluding Unscientific Postscript*, 21.
19. See Gottfried Leibniz, *New Essays on Human Understanding* (trans. Alfred Gideon Langley; Chicago: Open Court, 1916), I.i, and *Monadology* (trans. Robert Latta; London: Oxford University Press, 1898), Section 33.

20. *Concluding Unscientific Postscript*, 21.
21. *Concluding Unscientific Postscript*, 23.
22. *Concluding Unscientific Postscript*, 23.
23. Lessing, 'On the Proof of the Spirit and of Power', 53.
24. Lessing, 'On the Proof of the Spirit and of Power', 54.
25. Lessing, 'On the Proof of the Spirit and of Power', 55.
26. Lessing, 'The Testament of John', *Lessing's Theological Writings*, 57–61.
27. *Concluding Unscientific Postscript*, 24.
28. *Concluding Unscientific Postscript*, 24–5.
29. Ernst Troeltsch, toward the end of the nineteenth century, drew explicit attention to the sharp distinction and incompatibility between the two methods that was increasingly assumed. See Ernst Troeltsch 'Historical and Dogmatic Method in Theology', *Religion in History: Ernst Troeltsch* (Edinburgh: T&T Clark, 1991), 11–32.
30. *Concluding Unscientific Postscript*, 27.
31. It is important to note in this connection that Kierkegaard is not an individualist. He does not conceive of the human being as an isolated self-contained entity along the lines sketched by Boethius or Descartes or Kant. The human being is, for Kierkegaard, essentially a relational being, existing before God and bound to one's neighbour. That conception of the human is evident especially in Kierkegaard's *Works of Love*, of which we will say more in chapter eight below, but can be obscured in some of his other works that strive to make it clear that Christianity 'attaches enormous importance to the individual subject' (*Concluding Unscientific Postscript*, 49). Concerning the need for personal response, Kierkegaard expressed great admiration for Lessing, for, despite the poverty of his account of Christianity, he at least understood that the question of Christian faith concerned him personally and individually. See *Concluding Unscientific Postscript*, 65.
32. *Journals*, VI/6356, $X^1$ A 138, n.d., 1849.
33. *Concluding Unscientific Postscript*, 73.
34. The term 'viable' is used here in its original sense of 'able to live', or 'able to be lived'.
35. Kierkegaard, *Journals*, I/484, IX A 207, n.d., 1848. For further commentary on this matter, see Sylvia Walsh, *Living Christianly: Kierkegaard's Dialectic of Christian Existence* (University Park, PA: Pennsylvania State University Press, 2005), 11–15.
36. In fact, Kierkegaard anticipated the post-modern recognition that no enquiry is wholly objective. He mocked the presumption of complete objectivity by suggesting that those guilty of such presumption have forgotten what it means to exist. That is, they have failed to recognize the impact upon their thinking of their own historical circumstances. It should also be noted, however, that Kierkegaard was not a relativist. We will return to his point later.
37. Kierkegaard, *Judge for Yourself!*, 191.

# Notes

38. See *Concluding Unscientific Postscript*, 133; 158; 159, and elsewhere.
39. Kierkegaard, *Concluding Unscientific Postscript*, 91.
40. Kierkegaard, *Fear and Trembling*, 39.
41. For an extensive account of this preference, see, Jørgen Bukdahl, *Søren Kierkegaard and the Common Man*.
42. *Concluding Unscientific Postscript*, 201.
43. Kierkegaard wrote a whole series of Discourses on the theme, 'purity of heart is to will one thing'. See *Upbuilding Discourses in Various Spirits*, 7–154.
44. The discourse is the second of 'Three Discourses at the Communion on Fridays' published in *Without Authority*, 127–34. See also here, 'One who prays aright struggles in prayer and is victorious – in that God is victorious', *Eighteen Upbuilding Discourses*, 377–401.
45. Kierkegaard, *Concluding Unscientific Postscript*, 202. Italics and emphasis original.
46. Kierkegaard, *Concluding Unscientific Postscript*, 202–3.
47. See here Kierkegaard's reflections on the text, 'No one can serve two masters', *Judge for Yourself!*, 147–209.
48. Kierkegaard, *Journals*, II/1154, XI² A 380, n.d., 1854–1855. See also *Journals*, II/1436, XI¹ A 5, n.d., 1854.
49. Kierkegaard, *Upbuilding Discourses in Various Spirits*, 255. Italics original.
50. *Point of View*, 93n.
51. *Concluding Unscientific Postscript*, 205. Note however that the precise reference of the term 'paradox' does vary in Kierkegaard's works, sometimes in distinction from the 'absurd'. In his *Journals* for instance he notes, 'That there is a difference between the absurd in *Fear and Trembling* and the paradox in *Concluding Unscientific Postscript* is quite correct. The first is the purely personal definition of existential faith— the other is faith in relationship to a doctrine. *Journals*, I/ 11, X⁶ B 80, n.d., 1850.
52. *Concluding Unscientific Postscript*, 205.
53. Further features of the paradox associated with Christian faith, particularly concerning the incarnation, will be explored in the following chapter.
54. *Concluding Unscientific Postscript*, 204.
55. *Concluding Unscientific Postscript*, 203.
56. *Journals*, I/187, X² A 119, n.d., 1849.
57. *Philosophical Fragments*, 43.
58. See for example, Mt. 22.2–14; Lk. 14.16–24, 26.
59. See 'A First and Last Explanation', *Concluding Unscientific Postscript*, 625–30.
60. *Practice in Christianity*, 19.
61. *Journals*, VI/6516, X² A 134, n.d., 1849.
62. *For Self Examination and Judge for Yourself!*, 71–87.
63. *For Self Examination*, 81.

64. *For Self Examination*, 77.
65. *Journals*, IV/4939, X⁴ A 538, n.d., 1852.

# Chapter 4

1. *Journals and Papers*, 1/284, II A 595, n.d., 1837.
2. Sylvia Walsh, *Kierkegaard: Thinking Christianly in an Existential Mode* (Oxford: Oxford University Press, 2009), 111.
3. Kierkegaard, *For Self-Examination*, 57.
4. Kierkegaard, 'He Was Believed in the World', *Christian Discourses*, 234.
5. Kierkegaard, *Christian Discourses*, 234–5.
6. *Journals*, III/3606, V B 40:11, n.d., 1844.
7. *Without Authority*, 240. Italics original. Arnold Come offers an extensive and instructive account of Kierkegaard's understanding of the authority by which Christian life and thought is established in *Kierkegaard as Theologian: Recovering My Self* (Montreal: McGill-Queens University Press, 1997), chapter 1.
8. *The Book on Adler*, 32. The same point is made by Vigilius Haufniensis, another of Kierkegaard's pseudonyms, who contends that dogmatics, like every science, 'must vigorously lay hold of its own beginning and not live in complicated relations with other sciences'. *The Concept of Anxiety*, 58.
9. *The Book on Adler*, 34.
10. *Journals and Papers*, 6/6431, X¹ A 510, n.d., 1849.
11. *Practice in Christianity*, 9–10.
12. Interestingly, actuality provides exceptions to the rule. For instance, if one globule of mercury is added to a second globule of mercury, the result will not be two globules but one. Accordingly, Albert Einstein once remarked that 'as far as the propositions of mathematics refer to reality, they are not certain; and as far as they are certain, they do not refer to reality'. A. Einstein, 'Geometry and Experience', *A. Einstein, Ideas and Opinions* (New York: Crown Publishers, 1954), 233.
13. *Philosophical Fragments*, 55. Elsewhere Kierkegaard writes: 'Christ [is] infinitely more important than his teaching. It is true only of a human being that his teaching is more important than he himself; to apply this to Christ is a blasphemy, inasmuch as it makes him into only a human being'. *Practice in Christianity*, 124.
14. *Journals and Papers*, 1/278, II A 93, 9 June 1837.
15. *Practice in Christianity*, 37.
16. *Practice in Christianity*, 41.
17. While there is much evidence for Kierkegaard's appreciation of Luther, and particularly of Luther's *theologia crucis*, a number of *Journal* entries indicate also his careful attention to Calvin, particularly through Paul

# Notes

Henry's *Das Leben Johann Calvins*, I–III (Hamburg: 1835–44). Elsewhere Kierkegaard quotes Calvin's commentary on II Corinthians, specifically on the point we are concerned with here, the weakness of Christ, and thus also of the Christian. See *Journals and Papers*, 2/1704, II A 146, 27 August 1837. Disagreement on certain points notwithstanding, one finds in Kierkegaard numerous emphases that echo Calvin's theology.

18. See *Journals and Papers*, 1/77, $X^3$ A 186, n.d., 1850.
19. *Philosophical Fragments*, 31, 32, 33, 55.
20. *Philosophical Fragments*, 32–3.
21. *Practice in Christianity*, 23 and passim.
22. *Practice in Christianity*, 39.
23. Kierkegaard writes, 'the fact that [Jesus] descended from heaven to take upon himself the form of a servant – this is not an accidental something which now is to be thrust into the background and forgotten.' *Journals and Papers*, I/322, IX A 59, n.d., 1848. See also I/321, IX A 57, n.d., 1848.
24. *Upbuilding Discourses in Various Spirits*. 223.
25. Influential proponents of this view include the contributors to the volume edited by John Hick and published in 1977, *The Myth of God Incarnate* (London: SCM Press) and members of 'The Jesus Seminar' who commonly present 'christologies' that are devoid of any ontological identification of Jesus with God.
26. *Journals*, II/1343, VI A 127, n.d., 1845. The citation in its original setting refers to the domestication of God but it applies equally well to Christology.
27. Caution is required in attributing particular arguments to Arius because his theology is known to us only in fragments of his own writing and through the counter arguments of his opponents. Whether or not Arius himself argued this way, however, the theology found among his followers is certainly characterized by resistance to the 'lofty' claim that the Son is one with the Father.
28. Both summative points concerning Arius's position are drawn from Rowan Williams' magisterial study, *Arius* (London: SCM Press, 2nd edn, 2001), 232.
29. See *Practice in Christianity*, 97.
30. *Practice in Christianity*, 97.
31. *Practice in Christianity*, 101.
32. *Journals*, III/3571, $X^3$ A 122.
33. *Journals*, 1/318; 1/322; 1/626; 2/1642; 2/1648; 2/1649 are examples.
34. *Practice in Christianity*, 25.
35. *Practice in Christianity*, 9.
36. *Practice in Christianity*, 9.
37. *Practice in Christianity*, 107.
38. *Practice in Christianity*, 123.
39. That other work being, in fact, *Practice in Christianity* No.1. Until shortly before its publication Kierkegaard regarded the parts as separate books. See note 45 *Practice in Christianity*, 388.

40. *Practice in Christianity*, 123–4.
41. This is a view with which Kierkegaard in *Philosophical Fragments* readily concurs. See the 'Interlude'.
42. G. W. Leibniz, *New Essays on the Human Understanding*, 170.
43. G. W. Leibniz, *Monadology and other Philosophical Writings*, §33, 236.
44. Baruch Spinoza, *Tractatus theologico-politicus* (trans. Samuel Shirley; Leiden: E. J. Brill, 1991), iv.
45. Lessing, 'On the Proof of the Spirit and of Power', 53.
46. Lessing, 'On the Proof of the Spirit and of Power', 55.
47. See Ernst Troeltsch, 'Historical and Dogmatic Method in Theology', especially 13–14.
48. The problem is equally apparent in the methodological proposals of such contemporary inquirers into the 'Jesus of history' as the famous (or infamous!) 'Jesus Seminar'. C. Stephen Evans's book, *The Historical Christ and the Jesus of Faith* (Oxford: Clarendon Press, 1996) responds to the historiography represented by the 'Jesus Seminar' and makes much use of insights drawn from the writing of Kierkegaard.
49. *Practice in Christianity*, 25.
50. *Practice in Christianity*, 26. In accordance with the Christian, trinitarian conception of God, one would prefer a slightly more careful statement of the claim that "Christ was God." In Christian thought, God is Father, Son and Holy Spirit, one being in three persons. This theological subtlety notwithstanding, the point and force of Anti-Climacus' discussion remains intact.
51. *Practice in Christianity*, 26.
52. *Practice in Christianity*, 120.
53. Kierkegaard writes in his *Journals* that '[w]hen the believer has faith, the absurd is not the absurd – faith transforms it.' *Journals*, 1/10, X⁶ B 79, n.d., 1850.
54. *Practice in Christianity*, 26.
55. See 'On the Proof of the Spirit and of Power' *passim*.
56. The defence of Cardan is found in the first of Lessing's published writings on theology, namely, the *Vindication of Hieronymous Cardanus*, published in 1754.
57. *Practice in Christianity,* 26–7.
58. *Practice in Christianity*, 27.
59. *Practice in Christianity*, 27. Kierkegaard is concerned to safeguard the same distinction when in *The Book on Adler* he writes, 'For that purpose it is of primary importance that an unshakeable qualitative difference be fixed between *the historical in Christianity* (the paradox that the eternal once came into existence in time, this paradoxical fact) and *the history of Christianity*, the history of its followers, etc. *The Book on Adler*, 38.
60. Richard Tarnas tells us that 'this was the celebrated reply of the French astronomer and mathematician Pierre Simon Laplace to Napoleon, when

questioned about the absence of God in his new theory of the solar system.' Richard Tarnas, *The Passion of the Western Mind. Understanding the
Ideas That Have Shaped Our World View* (New York: Ballantine Books,
1991), 488.

61. *Practice in Christianity*, 29.
62. See Gordon E. Michalson, 'Lessing, Kierkegaard and the "Ugly Ditch":
    A Reexamination', 334 and 'Theology, Historical Knowledge and the
    Contingency-Necessity Distinction', 97. For similar views, see K. E.
    Løgstrup, 'Christentum ohne den historischen Jesus', *Orbis Litterarum* 10
    (1995), 156–65.
63. See *Practice in Christianity*, 31–2.
64. *Practice in Christianity*, 30.
65. *Practice in Christianity*, 25.
66. *Practice in Christianity*, 33.
67. See, for example, Karl Barth 'Faith as Knowledge', *Dogmatics in Outline*
    (trans. G. T. Thomson; London: SCM Press, 1949), 22–7 and Michael
    Polanyi, *Personal Knowledge: Towards a Post-Critical Philosophy* (London:
    Routledge & Kegan Paul, 1958).
68. *Practice in Christianity*, 25.
69. Witness, for instance, the contemporary claim of Philip Davies that
    the study of the biblical literature in the academy must be undertaken
    within a 'non-theological paradigm'. Such a view is set forth by Davies
    in the book, *In Search of Ancient Israel* (Sheffield: Sheffield Academic
    Press, 1992), and again in *Whose Bible is it Anyway?* (JSOTSup, 204;
    Sheffield: Sheffield Academic Press, 1995). I owe the references to Craig
    Bartholomew: '*Warranted* Biblical Interpretation: Alvin Plantinga's "Two
    (or More) Types of Scripture Scholarship"', *'Behind the Text' History and
    Biblical Interpretation* (eds. Craig Bartholomew, C. Stephen Evans, Mary
    Healy, Murray Rae; Grand Rapids: Zondervan and Carlisle: Paternoster
    Press, 2003), 58–78.
70. *Practice in Christianity*, 36.
71. *Practice in Christianity*, 35.
72. *Practice in Christianity*, 36.
73. *Practice in Christianity*, 36.
74. See especially, *For Self-Examination* and *Judge for Yourself!* and the Journal
    entries under 'Imitation': *Journals*, II/1833–1940).
75. *Practice in Christianity*, 40.
76. *Practice in Christianity*, 237.
77. *Practice in Christianity*, 171.
78. James Collins correctly notes the importance of Kierkegaard always
    speaking of *becoming* contemporaneous with Christ and *becoming* a
    Christian. 'Progress toward holiness is never brought to an end in
    history, and yet God's will is that each of us strive to become holy'.
    James Collins, *The Mind of Kierkegaard* (London: Secker and Warburg,
    1954), 229.
79. *Practice in Christianity*, 65.

80. The point is made by Merold Westphal: 'The ethical tells us to be generous out of our abundance, whereas the religious, understood as contemporaneity with Christ, makes a more radical demand.' Merold Westphal, *Kierkegaard's Critique of Reason and Society* (University Park, PA: The Pennsylvania State University Press, 1991), 26.
81. *Practice in Christianity*, 13.
82. See *For Self-Examination*, 25–51.
83. *Practice in Christianity*, 65.
84. *Journals*, I/695, X$^3$ A 653, n.d., 1850.
85. *Journals*, I/694, X$^2$ A 253, n.d., 1849.
86. *Practice in Christianity*, 12.
87. See especially *Philosophical Fragments*, 69.
88. *Journals*, I/694, X$^2$ A 253, n.d., 1849.
89. *Journals*, II/1785, X$^3$ A 268, n.d., 1850.
90. *Philosophical Fragments*, 62.
91. *Philosophical Fragments*, 59.

# Chapter 5

1. 'Letter 68' in *Letters and Documents*, 137.
2. 'Preface' to 'Two Discourses at the Communion on Fridays', *Without Authority*, 165.
3. We should note, however, Julia Watkin's claim that there is a degree of fluidity in the demarcation of these categories. See Watkin, *Kierkegaard*, 53.
4. Judge William is committed to an ethical life-view and his papers, gathered together by the editor of *Either/Or*, Victor Eremita, consist of a series of 'Letters to A' seeking to persuade 'A' to move from an aesthetic to an ethical view of life.
5. *Either/Or* II, 147.
6. See the comment in chapter one above on Kierkegaard's critique of Hans Christian Andersen's 'total lack' of a life-view.
7. *Either/Or* II, 179.
8. *Concluding Unscientific Postscript*, 252.
9. *Concluding Unscientific Postscript*, 274.
10. *Either/Or* II, 178.
11. *Either/Or* II, 179.
12. *Either/Or* II, 181.
13. *Either/Or* II, 180.
14. *Either/Or* II, 182.
15. *Either/Or* II, 291–2.
16. *Either/Or* I, 295–8.
17. Judge William notes also a certain affinity between his view and Aristotle's commendation of friendship as 'the point of departure for

his entire ethical view of life' and comments that Aristotle's conception is 'superior to the modern [Kantian] one, which bases justice upon the abstract-categorical; he bases it upon the social', *Either/Or* II, 322.

18. Allen W. Wood, 'Hegel's Ethics', *The Cambridge Companion to Hegel* (ed. Frederick C. Beiser; Cambridge: Cambridge University Press, 1993), 211–33, 215.

19. Anthony Rudd, *Kierkegaard and the Limits of the Ethical* (Oxford: Clarendon Press, 1993), 16.

20. *Either/Or* II, 294.

21. John D. Zizioulas, *Being as Communion: Studies in Personhood and the Church* (London: Darton, Longman and Todd, 1985), 47.

22. *Stages on Life's Way*, 476.

23. Rom. 3:23.

24. See *Either/Or* II, 339–54.

25. *Luther's Works*, Weimar Edition 45:482, American edition 24:23–4. Cited by George Yule in 'Luther's Attack on the Latin Heresy', *Christ in our Place: The Humanity of God in Christ for the Reconciliation of the World* (eds Trevor Hart and Daniel Thimell; Exeter: The Paternoster Press, 1989), 224–52, 227.

26. *Either/Or* II, 352.

27. *Either/Or* II, 10.

28. *Either/Or* II, 260.

29. David Gouwens, *Kierkegaard as Religious Thinker* (Cambridge: Cambridge University Press, 1996), 109.

30. See Gouwens, *Kierkegaard as Religious Thinker*, 108.

31. *Concluding Unscientific Postscript*, 267–8.

32. *Concluding Unscientific Postscript*, 269.

33. *Philosophical Fragments*, 47. The point is reiterated in The Concept of Anxiety where Vigilius Haufniensis advises that 'sin does not properly belong in any science but is the subject of the sermon' (p. 16), and again in *The Sickness Unto Death* where we read, 'neither paganism nor the natural man knows what sin is . . . [Christianity] assumes that there has to be a revelation from God to show what sin is' (p. 89).

34. *Philosophical Fragments*, 15.

35. *The Concept of Anxiety*, 56–7.

36. *The Concept of Anxiety*, 57–8.

37. *The Concept of Anxiety*, 58.

38. *The Concept of Anxiety*, 27.

39. *The Concept of Anxiety*, 60.

40. *The Sickness Unto Death*, 13.

41. We do well to remember here the words of John's Gospel: 'And this is eternal life, that they may know you, the only true God, and Jesus Christ whom you have sent' (Jn.17.3).

42. In contrast with some of the other pseudonyms, it is generally true that Kierkegaard approves all that Anti-Climacus has to say. He is distinguished from Kierkegaard himself not by the content of what he has to

say, but by the authority with which he says it. Anti-Climacus represents the view point of a Christian 'on an extraordinary level' whereas, by his own confession, Kierkegaard manages 'to be only a very simple Christian'. *Journals*, VI/6431, X¹ A 510, n.d., 1849.

43. *The Sickness Unto Death*, 13.
44. Saint Augustine, *Confessions* (Bk 1, 1.1.; trans. A. C. Outler; London: SCM Press, 1955), 31.
45. *The Concept of Anxiety*, 61.
46. See Fyodor Dostoyevsky, *The Brothers Karamazov* (trans. David Magarshak; London: Penguin Books, 1958), 288–311.
47. *The Sickness Unto Death*, 6.
48. See *Eighteen Upbuilding Discourses*, 297ff.
49. *The Sickness Unto Death*, 49.
50. *The Sickness Unto Death*, 50–60.
51. See, for example, the 'Three Devotional Discourses' in *Without Authority* and Part I of *Christian Discourses*.
52. *The Sickness Unto Death*, 60–67.
53. *The Sickness Unto Death*, 61.
54. *The Sickness Unto Death*, 63.
55. See especially *Lectures on Romans, Luther's Works* (vol. 25; St Louis: Concordia Publishing House, 1972), 345.
56. On which, see Matt Jenson, *The Gravity of Sin: Augustine, Luther and Barth on Homo Incurvatus in Se* (London: T&T Clark, 2006).
57. *The Sickness Unto Death*, 67.
58. *The Sickness Unto Death*, 67.
59. *The Sickness Unto Death*, 68; 69.
60. *The Sickness Unto Death*, 5. The same metaphor is used by Luther in his diagnosis of humanity's sinful condition. See *Lectures on Romans, Luther's Works*, vol. 25, 260.
61. *Journals*, IV/3915, III C 1, n.d., 1840–41.
62. *The Sickness Unto Death*, 6.
63. *Journals*, IV/3915, III C 1, n.d., 1840–41.
64. *The Sickness Unto Death*, 113.
65. *The Sickness Unto Death*, 113–14.
66. Karl Barth, *Church Dogmatics*, IV.2 (Edinburgh: T&T Clark, 1958), 27.
67. The Sickness Unto Death, 114.
68. Sylvia Walsh observes a similar attitude in Kierkegaard himself: 'Like the believer, Kierkegaard is content to rest in faith and concern himself only with the meaning of the death and atonement of Christ for the believer, which is the believer's personal reconciliation with God in and through Christ.' *Kierkegaard: Thinking Christianly in Existential Mode*, 133.
69. *The Sickness Unto Death*, 120. Anti-Climacus does not deny 'the teaching about the sin of the race' but he does lament its misuse, its use in providing absolution for the individual. We are each of us guilty before God, and God is concerned with each of us, especially.

Notes

70. *The Sickness Unto Death*, 122.
71. *The Sickness Unto Death*, 128.
72. *The Sickness Unto Death*, 131. The point of my emphasis is that Christ is the one through whom and in whom all things came to be, and through whom God was pleased to reconcile all things. See Col. 1.15–20.
73. *The Sickness Unto Death*, 89.
74. *The Sickness Unto Death*, 89.
75. *Journals*, II/1216, VIII¹ A 675, n.d., 1848.
76. For a critique of the Western *ordo salutis* and its attendant epistemology, see Alan J. Torrance, *Persons in Communion: Trinitarian Description and Human Participation* (Edinburgh: T&T Clark, 1996), 59–70.
77. *Journals*, II/1206, VII¹ A 167, n.d., 1846.
78. John Calvin, *Institutes of the Christian Religion* (trans. John Allen; Philadelphia: Presbyterian Board of Christian Education, 1936), III.3.2.
79. 'Letter to John Staupitz', *Works of Martin Luther* (trans. and ed. Adolph Spaeth, L. D. Reed, Henry Eyster Jacobs et al.; vol. 1; Philadelphia: A. J. Holman Company, 1915), 39–43.
80. *Christian Discourses*, 298. Cf. *Without Authority*, 155.
81. *Without Authority*, 58.
82. *Without Authority*, 59.
83. See especially, Jürgen Moltmann, *The Crucified God* (trans. R.A. Wilson and John Bowden; London: SCM Press, 1974).
84. *Without Authority*, 116.
85. *Without Authority*, 122.
86. *Without Authority*, 123.
87. *Without Authority*, 123.
88. *Without Authority*, 123.
89. *Without Authority*, 169.
90. *Without Authority*, 173.
91. *Without Authority*, 175.
92. *Without Authority*, 173.
93. Karl Barth, *Church Dogmatics*, III.1 (Edinburgh: T&T Clark, 1958), 384.
94. *Journals*, II/1471, X² A 189, n.d., 1849.
95. I owe this phrase to R. S. Thomas's poem 'The Kingdom', *Later Poems* (London: Macmillan, 1983), 35.
96. *Eighteen Upbuilding Discourses*, 325.
97. *Concluding Unscientific Postscript*, 561.

Chapter 6

1. *Practice in Christianity*, 7.
2. 'The severity of [Kierkegaard's] demands' is a phrase taken from Karl Barth's portrayal of Kierkegaard, See Barth, 'Kierkegaard and the

Theologians', *Fragments Grave and Gay* (London: Fontana, 1971), 102–4, 103. The further critique of Kierkegaard offered in Barth's partially favourable review of Kierkegaard, indicates that Barth missed in Kierkegaard's writings the profound reliance upon grace that, in Kierkegaard's view, lies at the heart of Christian life.

3. *Practice in Christianity*, 7.
4. Barth, 'Kierkegaard and the Theologians', 103–4. See also, 'A Thank-You and a Bow – Kierkegaard's Reveille', *Fragments Grave and Gay*, 95–101.
5. *Practice in Christianity*, 7.
6. Barth, 'Kierkegaard and the Theologians', 102.
7. See, especially, Rom. 4.
8. Gen. 17.5, 8.
9. *Concluding Unscientific Postscript*, 429.
10. *The Sickness Unto Death*, 129n.
11. David McCracken, *The Scandal of the Gospels: Jesus, Story and Offense* (New York: Oxford University Press, 1994), 41.
12. Henry E. Allison, 'Christianity and Nonsense', *Søren Kierkegaard: Critical Assessments of Leading Philosophers* (eds Daniel W. Conway and K. E. Gover; vol. III; London: Routledge, 2002), 7–29, 16. Reprinted from *The Review of Metaphysics* 20.3 (1967), 39–58.
13. *Journals*, I/334, X[1] A 279, n.d., 1849. See also the prayer preceding the discourse 'Christ as the Prototype' in *Judge For Yourself!*, 147.
14. *For Self-Examination and Judge For Yourself!*, 25.
15. *For Self-Examination and Judge For Yourself!*, 25 (Italics original).
16. See Chapter 3 above.
17. *For Self-Examination and Judge For Yourself!*, 25–6.
18. *The Book on Adler*, 64.
19. In his *Journals* Kierkegaard writes, 'What holds true for the apostles, who were very simple men of the poorest class (for in this way their *authority* was all the more accentuated; they were nothing in themselves, not geniuses, not councilmen or state governors, but fishermen – therefore all of their *authority* was from God), holds true also for the bad Greek of the New Testament'. *Journals*, I/182, VIII[1] A 225, n.d., 1847 (Italics original).
20. See, *For Self-Examination and Judge For Yourself!*, 47–51.
21. *For Self-Examination and Judge For Yourself!*, 27.
22. *For Self-Examination and Judge For Yourself!*, 29.
23. *For Self-Examination and Judge For Yourself!*, 35 (Italics original).
24. *For Self-Examination and Judge For Yourself!*, 43.
25. Paul S. Minear and Paul S. Morimoto, *Kierkegaard and the Bible: An Index* (Princeton, NJ: Princeton Theological Seminary, 1953), 8. Cited in 'Timothy Houston Polk', *The Biblical Kierkegaard, Reading by the Rule of Faith* (Macon, GA: Mercer University Press, 1997), 1.
26. See the preceding note. George Pattison's protestations notwithstanding, I think there is ample evidence in support of Polk's basic contentions

that Kierkegaard advocates the reading of Scripture according to the rule of faith, that the rule of faith is to be construed in terms of love for God, that Scripture exists for religious use, and that such reading is characterized by trust in the authoritative status of the canon as a whole. For Pattison's dubious critique of these claims, see his review of Polk's work in *Literature and Theology*, 13.1 (March 1999), 90–1. Pattison's reservations about whether Kierkegaard conceives such reading in an ecclesial context have more credence, however.

27. The citation comes from Stanley Fish, *Is There a Text in This Class? The Authority of Interpretive Communities* (Cambridge, MA: Harvard University Press, 1980), 170, and appears in Polk, *The Biblical Kierkegaard*, 8–9.

28. *Journals*, III/2501, X¹ A 630, n.d.

29. *Journals* III/3403, VII¹ A 56, n.d., 1846 (Emphases original).

30. Again, see Barth's critique referred to above.

31. *Without Authority*, 137.

32. *Journals*, III/3441, X² A 77, n.d., 1849.

33. See, for example, John Calvin who provides one of the classic Reformation statements of the mediatorial and priestly role of Christ in his *Institutes of the Christian Religion*, Book II, Chapter 12.

34. *Without Authority*, 149.

35. Kierkegaard, *Without Authority*, 123–4.

36. See Kierkegaard, *Christian Discourses*, 270–1.

37. *Journals*, II/591, X¹ A 271, n.d., 1849.

38. Merold Westphal, *Kierkegaard's Critique of Reason and Society*, vii.

39. *Fear and Trembling*, 28.

40. *Fear and Trembling*, 54.

41. Immanuel Kant, *Critique of Practical Reason* (trans. Lewis White Beck; New York: Macmillan, 1956), 30.

42. On which, see Allen W. Wood, 'Hegel's Ethics'.

43. It is however the case that Hegel rejected the individualism and abstraction of Kant's conception of practical reason and set forth instead an understanding of reason informed by the concrete relations of a particular social order. See Hegel's *Philosophy of Right* (trans. T. M. Knox; Oxford: Clarendon Press, 1942).

44. *Fear and Trembling*, 54.

45. *Fear and Trembling*, 54.

46. *Fear and Trembling*, 54.

47. Kant, *Religion Within the Limits of Reason Alone* (trans. Theodore M. Greene and Hoyt H. Hudson; New York: Harper, 1960), 78. Admittedly Kant struggles with the notion that faith in a vicarious atonement might also be a pre-requisite of salvation (e.g. 108) but his offense at this apparent violation of individual autonomy leads him to banish such a notion to the realm of the 'theoretical concept' while having no practical import.

48. Kant, *Religion Within the Limits of Reason Alone*, 175.

49. Kant, *Critique of Practical Reason*, Pailin, 32

50. Kant, *Der Streit der Facultäten*, cited by David A. Pailin, 'Abraham and Isaac: A Hermeneutical Problem before Kierkegaard', *Kierkegaard's 'Fear and Trembling': Critical Appraisals* (ed. Robert L. Perkins; Alabama: University of Alabama Press, 1981), 10–42, 32.

51. For a more detailed defence see Alastair McKinnon, 'Kierkegaard: "Paradox" and Irrationalism', *Essays on Kierkegaard* (ed. Jerry H. Gill; Minneapolis: Burgess Publishing Co., 1969), 102–12. My own attempt at a more detailed defence can be found in *Kierkegaard's Vision of the Incarnation: By Faith Transformed* (Oxford: Clarendon Press, 1997).

52. *Journals*, I/10, X$^6$ B 79, n.d., 1850.

53. Ludwig Wittgenstein, *Tractatus Logico-Philosophicus* (trans. C. K. Oden; London: Routledge & Kegan Paul Ltd, 1922), 7.

54. *Fear and Trembling*, 82.

55. *Fear and Trembling*, 115.

56. Peter van Inwagen, 'Is it possible to prove that God does not exist?', F. D. Maurice Lectures presented at King's College, London in March 1999.

57. Kierkegaard himself discusses in this same vein the 'remarkable teaching' recorded in Lk. 14.26, 'If any one comes to me and does not hate his own father and mother and wife and children and brothers and sisters, yes, and even his own life, he cannot be my disciple'. *Fear and Trembling*, 72–3.

58. The point is taken from Anthony Rudd's study, *Kierkegaard and the Limits of the Ethical*, 148.

59. Paul Holmer, 'About Being a Person: "Fear and Trembling"', *Kierkegaard's* Fear and Trembling: *Critical Appraisals* (ed. Robert L. Perkins; Alabama: University of Alabama Press, 1981), 81–99.

60. The formation and judgement of one's life before God is frequently referred to by Kierkegaard as a 'spiritual trial' (*anfoegtelse*). For more extensive treatment of Kierkegaard's conception of such trial, see Simon Podmore, *Anatomy of the Abyss: A Kierkegaardian Vision of the Self Before God* (Indiana: Indiana University Press, 2010).

61. Published in New Zealand by the Spiral Collective, 1984.

62. *Fear and Trembling*, 33.

63. This point is made by Julia Watkin on whose discussion I am relying here. See Watkin, 89.

64. *The Book on Adler*, 159n.

# Chapter 7

1. *Works of Love*, 3.

2. See, for example, Alasdair MacIntyre, *A Short History of Ethics* (London: Routledge, 2nd edn, 1998), 208–11; Roger S. Gottlieb, 'Kierkegaard's Ethical Individualism', *Monist* 62.3 (July 1979), 351–67.

3. See especially the work of John Zizioulas, *Being as Communion: Studies in Personhood and the Church* (London: Darton, Longman and Todd, 1985). Feminist theologians, such as Letty Russell, *Becoming Human* (Philadelphia: Westminster Press, 1982); *Church in the Round* (Louisville: Westminster John Knox Press, 1993) have played prominent roles in the recovery of a social conception of the person. Other important works include, Alistair I. McFadyen, *The Call to Personhood* (Cambridge: Cambridge University Press, 1990); Alan J. Torrance, *Persons in Communion*; Stanley J. Grenz, *The Social God and the Relational Self* (Louisville: Westminster John Knox Press, 2001). In philosophy, John Macmurray's book *Persons in Relation* (London: Faber & Faber, 1961) has also been influential.

4. *Journals*, V/5972, VIII[1] A 4, January 1847.

5. Merold Westphal and J. Martin Matuštík (eds), *Kierkegaard in Post/ Modernity* (Bloomington: Indiana University Press, 1995), ix.

6. See *Fear and Trembling*, 82–120.

7. *Works of Love*, 14.

8. M. Jamie Ferreira, *Love's Grateful Striving: A Commentary on Kierkegaard's Works of Love* (New York: Oxford University Press, 2001).

9. *Works of Love*, 383–4.

10. Ferreira, *Love's Grateful Striving*, 247.

11. *Works of Love*, 3–4.

12. Ferreira, *Love's Grateful Striving*, 17.

13. Ferreira, *Love's Grateful Striving*, 18 (Upper case original).

14. *Works of Love*, 18.

15. *Works of Love*, 9.

16. *Works of Love*, 44. Almost a century before Swedish theologian Anders Nygren's renowned two volume work *Agape and Eros*, Kierkegaard here contrasts eros (*Elskov*) with agape, for which he uses the Danish term *Kjerlighed*.

17. For recent discussions of the matter, see Sharon Krishek, 'Two Forms of Love: The Problem of Preferential Love in Kierkegaard's *Works of Love*', *Journal of Religious Ethics*, 36.4 (2008) 595–617, and C. Stephen Evans, *Kierkegaard's Ethic of Love: Divine Commands and Moral Obligations* (Oxford: Oxford University Press, 2004), especially Chapter 9.

18. *Works of Love*, 68.

19. Theodor W. Adorno, 'On Kierkegaard's Doctrine of Love', *Studies in Philosophy and Social Science* 8 (1939–40), 413–29, 418–9. Cited in Ferreira, *Love's Grateful Striving*, 54.

20. Ferreira, *Love's Grateful Striving*, 54.

21. Ferreira, *Love's Grateful Striving*, 55.

22. *Works of Love*, 19.

23. See *Works of Love*, Chapter IV.

24. Among numerous works by Levinas, see especially, *Otherwise than Being or Beyond Essence* (trans. A. Lingis; The Hague: Martinus Nijhoff, 1981); *Totality and Infinity* (trans. A. Lingis; Pittsburgh: Duquesne University

Press, 1969) and *Humanism of the Other* (trans. Nidra Poller; Chicago: University of Illinois Press, 2003).

25. *Works of Love*, 60.
26. *Works of Love*, 89.
27. *Works of Love*, 60.
28. *Works of Love*, 82.
29. *Works of Love*, 83.
30. *Works of Love*, 83–4.
31. *Works of Love*, 96.
32. *Works of Love*, 107 (Italics original).
33. This question is raised by Ferreira, *Love's Grateful Striving*, 71.
34. *Works of Love*, 10.
35. See *Works of Love*, 108. Cf. 110: '. . . with Christianity came the divine explanation of what love is.'
36. *Works of Love*, 112.
37. *Works of Love*, 114.
38. *For Self-Examination*, 24.
39. Vernard Eller, *Kierkegaard and Radical Discipleship A New Perspective* (Princeton, NJ: Princeton University Press, 1968), 168.
40. Karl Barth, 'A Thank-You and a Bow – Kierkegaard's Reveille', *Fragments Grave and Gay*, 99.
41. *For Self-Examination*, 15.
42. *For Self-Examination*, 15.
43. *Judge For Yourself!*, 193.
44. James Collins twice observes that Kierkegaard saw his own position as a corrective to the errors of his age and not as a refutation of Luther. See James Collins, *The Mind of Kierkegaard*, 236, 242. On the same theme see also Julia Watkin, *Kierkegaard*, 34, 95; David Gouwens, *Kierkegaard as Religious Thinker*, 48, 128.
45. *Judge For Yourself!*, 194.
46. *Judge For Yourself!*, 147.
47. *Judge For Yourself!*, 191.
48. *Judge For Yourself!*, 151.
49. *Judge For Yourself!*, 151.
50. *Judge For Yourself!*, 152.
51. *Journals*, II/1477, $X^3$ A 106, n.d., 1850. Compare the claim, '. . . for what man does on his own never becomes more than a fig leaf'. *Journals*, IV/4959, II A 453, n.d.
52. *Judge For Yourself!*, 152.
53. *Judge For Yourself!*, 153.
54. The echo of this early work indicates that if, as Alastair McKinnon argues, there is in Kierkegaard's authorship as a whole a progress towards the final resolution of the question of grace and works in *Judge for Yourself!*, written in 1851, then that resolution is to be understood as a refinement of rather than a departure from the position already reached in 1842 with the writing of *Either/Or*. McKinnon makes the remark in

an unpublished paper, 'Model and Redeemer in Kierkegaard's Religious Writings', 1980.

55. *Judge For Yourself!*, 153. Sylvia Walsh thus observes, along with other commentators, that 'the primary function of the prototype is to teach us how greatly we are in need of grace.' Sylvia Walsh, *Living Poetically: Kierkegaard's Existential Aesthetics* (University Park, PA: The Pennsylvania State University Press, 1994), 237.

56. Here one does detect a significant change in Kierkegaard's thought. At the time of the writing of *Fear and Trembling* in 1843, Kierkegaard, under the guise of Johannes de Silentio, could argue that 'those who carry the treasure of faith' had no distinguishing external marks, 'they have a striking resemblance to bourgeois philistinism'. (*Fear and Trembling*, 38). When imagining such a one Silentio remarks, 'Good Lord, is this the man, is this really the one – he looks just like a tax collector!' (p. 39). In the later period of his authorship, however, when the attack upon Christendom becomes more direct and more vociferous, Kierkegaard increasingly insists that the person of authentic Christian faith will stand out from the crowd. Suffering, that is, taking up one's cross, even to the point of martyrdom, is the distinguishing mark.

57. *Judge For Yourself!*, 188.

58. *Judge For Yourself!*, 156.

59. *Judge For Yourself!*, 156–7.

60. *Judge For Yourself!*, 156.

61. *Judge For Yourself!*, 166.

62. *Judge For Yourself!*, 166–7.

63. The German work *Nachfolge* is more commonly known under the earlier English title, *The Cost of Discipleship*, but appears in a new English translation simply as *Discipleship* (Dietrich Bonhoeffer Works, vol. 4). *Nachfolge* means in German, simply 'following after', an exact equivalent of the Danish *Efterfølgelse*, used by Kierkegaard in *Judge for Yourself!*.

64. Dietrich Bonhoeffer, *Discipleship* (trans. Barbara Green and Reinhard Krauss; Minneapolis: Fortress Press, 2001), 9.

65. Bonhoeffer, *Discipleship*, 39.

66. Bonhoeffer, *Discipleship*, 43.

67. Bonhoeffer, *Discipleship*, 43.

68. Bonhoeffer, *Discipleship*, 43.

69. While Bonhoeffer's original text makes little explicit reference to Kierkegaard, the 1989 German edition, edited by Martin Kuske and Ilse Tödt, provides in the notes extensive indications of where Bonhoeffer is drawing on Kierkegaard. See Dietrich Bonhoeffer, *Nachfolge* (München: Chr. Kaiser Verlag, 1989). So too does Volume 4 of Dietrich Bonhoeffer Works, the new English translation from which I have been quoting. The debt to Kierkegaard is also discussed in the 'Editor's Introduction to the English Edition'. *Discipleship*, 1–33.

70. Bonhoeffer, *Discipleship*, 49–50. Compare Kierkegaard: 'There is always a secular mentality that no doubt wants to have the name of being Christian but wants to become a Christian as cheaply as possible. This secular mentality became aware of Luther. It listened; for safety's sake it listened once again lest it should have heard wrongly; thereupon it said, 'Excellent! This is something for us. Luther says: It depends on faith alone. He himself does not say that his life expresses works, and since he is now dead it is no longer an actuality. So we take his words, his doctrine – and we are free from all works – long live Luther!'" *For Self-Examination*, 16.

71. Bonhoeffer, *Discipleship*, 87 – famously rendered by R. H. Fuller in the first English translation as, 'When Christ calls a man he bids him come and die'.

72. See *Judge For Yourself!*, 168–9, and Bonhoeffer, *Discipleship*, 46–8.

73. Compare Rom. 5.3.

74. *Judge For Yourself!*, 207–8.

75. Note well that Kierkegaard is not recommending subjectivism. His category of the subjective is properly understood as 'the personal'.

76. *Judge For Yourself!*, 209 (Italics original).

77. See *Judge For Yourself!*, 152 on the atonement and 153 on grace.

78. *Judge For Yourself!*, 159.

79. *Journals*, II/1469, $X^1$ A 507, n.d., 1849.

80. See *Judge For Yourself!*, 196.

81. Kierkegaard remarks both in *For Self-Examination* and in *Judge For Yourself!*, that the error in monasticism was not the works themselves but the idea that the works were meritorious. See *For Self-Examination*, 15; *Judge For Yourself!*, 192. Anthony Rudd writes perceptively on this matter: 'The cause for "fear and trembling". . . is not that I must perform the terribly strenuous task of relating to the absolute *telos* through my own efforts, but that I must constantly bear in mind that my own efforts have no merit and can achieve nothing. This attitude produces not a crushed passivity, but a freedom to live beyond the terror of the law . . .' Rudd, *Kierkegaard and the Limits of the Ethical*, 171.

82. Compare the claim, 'The absence of striving makes it obvious that one does not have faith.' *Journals*, II/1140, $X^3$ A 323, n.d.

83. Bonhoeffer, *Discipleship*, 63.

84. *Judge For Yourself!*, 208.

85. *For Self-Examination*, 17.

86. *For Self-Examination*, 17; cf. *Judge For Yourself!*, 193.

87. *Journals*, III/3506, $X^3$ A 246, n.d., 1850; cf. *Journals*, III/3499, $X^3$ A 59, n.d., 1850.

88. *Judge For Yourself!*, 189.

89. *For Self-Examination*, 68.

90. *For Self-Examination*, 69.

91. *For Self-Examination*, 70. Bonhoeffer again repeats Kierkegaard's insight. The reason for doubt is disobedience, Bonhoeffer contends, and he thus

recommends that the pastor advise the doubter, '[y]our trouble is your sin.' *Discipleship*, 68, See also the whole of Chapter 2, 'The Call to Discipleship'.

92. Karl Barth, *Church Dogmatics*, IV.2, 780.

93. Barth, *Church Dogmatics*, IV.2, 781.

94. Barth, *Church Dogmatics*, IV.2, 781.

95. Barth, *Church Dogmatics*, IV.2, 782.

96. Paul Martens, '"You Shall Love": Kant, Kierkegaard and the Interpretation of Matthew 22:39' in *International Kierkegaard Commentary: Works of Love* (IKC 16; ed. Robert L. Perkins; Macon, GA: Mercer University Press, 1999), 57–78, 77.

97. *Judge For Yourself!*, 182–3. Compare Kierkegaard's remark in the Journals: 'There is an infinitely radical, qualitative difference between God and man. This means, or the expression for this is: the human person achieves absolutely nothing; it is God who gives everything; it is he who brings forth a person's faith etc. This is grace and this is Christianity's major premise.' *Journals*, II/1383, X$^1$ A 59, n.d., 1849.

98. *Judge For Yourself!*, 183–4.

99. *Judge For Yourself!*, 185.

100. *Journals*, I/983, X$^2$ A 208, n.d., 1849.

101. *For Self-Examination*, 77.

102. *For Self-Examination*, 85. The citation here alludes, of course, to 1 Cor. 13, upon which Kierkegaard offers extensive reflection in the second series of Discourses in *Works of Love*.

103. *For Self-Examination*, 85–6.

104. *For Self-Examination*, 86.

105. See especially, again, the 'First Series' of discourses in *Works of Love*, though note well that Kierkegaard himself recognizes that to speak of a *duty* to love is an apparent contradiction. *Works of Love*, 24. Barth is not therefore drawing our attention to something that Kierkegaard himself has not already thought of.

106. In the Journals Kierkegaard comments, 'The Spirit is the Comforter. It is not only vitalizing, enabling power for "dying to the world"—but is also the Comforter in relation to "imitation."' *Journals*, II/1919, X$^5$ A 44, n.d., 1852.

107. *Judge For Yourself!*, 159.

108. *Works of Love*, 41.

109. Polk here refers the 1962 translation of *Works of Love*. The corresponding pagination in the 1995 translation is 41, 61; cf. 189.

110. Timothy Polk, *The Biblical Kierkegaard*, 46–7. It is remarkable that Barth attributes the supposed error in Kierkegaard to a misunderstanding of the future sense of the Greek *agapeseis* (*Church Dogmatics*, IV.2, 782) when, as Polk has shown, Kierkegaard himself draws out the promissory character of the commandment.

111. *Works of Love*, 43.

112. *Works of Love*, 189.

113. David Gouwens, *Kierkegaard as Religious Thinker*, 195. I commend Gouwens' entire discussion of Barth's critique of Kierkegaard, 188–97.
114. Timothy Polk, *The Biblical Kierkegaard*, 46.
115. In a passage headed 'Works', in which Kierkegaard describes the failures of Christendom, he writes that he nevertheless believes 'these millions of Christians will all be saved.' *Journals*, IV/4524, X⁴ A 639, n.d., 1852.
116. See, for example, Rom. 6.
117. See, for example, Calvin's *Institutes of the Christian Religion* II, vii.

Chapter 8

1. *Journals*, II/2379, XI² A 39, n.d., 1854.
2. Howard, V. and Edna H. Hong, 'Historical Introduction' to Kierkegaard, *The Moment and Late Writings*, xvii–xviii.
3. *Journals*, I/708, X⁴ A 15, n.d., 1851.
4. *Journals*, VI/6467, X¹ A 640, n.d., 1849.
5. Richard John Neuhaus, 'Kierkegaard for Grownups', *First Things* No. 146 (October 2004), 27–33.
6. F. D. E. Schleiermacher, *The Christian Faith* (Eng. trans.; Edinburgh: T&T Clark, 1928), 385.
7. The structure of this self-projection, the emergence of finite mind and its return to its essential unity with Absolute Mind is dialectical, a pattern of movement which proceeds from a starting point (the thesis) to another which stands over against it (the antithesis) and then moves on to a third stage in which the two are reconciled and reintegrated on a higher level (the synthesis). See A. I. C. Heron, *A Century of Protestant Theology* (London: Lutterworth Press, 1980), 39.
8. I take the point from Robert L. Perkins, *Søren Kierkegaard* (London: Lutterworth Press, 1969), 42–3.
9. Perkins, *Søren Kierkegaard*, 41.
10. From the Preface to 'Two Discourses at the Communion on Fridays', *Without Authority*, 165. Elsewhere he speaks of 'the most noble Avenue of the Church Fathers, in whose shade I still at times find rest.' *Journals*, I/583, II A 750, n.d., 1838.
11. *Journals*, II/2370, V B 1:2, n.d., 1844.
12. Only Hegel appears as often as Luther but Hegel was a philosopher rather than a theologian and, of course, Kierkegaard regarded Hegel as having departed from the 'old familiar text'. Not so, in the main, with Luther. Indeed, as Regin Prenter observes, in the published works, as distinct from the Journals, 'Luther is always represented as an ally of Kierkegaard and never an antagonist'. Regin Prenter, 'Luther and Lutheranism', *Bibliotheca Kierkegaardiana, Vol. 6: Kierkegaard and Great Traditions* (eds

# Notes

Niels Thulstrup and Marie Mikulová Thulstrup; Copenhagen: C. A. Reitzels Boghandel, 1981), 136.

13. See *Journals*, III/2463, VIII¹ A465, n.d., 1847.
14. Walter Lowrie, *Kierkegaard* (2 vols.; New York: Harper and Brothers, 1962), vol. 1, 164.
15. Hinkson's account of Hamann's influence can be found in 'Kierkegaard's Theology: Cross and Grace', PhD Dissertation, University of Chicago, 1993, especially Chapter 3. See also Craig Hinkson, 'Luther and Kierkegaard: Theologians of the Cross', *International Journal of Systematic Theology*, 3.1 (March 2001), 27–45, and John R. Betz, 'Hamann Before Kierkegaard: A Systematic Theological Oversight', *Pro Ecclesia* XVI.3 (2007), 299–333. At note 5 (p. 301) of his article Betz lists a number of other scholars who have written on the relation between Hamann and Kierkegaard. For a contrary view of the importance of Hamann's influence, however, see Stephen N. Dunning 'Kierkegaard's "Hegelian" Response to Hamann', *Thought* 55:218 (September 1980), 259–70.
16. M. Jamie Ferreira, *Love's Grateful Striving*, 19.
17. *Journals*, II/1841, VIII¹ A 432, n.d., 1847.
18. *Christian Discourses*, 187.
19. *Journals*, III/2461, VII¹ A 209, n.d., 1846.
20. Bruce Kirmmse's *Encounters with Kierkegaard*, provides a rich compendium of the reception of Kierkegaard and his works by his contemporaries.
21. See, Paul Roubiczek, *Existentialism: For and Against* (Cambridge: Cambridge University Press, 1964).
22. See, for example, Michael Weston, *Kierkegaard and Modern Continental Philosophy: An Introduction* (London: Routledge, 1994).
23. Spencer, Herbert, *Social Statics* [1851] (New York: Robert Schalkenbach Foundation, 1954), 60.
24. See, for example, Alisdair Heron, *A Century of Protestant Theology* (London: Lutterworth Press, 1980).
25. A number of scholars have, over the years, offered useful accounts of Barth's relation to Kierkegaard. Philip Ziegler's recent article, 'Barth's Criticism's of Kierkegaard – A Striking Out at Phantoms', *International Journal of Systematic Theology* 9.4 (May 2007), 434–51, is particularly to be recommended.
26. The observation is drawn from Elmer H. Duncan, *Søren Kierkegaard, Makers of the Modern Theological Mind* (Waco: Word Books, 1976), 126.
27. Watkin, *Kierkegaard*, 103.
28. I take the point from Sylvia Walsh, *Kierkegaard: Thinking Christianly in an Existential Mode*, 205.
29. Louis Dupré, *Kierkegaard as Theologian* (London: Sheed and Ward, 1964); Erich Przywara, *Das Geheimnis Kierkegaards* (München: Oldenbourg, 1929).
30. Again, the point is taken from Sylvia Walsh, *Kierkegaard: Thinking Christianly in an Existential Mode*, 205. See further Simon Podmore, 'The

Dark Night of Suffering and the Darkness of God: God-forsakenness or Forsaking God in "The Gospel of Sufferings"', *International Kierkegaard Commentary, vol. 15: Upbuilding Discourses in Various Spirits* (ed. Robert L. Perkins; Macon, GA: Mercer University Press, 2005), 229–56.

31. Jack Mulder, Jr., *Kierkegaard and the Catholic Tradition: Conflict and Dialogue* (Bloomington, IN: Indiana University Press, 2010).

# Bibliography

## Works by Kierkegaard

*Christian Discourses, The Crisis and a Crisis in the Life of an Actress* (ed. and trans. Howard V. Hong and Edna H. Hong; Princeton, NJ: Princeton University Press, 1997).

*Concluding Unscientific Postscript* (2 vols; ed. and trans. Howard V. Hong and Edna H. Hong; Princeton, NJ: Princeton University Press, 1992).

*Early Polemical Writings* (Princeton, NJ: Princeton University Press, 1990).

*Edifying Discourses* (ed. and trans. Howard V. Hong and Edna H. Hong; Princeton, NJ: Princeton University Press, 1990).

*Eighteen Upbuilding Discourses* (ed. and trans. Howard V. Hong and Edna H. Hong; Princeton, NJ: Princeton University Press, 1990).

*Either/Or* (2 vols; ed. and trans. Howard V. Hong and Edna H. Hong; Princeton, NJ: Princeton University Press, 1987).

*Fear and Trembling and Repetition* (ed. and trans. Howard V. Hong and Edna H. Hong; Princeton, NJ: Princeton University Press, 1983).

*For Self-Examination and Judge for Yourself!* (ed. and trans. Howard V. Hong and Edna H. Hong; Princeton, NJ: Princeton University Press, 1990).

*Journals and Papers* (ed. and trans. Howard V. Hong and Edna H. Hong; 6 vols; Bloomington, IN: Indiana University Press, 1967–78).

*Kierkegaard's Journals and Notebooks* (vols 1–2; ed. Niels Jørgen Cappelørn et al.; Princeton, NJ: Princeton University Press, 2007–2008).

*Letters and Documents* (trans. Henrik Rosenheimer; Princeton, NJ: Princeton University Press, 1978).

*Philosophical Fragments and Johannes Climacus* (ed. and trans. Howard V. Hong and Edna H. Hong; Princeton, NJ: Princeton University Press, 1985).

*Practice in Christianity* (ed. and trans. Howard V. Hong and Edna H. Hong; Princeton, NJ: Princeton University Press, 1991).

*Prefaces, Writing Sampler* (ed. and trans. Todd W. Nichol; Princeton, NJ: Princeton University Press, 1997).

*Stages on Life's Way* (ed. and trans. Howard V. Hong and Edna H. Hong; Princeton, NJ: Princeton University Press, 1988).

*The Book on Adler* (ed. and trans. Howard V. Hong and Edna H. Hong; Princeton, NJ: Princeton University Press, 1998).

*The Concept of Anxiety* (ed. and trans. Reidar Thomte; Princeton, NJ: Princeton University Press, 1980).

*The Concept of Irony* (ed. and trans. Howard V. Hong and Edna H. Hong; Princeton, NJ: Princeton University Press, 1989).

# Bibliography

*The Corsair Affair and Articles Related to the Writings* (ed. and trans. Howard V. Hong and Edna H. Hong; Princeton, NJ: Princeton University Press, 1982).

*The Moment and Late Writings* (ed. and trans. Howard V. Hong and Edna H. Hong; Princeton, NJ: Princeton University Press, 1998).

*The Point of View of my Work as an Author* (ed. and trans. Howard V. Hong and Edna H. Hong; Princeton, NJ: Princeton University Press, 1998).

*The Sickness Unto Death* (ed. and trans. Howard V. Hong and Edna H. Hong; Princeton, NJ: Princeton University Press, 1980).

*Three Discourses on Imagined Occasions* (ed. and trans. Howard V. Hong and Edna H. Hong; Princeton, NJ: Princeton University Press, 1993).

*Upbuilding Discourses in Various Spirits* (ed. and trans. Howard V. Hong and Edna H. Hong; Princeton, NJ: Princeton University Press, 1993).

*Works of Love* (ed. and trans. Howard V. Hong and Edna H. Hong; Princeton, NJ: Princeton University Press, 1995).

## Other Works

Adorno, Theodor W., 'On Kierkegaard's Doctrine of Love', *Studies in Philosophy and Social Science* 8 (1939–40), 413–29.

Allison, Henry E., 'Christianity and Nonsense', *Søren Kierkegaard: Critical Assessments of Leading Philosophers* (vol. III; eds Daniel W. Conway and K. E. Gover; London: Routledge, 2002), 7–29.

Augustine, *Confessions* (trans. A.C. Outler; London: SCM Press, 1955).

Barth, Karl, *Dogmatics in Outline* (trans. G. T. Thomson; London: SCM Press, 1949).

—*Church Dogmatics*, IV.2 (Edinburgh: T&T Clark, 1958).

—*Church Dogmatics*, III.1 (Edinburgh: T&T Clark, 1958).

—*Fragments Grave and Gay* (London: Fontana, 1971).

Bartholomew, Craig, '*Warranted* Biblical Interpretation: Alvin Plantinga's "Two (or More) Types of Scripture Scholarship"', '*Behind the Text' History and Biblical Interpretation* (eds Craig Bartholomew, C. Stephen Evans, Mary Healy, Murray Rae; Grand Rapids Zondervan and Carlisle: Paternoster Press, 2003), 58–78.

Betz, John R., 'Hamann Before Kierkegaard: A Systematic Theological Oversight', *Pro Ecclesia* XVI.3 (2007), 299–333.

Bonhoeffer, Dietrich, *Nachfolge* (München: Chr. Kaiser Verlag, 1989).

—*Discipleship* (trans. Barbara Green and Reinhard Krauss; Minneapolis: Fortress Press, 2001).

Bukdahl, Jørgen, *Søren Kierkegaard and the Common Man* (trans. Bruce H. Kirmmse; Grand Rapids: Eerdmans, 2001).

Calvin, John, *Institutes of the Christian Religion* (trans. John Allen; Philadelphia, PN: Presbyterian Board of Christian Education, 1936).

Collins, James, *The Mind of Kierkegaard* (London: Secker and Warburg, 1954).

# Bibliography

Come, Arnold, *Kierkegaard as Theologian: Recovering My Self* (Montreal: McGill-Queens University Press, 1997).

Davies, Philip, *In Search of Ancient Israel* (Sheffield: Sheffield Academic Press, 1992).

—*Whose Bible is it Anyway?* (JSOTSup, 204; Sheffield: Sheffield Academic Press, 1995).

Dewey, Bradley R., 'Seven Seducers: A Typology of Interpretations of the Aesthetic Stage in Kierkegaard's "The Seducer's Diary"', *International Kierkegaard Commentary, vol. 3 Either/Or I* (ed. Robert L. Perkins; Macon, GA.: Mercer University Press, 1995), 159–99.

Dostoyevsky, Fyodor, *The Brothers Karamazov* (trans. David Magarshak; London: Penguin Books, 1958).

Duncan, Elmer H., *Søren Kierkegaard, Makers of the Modern Theological Mind* (Waco: Word Books, 1976).

Dunning, Stephen N., 'Kierkegaard's "Hegelian" Response to Hamann', *Thought* 55:218 (September 1980), 259–70.

Dupré, Louis, *Kierkegaard as Theologian* (London: Sheed and Ward, 1964).

Einstein, Albert, 'Geometry and Experience', *A. Einstein, Ideas and Opinions* (New York: Crown Publishers, 1954).

Eller, Vernard, *Kierkegaard and Radical Discipleship A New Perspective* (Princeton, NJ: Princeton University Press, 1968).

Evans, C. Stephen, *The Historical Christ and the Jesus of Faith* (Oxford: Oxford Clarendon Press, 1996).

—*Kierkegaard's Ethic of Love: Divine Commands and Moral Obligations* (Oxford: Oxford University Press, 2004).

Ferreira, M. Jamie, *Love's Grateful Striving: A Commentary on Kierkegaard's Works of Love* (New York: Oxford University Press, 2001).

Fish, Stanley, *Is There a Text in This Class? The Authority of Interpretive Communities* (Cambridge, MA: Harvard University Press, 1980).

Garff, Joakim, *Søren Kierkegaard: A Biography* (trans. Bruce H. Kirmmse; Princeton, NJ: Princeton University Press, 2005).

Gottlieb, Roger S., 'Kierkegaard's Ethical Individualism', *Monist* 62.3 (July 1979), 351–67.

Gouwens, David, *Kierkegaard as Religious Thinker* (Cambridge: Cambridge University Press, 1996).

Grenz, Stanley J., *The Social God and the Relational Self* (Louisville, KY: Westminster John Knox Press, 2001).

Hannay, Alastair, *Kierkegaard: A Biography* (Cambridge: Cambridge University Press, 2001).

Hegel, G. W. F., *Philosophy of Right* (trans. T. M. Knox; Oxford: Clarendon Press, 1942).

Henry, Paul, *Das Leben Johann Calvins*, I–III (Hamburg: Friedrich Perthes, 1835–44).

Heron, A. I. C., *A Century of Protestant Theology* (London: Lutterworth Press, 1980).

Hick, John (ed.) *The Myth of God Incarnate* (London, SCM Press, 1977).

# Bibliography

Hinkson, Craig, 'Kierkegaard's Theology: Cross and Grace', PhD Dissertation (University of Chicago, 1993).

—'Luther and Kierkegaard: Theologians of the Cross', *International Journal of Systematic Theology* 3.1 (March 2001), 27–45.

Holmer, Paul, 'About Being a Person: "Fear and Trembling"', *Kierkegaard's 'Fear and Trembling: Critical Appraisals* (ed. Robert L. Perkins; Alabama: University of Alabama Press, 1981), 81–99.

Hulme, Keri, *The Bone People* (New Zealand: The Spiral Collective, 1984).

Jenson, Matt, *The Gravity of Sin: Augustine, Luther and Barth on Homo Incurvatus in Se* (London: T&T Clark, 2006).

Kant, Immanuel, *Critique of Practical Reason* (trans. Lewis White Beck; New York: Macmillan, 1956).

—*Religion Within the Limits of Reason Alone* (trans. Theodore M. Greene and Hoyt H. Hudson; New York: Harper, 1960).

—*Der Streit der Facultäten,* ed. Pierro Gioranetti (Hamburg: Felix Meiner Verlag, 2005).

Kirmmse, Bruce H. (ed.), *Encounters with Kierkegaard: A Life as Seen by His Contemporaries* (Princeton, NJ: Princeton University Press, 1996).

Krishek, Sharon, 'Two Forms of Love: The Problem of Preferential Love in Kierkegaard's *Works of Love'*, *Journal of Religious Ethics* 36.4 (2008), 595–617.

Leibniz, Gottfried, *New Essays on Human Understanding* (trans. Alfred Gideon Langley; Chicago: Open Court, 1916).

—*Monadology* (trans. Robert Latta; London: Oxford University Press, 1898).

Lessing, G. E., 'On the Proof of the Spirit and of Power', *Lessing's Theological Writings* (ed. Henry Chadwick; London: Adam and Charles Black, 1956).

Levinas, Emmanuel, *Totality and Infinity* (trans. A. Lingis; Pittsburgh: Duquesne University Press, 1969).

—*Otherwise than Being or Beyond Essence* (trans. A. Lingis; The Hague: Martinus Nijhoff, 1981).

—*Humanism of the Other* (trans. Nidra Poller; Chicago: University of Illinois Press, 2003).

Løgstrup, K. E., 'Christentum ohne den historischen Jesus', *Orbis Litterarum* 10 (1995), 156–65.

Lowrie, Walter, *Kierkegaard* (2 vols; New York: Harper and Brothers, 1962).

Luther, Martin, *Luther's Works* (vol. 25; St Louis: Concordia Publishing House, 1972).

—'Letter to John Staupitz', *Works of Martin Luther* (ed. and trans. Adolph Spaeth, L. D. Reed, Henry Eyster Jacobs et al.; Philadelphia: A. J. Holman Company, 1915).

MacIntyre, Alasdair, *A Short History of Ethics* (London: Routledge, 2nd edn, 1998).

Macmurray, John, *Persons in Relation* (London: Faber & Faber, 1961).

Martens, Paul, '"You Shall Love": Kant, Kierkegaard and the Interpretation of Matthew 22:39', *International Kierkegaard Commentary: Works of Love* (IKC 16; ed. Robert L. Perkins; Macon, GA: Mercer University Press, 1999), 57–78.

# Bibliography

Martenson, Hans Lassen, *Af mit Levnet* I–III (Copenhagen: Gyldendalske Boghandel Nordisk Forlag, 1882–83).

McCracken, David, *The Scandal of the Gospels: Jesus, Story and Offense* (New York: Oxford University Press, 1994).

McFadyen, Alistair I., *The Call to Personhood* (Cambridge: Cambridge University Press, 1990).

McKinnon, Alastair, 'Kierkegaard: "Paradox" and Irrationalism', *Essays on Kierkegaard* (ed. Jerry H. Gill; Minneapolis: Burgess Publishing Co., 1969), 102–12.

—'Model and Redeemer in Kierkegaard's Religious Writings' (Unpublished Paper, 1980).

Michalson Jr., G. E., 'Lessing, Kierkegaard, and the "Ugly Ditch": A Reexamination', *The Journal of Religion* 59.3 (1979), 324–34.

—'Theology, Historical Knowledge and the Contingency-Necessity Distinction', *International Journal for Philosophy of Religion* 14.2 (1983), 87–98.

Minear, Paul S. and Morimoto, Paul S., *Kierkegaard and the Bible: An Index* (Princeton, NJ: Princeton Theological Seminary, 1953).

Moltmann, Jürgen, *The Crucified God* (trans. R.A. Wilson and John Bowden; London: SCM Press, 1974).

Mulder, Jr., Jack, *Kierkegaard and the Catholic Tradition: Conflict and Dialogue* (Bloomington, IN: Indiana University Press, 2010).

Neuhaus, Richard John, 'Kierkegaard for Grownups', *First Things*, no. 146 (October 2004), 27–33.

Nygren, Anders, *Agape and Eros* (trans. Philip S. Watson; Chicago: University of Chicago Press, 1982).

Pailin, David A., 'Abraham and Isaac: A Hermeneutical Problem before Kierkegaard', *Kierkegaard's 'Fear and Trembling': Critical Appraisals* (ed. Robert L. Perkins; Alabama: University of Alabama Press, 1981), 10–42.

Pattison, George, 'Review of Timothy Houston Polk, *The Biblical Kierkegaard, Reading by the Rule of Faith'*, *Literature and Theology* 13.1 (March 1999), 90–1.

Perkins, Robert L., *Søren Kierkegaard* (London: Lutterworth Press, 1969).

Podmore, Simon, *Anatomy of the Abyss: A Kierkegaardian Vision of the Self Before God* (Bloomington, IN: Indiana University Press, 2010).

—'The Dark Night of Suffering and the Darkness of God: God-forsakeness or Forsaking God in "The Gospel of Sufferings"', *International Kierkegaard Commentary, vol. 15: Upbuilding Discourses in Various Spirits* (ed. Robert L. Perkins; Macon, GA: Mercer University Press, 2005), 229–56.

Polanyi, Michael, *Personal Knowledge: Towards a Post-Critical Philosophy* (London: Routledge & Kegan Paul, 1958).

Polk, Timothy Houston, *The Biblical Kierkegaard, Reading by the Rule of Faith* (Macon, Georgia: Mercer University Press, 1997).

Prenter, Regin, 'Luther and Lutheranism', *Bibliotheca Kierkegaardiana, Vol. 6: Kierkegaard and Great Traditions* (eds Niels Thulstrup and Marie Mikulová Thulstrup; Copenhagen: C.A. Reitzels Boghandel, 1981).

Przywara, Erich, *Das Geheimnis Kierkegaards* (München: Oldenbourg, 1929).

Rae, Murray, *Kierkegaard's Vision of the Incarnation: By Faith Transformed* (Oxford: Clarendon Press, 1997).

# Bibliography

Roubiczek, Paul, *Existentialism: For and Against* (Cambridge: Cambridge University Press, 1964).

Rudd, Anthony, *Kierkegaard and the Limits of the Ethical* (Oxford: Clarendon Press, 193).

Russell, Letty, *Becoming Human* (Philadelphia: Westminster Press, 1982).

—*Church in the Round* (Louisville, KY: Westminster John Knox Press, 1993).

Schleiermacher, F.D.E., *The Christian Faith* (ET; Edinburgh: T&T Clark, 1928).

Spencer, Herbert, *Social Statics* [1851] (New York: Robert Schalkenbach Foundation, 1954).

Spinoza, Baruch, *Tractatus theologico-politicus* (trans. Samuel Shirley; Leiden: E.J. Brill, 1991).

Tarnas, Richard, *The Passion of the Western Mind. Understanding the Ideas That Have Shaped Our World View* (New York: Ballantine Books, 1991).

Thomas, R. S., *Later Poems* (London: Macmillan, 1983).

Torrance, Alan J., *Persons in Communion: Trinitarian Description and Human Participation* (Edinburgh: T&T Clark, 1996).

Troeltsch, Ernst, 'Historical and Dogmatic Method in Theology' in *Religion in History: Ernst Troeltsch* (Edinburgh: T&T Clark, 1991), 11–32.

Van Inwagen, Peter, 'Is it possible to prove that God does not exist?', F. D. Maurice Lectures (London: King's College, March 1999).

Walsh, Sylvia, *Living Poetically: Kierkegaard's Existential Aesthetics* (University Park, PA: The Pennsylvania State University Press, 1994).

—*Living Christianly: Kierkegaard's Dialectic of Christian Existence* (University Park, PA: The Pennsylvania State University Press, 2005).

—*Kierkegaard: Thinking Christianly in an Existential Mode* (Oxford: Oxford University Press, 2009).

Watkin, Julia, *Kierkegaard* (London: Geoffrey Chapman, 1997).

Weston, Michael, *Kierkegaard and Modern Continental Philosophy: An Introduction* (London: Routledge, 1994).

Westphal, Merold, *Kierkegaard's Critique of Reason and Society* (University Park, PA: The Pennsylvania State University Press, 1991).

Westphal, Merold and Matuštík, J. Martin (eds), *Kierkegaard in Post/Modernity* (Bloomington, IN: Indiana University Press, 1995).

Williams, Rowan, *Arius* (London: SCM Press, 2nd edn, 2001).

Wittgenstein, Ludwig, *Tractatus Logico-Philosophicus* (trans. C. K. Oden; London: Routledge & Kegan Paul Ltd, 1922).

Wood, Allen W., 'Hegel's Ethics', *The Cambridge Companion to Hegel* (ed. Frederick C. Beiser; Cambridge: Cambridge University Press, 1993), 211–33.

Yule, George, 'Luther's Attack on the Latin Heresy', *Christ in our Place: The Humanity of God in Christ for the Reconciliation of the World* (eds Trevor Hart and Daniel Thimell; Exeter: The Paternoster Press, 1989), 224–52.

Ziegler, Philip, 'Barth's Criticism's of Kierkegaard – A Striking Out at Phantoms', *International Journal of Systematic Theology*, 9.4 (May 2007), 434–51.

Zizioulas, John D., *Being as Communion: Studies in Personhood and the Church* (London: Darton, Longman and Todd, 1985).

# Index

# Index

# Index

# Index